PRAISE FO
Lives of American Women

"Finally! The majority of students—by which I mean women—will have the opportunity to read biographies of women from our nation's past. (Men can read them too, of course!) The 'Lives of American Women' series features an eclectic collection of books, readily accessible to students who will be able to see the contributions of women in many fields over the course of our history. Long overdue, these books will be a valuable resource for teachers, students, and the public at large."

—COKIE ROBERTS,
author of *Founding Mothers* and *Ladies of Liberty*

"Just what any professor wants: books that will intrigue, inform, and fascinate students! These short, readable biographies of American women—specifically designed for classroom use—give instructors an appealing new option to assign to their history students."

—MARY BETH NORTON,
Mary Donlon Alger Professor of American History,
Cornell University

"For educators keen to include women in the American story, but hampered by the lack of thoughtful, concise scholarship, here comes 'Lives of American Women,' embracing Abigail Adams's counsel to John—'remember the ladies.' And high time, too!"

—LESLEY S. HERRMANN,
Executive Director, The Gilder Lehrman
Institute of American History

"Students both in the general survey course and in specialized offerings like my course on U.S. women's history can get a great understanding of an era from a short biography. Learning a lot about a single but complex character really helps to deepen appreciation of what women's lives were like in the past."

—PATRICIA CLINE COHEN,
University of California, Santa Barbara

"Biographies are, indeed, back. Not only will students read them, biographies provide an easy way to demonstrate particularly important historical themes or ideas. . . . Undergraduate readers will be challenged to think more deeply about what it means to be a woman, citizen, and political actor. . . . I am eager to use this in my undergraduate survey and specialty course."

—JENNIFER THIGPEN,
Washington State University, Pullman

"These books are, above all, fascinating stories that will engage and inspire readers. They offer a glimpse into the lives of key women in history who either defied tradition or who successfully maneuvered in a man's world to make an impact. The stories of these vital contributors to American history deliver just the right formula for instructors looking to provide a more complicated and nuanced view of history."

—ROSANNE LICHATIN,
2005 Gilder Lehrman Preserve
America History Teacher of the Year

"The *Lives of American Women* authors raise all of the big issues I want my classes to confront—and deftly fold their arguments into riveting narratives that maintain students' excitement."

—WOODY HOLTON,
author of *Abigail Adams*

Lives of American Women

Carol Berkin, Series Editor

Westview Press is pleased to launch Lives of American Women. Selected and edited by renowned women's historian Carol Berkin, these brief, affordably priced biographies are designed for use in undergraduate courses. Rather than a comprehensive approach, each biography focuses instead on a particular aspect of a woman's life that is emblematic of her time, or which made her a pivotal figure in the era. The emphasis is on a "good read," featuring accessible writing and compelling narratives, without sacrificing sound scholarship and academic integrity. Primary sources at the end of each biography reveal the subject's perspective in her own words. Study Questions and an Annotated Bibliography support the student reader.

Dolley Madison: The Problem of National Unity by Catherine Allgor

Lillian Gilbreth: Redefining Domesticity by Julie Des Jardins

Alice Paul: Equality for Women by Christine Lunardini

Rebecca Dickinson: Independence for a New England Woman by Marla Miller

Sarah Livingston Jay: Model Republican Woman by Mary-Jo Kline

Betsy Mix Cowles: Bold Reformer by Stacey Robertson

Sally Hemings: Given Her Time by Jon Kukla

Shirley Chisholm: Catalyst for Change by Barbara Winslow

Margaret Sanger: Freedom, Controversy and the Birth Control Movement by Esther Katz

Barbara Egger Lennon: Teacher, Mother, Activist by Tina Brakebill

Anne Hutchinson: A Dissident Woman's Boston by Vivian Bruce Conger

Angela Davis: Radical Icon by Robyn Spencer

Catharine Beecher: The Complexity of Gender in 19th Century America by Cindy Lobel

Julia Lathrop: Social Service and Progressive Government by Miriam Cohen

Mary Pickford: Women, Film and Selling Girlhood by Kathy Feeley

Elizabeth Gurley Flynn: The Making of the Modern Woman by Lara Vapnek

Alice
Paul

Equality for Women

CHRISTINE LUNARDINI

LIVES OF AMERICAN WOMEN
Carol Berkin, Series Editor

WESTVIEW
PRESS
A Member of the Perseus Books Group

This book is dedicated, with love and gratitude and my thanks for always being there, to Patricia Lunardini Donahue, Noah Callahan-Bever, and Chloe Callahan-Flintoft.

Westview Press was founded in 1975 in Boulder, Colorado, by notable publisher and intellectual Fred Praeger. Westview Press continues to publish scholarly titles and high-quality undergraduate-and graduate-level textbooks in core social science disciplines. With books developed, written, and edited with the needs of serious nonfiction readers, professors, and students in mind, Westview Press honors its long history of publishing books that matter.

Find us on the World Wide Web at www.westviewpress.com.
Every effort has been made to secure required permissions for all text, images, maps, and other art reprinted in this volume.

Westview Press books are available at special discounts for bulk purchases in the United States by corporations, institutions, and other organizations. For more information, please contact the Special Markets Department at the Perseus Books Group, 2300 Chestnut Street, Suite 200, Philadelphia, PA 19103, or call (800) 810-4145, ext. 5000, or e-mail special.markets@perseusbooks.com.

Library of Congress Cataloging-in-Publication Data
Lunardini, Christine A., 1941-
  Alice Paul : equality for women / Christine Lunardini.
    p. cm.—(Lives of American women)
  Includes bibliographical references and index.
  ISBN 978-0-8133-4761-5 (pbk. : alk. paper)—ISBN 978-0-8133-4762-2
(e-book) 1. Paul, Alice, 1885–1977. 2. Suffragists—United States—
Biography. 3. Women—Suffrage—United States—History. 4. Women's
rights—United States—History. I. Title.
  HQ1413.P38L86 2013
  324.6'23092—dc23
  [B]
                                                              2012032769
10 9 8 7 6 5 4 3 2 1

CONTENTS

SERIES EDITOR'S
FOREWORD

When women gathered at Seneca Falls in 1848, their agenda was truly radical: they were challenging the norms and the values of their society. In an era when men and women were assigned separate spheres and full citizenship was available only to adult white males, these women called for nothing less than equal economic, educational, and political equality—and a dramatic shift in established notions of the intellectual and moral differences between the sexes.

The right to vote, or suffrage, was only one of the Seneca Falls convention's radical demands. But as the decades went by, many of the women who devoted time and energy to women's rights took a narrower view of their agenda. By the time Alice Paul was born in 1885, winning the vote had become the central, if not the only, goal of the movement. In Paul, however, the spirit of Seneca Falls lived on. Over her remarkable lifetime, she campaigned tirelessly for full equality of the sexes. For Paul, suffrage was only a first step; the ultimate goal had to be a nation fully committed to gender equality. This, she argued, could be achieved only through the passage of an equal rights amendment.

As a leader of the feminist movement in the early twentieth century, Paul brought to her campaigns a rare combination of unshakable conviction, willing personal sacrifice, and remarkable political savvy. She had a flair for the dramatic—and knew how to mobilize support and gain national attention for her cause. It was Paul who organized the first major suffrage parade down the streets of Washington, DC, and it was Paul who brought national attention to the plight of suffrage demonstrators who had been arrested and jailed by organizing a hunger strike within the prison.

As Christine Lunardini shows us, Paul's feminism was rooted in her Quaker upbringing within a family that assumed a daughter had as great an obligation to improve the world as a son. Throughout her lifetime, Paul attracted devoted followers and allies who respected her tireless work, first for suffrage and then for the equal rights amendment. Yet Paul had as many critics as she had admirers. Her tactics shocked other leaders of the suffrage movement, and her refusal to compromise drove a wedge between her and mainstream women's organizations. Like many visionaries, Paul was controversial in her own lifetime—and remains controversial in the histories written about the women's movement.

Paul's successes illustrate how effective leadership can both harness and shape changes in the social and political climate of a nation, but Paul's failures may be equally instructive. The debate over the equal rights amendment reminds us that the women's movement did not speak with one voice. Feminists were divided on many issues, including the wisdom of the amendment, which would have eliminated special protection for women in the workplace. What might have been a principled stand for white middle- and upper-class women was seen as a threat to the health of working women. The failure of the equal rights amendment thus reminds us that race and class always intersect with gender, making a universal women's agenda difficult, if not impossible.

Alice Paul's story also reminds us that rights we take for granted today were once resisted and were won only through struggle. In her own lifetime, Paul was labeled a "militant" and criticized as a "radical." Today, her insistence that women, no less than men, deserve a place in every facet of American social, political, and economic life defines the reality we see around us. How this change came about—and who the agents of that change were—is central to understanding the twentieth and twenty-first centuries in America.

In examining and narrating the lives of women both famous and obscure, Westview's "Lives of American Women" series populates our national past more fully and more richly. Each story told is the story not simply of an individual but of the era in which she lived, the events in which she participated, and the experiences she shared with her contemporaries. Some of these women will be familiar to the reader; others may not appear at all in the history books that focus on the powerful, the brilliant, or the privileged. But each of these women is worth knowing. In their personal odysseys, American history comes alive.

—*Carol Berkin*

AUTHOR'S PREFACE

As an undergraduate at Mount Holyoke College, I discovered the National Woman's Party while searching for a senior thesis topic. I soon realized that Alice Paul was the real story. Even a superficial investigation of Paul left me with a question: Given the awe-inspiring nature of her accomplishments on behalf of American women, why was she almost always marginalized by historians of women's history? Most of the histories written about the suffrage campaign viewed Paul either as a nuisance who threatened to delay the vote for women or as a well-meaning but ineffective suffragist. Even William Chafe, one of the very few historians who recognized Paul as a truly charismatic figure in the movement, tended to praise Carrie Chapman Catt's leadership. Catt, the president of the National American Woman Suffrage Association, unfairly garnered the lion's share of credit for passage of the Nineteenth Amendment.

After graduating from MHC and beginning graduate studies at Princeton University, I continued to be fascinated with Alice Paul. My adviser (Chair Professor Arthur S. Link, the great Wilsonian scholar) offered his enthusiastic approval for my thesis topic. My original thesis dealt with the National Woman's Party and the suffrage campaign. Very few of Alice Paul's personal papers were available at the time I was studying these topics. In the intervening years, however, many more of Paul's public and private papers have been made available in various library collections. The National Woman's Party archives, the Schlesinger Library in Cambridge, and the Library of Congress, among others, now include Paul's papers.

I was recently handed a second opportunity to produce another Alice Paul volume. This one would focus much more on Alice herself. She was—and is—a heroic figure in American history. She dedicated her life to working for equality for women, not only in America but throughout the world. She also happened to be extremely intelligent and charismatic. Don't be surprised, after reading about Alice Paul and everything she accomplished, if you find yourself asking, "What can *I* do to promote equality for women?"

I am grateful to the following people for this opportunity to revisit Alice Paul. First and foremost, I would like to thank senior editors Priscilla McGeehan and Carol Berkin for making sure that the Lives of American Women series found a home with such a distinguished publisher. Priscilla worked tirelessly on behalf of all of us authors to make sure that happened. In addition, she has proved to be a wonderfully supportive editor. Her encouragement throughout made it so much easier to get done what had to be done. Carol, too, was very helpful, providing practical advice on producing a manuscript that would be readable and exciting. I thank her for that. The suggestions from readers of the proposal and the manuscript added materially to the book. For alerting me to issues and questions that I had to rethink, I am indebted to Amy Bix (Iowa State University), Wendy Castro (University of Central Arkansas), Megan Elias (Queensboro Community College), Jane Gerhard (Mount Holyoke College), Elizabeth Pleck (University of Illinois), and Veronica Wilson (University of Pittsburgh). I would also like to thank my longtime friend and colleague Professor Catherine Clinton of Queens College, Belfast, Ireland, for suggesting my name to Priscilla and Carol. From our graduate-school days at Princeton to the present, Catherine has pointed me in the direction of several projects—including some collaborative efforts—that have proved to be personally satisfying. Thank you, Catherine. My thanks to Sandra Beris, senior project editor at The Perseus Books Group; and a special thanks to copyeditor Christine Arden. Her attention to the small details in the manuscript resulted in an infinitely better final product. In this case, the luck of the draw made all the difference and I am truly appreciative.

Members of my family have been more than generous in their support and encouragement, including my sister Pat Donahue as well as Kevin, Kate, Sarah, and Luke Donahue. My sister-in-law Donna Lunardini has also been unfailingly encouraging throughout. My niece Abby Lunardini Owens remains my political touchstone in a world gone right. I have three wonderful godchildren who mean more to me than I can express and whose thoughtfulness and support never cease to amaze: Noah Callahan-Bever, editor in chief of *Complex Magazine;* Chloe Callahan-Flintoft, who graduated from Trinity College Dublin and is now a master's candidate in statistics at Baruch College in New York City; and Sheila Callahan-Victore, a sophomore at Tufts University in Boston.

Everything that is right about this volume I owe in great measure to these professional colleagues, friends, and family members. Everything that is not what it should be is solely my responsibility.

—Christine Lunardini
Roseville, California

1

Becoming Alice Paul

Alice Paul, the oldest child of William and Tacie Paul, was born in 1885. The struggle for women's rights, begun in 1848, had expanded over the years but could count only a handful of suffrage states where women were allowed to vote. No one, least of all Alice's parents, could foresee that this tiny addition to the American population was destined to change all of that.

William Mickle Paul married Tacie Haines Parry in 1881. He was just thirty years old but already a successful businessman and community leader in what is now Moorestown, New Jersey. A cofounder and the president of the Burlington County Trust Company, Paul sat on the Board of Directors of several area companies and invested in real estate. Both he and his new wife were descended from illustrious and influential colonial leaders. William could claim no less than John Winthrop, the first governor of the Massachusetts Bay Colony. Winthrop's vision of Massachusetts as the "city on a hill," which would shine as a beacon for all to follow, helped shape the character of the New World colonies. Another of William Paul's ancestors had been jailed in England because of his Quaker religious beliefs. After his release he, too, made his way to the New World, the first Paul to do so, and settled in New Jersey. The community, originally named Paulsboro and later renamed Moorestown, was located in Burlington County, bordering Pennsylvania, less than ten miles from Philadelphia. By the time William was born in 1850, Burlington County had become home to a thriving

Quaker community. It is likely that William attended the same Friends School in Cinnaminson, New Jersey, as his future wife.

Tacie Parry Paul, born in Cinnaminson, could, like William, trace her ancestors back to the earliest colonial settlers. On her side of the family, her lineage went all the way back to William Penn, the founder of Pennsylvania Colony. After graduating from the Cinnaminson Friends School, Tacie was one of the first women to attend Swarthmore College. Her father, Judge William Parry, cofounded Swarthmore, along with, among others, Lucretia Mott, one of the most influential abolitionists in the years leading up to the Civil War and a longtime women's rights advocate. Judge Parry raised much of the funding for the school. Tacie would have been one of the first women graduates of Swarthmore had she not left during her final year to marry William Paul. At that time, married women were not allowed to attend school. Perhaps to lessen her father's disappointment, Tacie promised that all of her children would spend at least a year at Swarthmore in order to benefit from a Quaker education.

William and Tacie subscribed wholeheartedly to gender equality, separation from materialistic society, a close relationship with nature, and working toward a better society. In accordance with a Quaker tenet, all members of the community were urged to find their "inner light"— namely, the motivation to act on their conscience and to influence the creation of a "better society" as they personally defined it. The broad strokes of a better society included beliefs in pacifism, nonviolent resolution of problems, equal justice, and personal growth. Two years after they were married, the Pauls purchased a sprawling working farm in Mt. Laurel, New Jersey, a few miles from Moorestown, which they promptly named Paulsdale Farm. The 170-plus-acre farm, complete with a large rambling farmhouse, was another measure of William's business success. From its enormous wraparound veranda, one could look out on a sweeping front yard, several barns and other buildings, and fields of various crops and animals. Although William considered himself a gentleman farmer, his hired hands did most of the actual farm work. The family also employed several Irish maids to help with the work in the main house. It was in this prosperous and peaceful setting that the Pauls' four children were born.

Alice Stokes Paul, named for her maternal grandmother, arrived on January 11, 1885. Her three younger siblings followed in fairly rapid succession: William (1886), Helen (1889), and Parry (1895). Growing up at Paulsdale Farm became a life lesson in the core beliefs of the elder Pauls. Though removed from the surrounding community, the farm was certainly not isolated. Relying on its bounty kept the Paul children close to nature, while their various chores taught them the virtues of perseverance and industry. The children enjoyed competitive games, but, in keeping with Quaker belief, music and dancing were not part of their young lives. They were very aware that their Irish maids went off to dances in town. As Alice noted years later, they assumed that only "a sort of common people" engaged in that kind of activity.[1] It is likely that William Paul was the more conservative parent when it came to music and dance. Shortly after his death, when Alice had already left for college, Tacie Paul purchased a harpsichord for the family home so her daughter Helen could take music lessons.

Alice also remembered at a very young age going with her mother to woman suffrage meetings at neighbors' homes. Since all of their relatives and friends were Quakers, she grew up accepting women's equality as a given and not as something up for debate. More than anything else, however, Alice loved to read. She loved the classics. If she was off on her own, more than likely she could be found at the local Friends Library. She recalls reading every line written by Charles Dickens "over and over and over again."[2] These early experiences were already beginning to reveal Paul's complex nature. On the one hand, she clearly believed the household staffs were commoners with lower social standings than the Pauls. On the other hand, she believed without question in equality for women and found great resonance in the social issues that Dickens wrote about, including the relationship between class and poverty.

Because her parents believed deeply in gender equality, they expected Alice to lead her younger siblings by example. Alice easily adapted to this position of responsibility. She strove to shine in her parents' eyes— and succeeded in doing so. Her father had ultimate confidence in his oldest daughter's ability to do whatever was asked of her. He observed more than once that "whenever there is anything hard and disagreeable to do, I bank on Alice."[3] And her mother's words of advice, which were repeated each time Alice was asked to take on a new task, stayed with her throughout her lifetime: "When you put your hand to the plow, you can't put it down until you get to the end of the row."[4] Her parents' teachings and her Quaker upbringing—combined with the worldviews of the many authors, such as Dickens, whose words she internalized— were strong influences in shaping her own worldview. They also helped to teach her how one should live life.

All four of the Paul children attended the Moorestown Friends School. And, in keeping with Tacie Paul's promise to her father, all four attended Swarthmore for at least one year. The younger Paul children, however, chose to transfer to different colleges after their year was up. Only Alice stayed at Swarthmore. She loved college life. She thrived on being a part of the intellectual community of teachers and fellow students that she found there. She also liked the atmosphere steeped in Quaker tradition. Her intelligence and thirst for knowledge ensured that she would do extremely well at Swarthmore. That fact may explain her siblings' preference for educational experiences elsewhere—an alternative preferable to having to live up to Alice's reputation!

After graduating at the top of her class from the Moorestown Friends School in 1901, Alice was more than ready for college. She did not yet have a clear idea of the path she would follow. She did know that, as soon as she enrolled at Swarthmore, she would have to declare her major. Most of the other women students were taking majors in subjects like English literature and Latin. Because she was so well-read and had done so well in these areas at the Friends School, Paul was determined to take the path less followed. She knew absolutely nothing about science or math. To her, the logical choice was to spend her time at Swarthmore learning about what she didn't know rather than concentrating on academic pursuits that were in her comfort zone. She chose biology as her major because, as she readily admitted, "this is the only way I will ever learn about [science]."[5] Her choice of a major in science revealed another of Paul's characteristics: the sense that there was little to be gained from redoing something already done. To be clear, pursuing a career in science had never really entered Paul's mind. Although she thought she should know as much as she could about science and higher mathematics, these subjects just didn't interest her as a career choice.

A few months into her freshman year at Swarthmore, Paul suffered a personal tragedy, probably the first in her young life. In the winter of 1901, her parents took a vacation trip to Florida. They stayed only two weeks and then quickly returned to New Jersey; as Paul would subsequently recall, her father's business activities kept him extremely busy. Soon after their return, Mr. Paul caught a cold that quickly became a very bad cold and then turned into pneumonia. In the blink of an eye he was gone, succumbing to the pneumonia and leaving Mrs. Paul with four young children. Alice had just turned sixteen. When asked many years later how she dealt with her father's death, Alice's response was vague at best: "I just remember that life went on."[6] For someone to have so vague a recollection about a seminal life event may seem odd at first glance. In fact, her response reflected another Paul characteristic. She consistently downplayed or was extremely vague about events in her life that, factually, had to have affected her deeply. Whether it was the death of her father or being force-fed as a suffrage prisoner or being committed to a psychiatric ward by the government because of her picketing activity, Paul's personal recollections of these events were often sketchy, if not dismissive. Were it not for the testimony of others who worked with her and ample printed coverage of her experiences, she might still be regarded historically as little more than a misguided eccentric. As late as the 1970s, many historians of the woman suffrage movement viewed her as marginal at best and counterproductive at worst.

Yet life did go on for Alice, and Swarthmore continued to suit her. At that time, the college enrolled about four hundred students. In keeping with Quaker beliefs, about half the students were women—a ratio that made Swarthmore stand out among coeducational schools of the day. Alice enjoyed participating in sports; she excelled at tennis, loved basketball, and played field hockey as well. A lifelong friend whom she met at Swarthmore, Mabel Vernon, remembered Alice as rather shy but very sports-oriented. In those days, Vernon noted, Alice was the picture of health. Despite her shyness, Alice enjoyed conspiring with her close friends to play pranks on fellow students. One night, she and her friends tied together several white sheets and hung them out the dorm window, hoping to shock passersby when they spotted the ghostly apparitions. In many ways, this early version of Alice Paul was the typical college coed of her day, stretching the boundaries of her experience and enjoying the camaraderie of her friends.

For the first time in her memory, Paul experienced music and dance, both of which she seemed to enjoy. For Quakers, consensus on all things was not as important as interpreting one's inner light. Those making the decisions at Swarthmore were comfortable with exposing their students to music and dance. Swarthmore students were encouraged to play musical instruments, and on Sunday evenings everyone could sing or listen to hymns performed by members of the community. Alice took dance classes and attended the college-sponsored dances for female students, the custom at Swarthmore. There were also weekly gatherings to which all students were invited. It was an opportunity to socialize, to chat with and get to know other students. Alice was also content to spend long hours reading and taking walks alone or with classmates along the Crum, a stream that bordered the Swarthmore campus.

Swarthmore students were expected to attend Quaker services each week and to take all their meals together as well. Students were assigned designated tables and seats when they arrived on campus. For four years they ate all their meals with the same group. Each table was presided over by a college dean, charged with instilling in her pupils proper etiquette as preparation for taking their place in polite society. Everyone said grace together, and then the male students would go out to the kitchen and bring in the food for the table. The dean signaled the end of each meal when "with great ceremony she rose and walked out and with great ceremony the students rose and walked out behind her. It was a very dignified and a very lovely regime."[7]

In her sophomore year Alice joined a debate society, probably because she did not think her public speaking skills were at all impressive. Debating would be an opportunity to improve upon them. Mabel Vernon first met Alice Paul when both were competing in an extemporaneous speaking contest at Swarthmore. Knowing her friend to be a gifted speaker, Paul sought out her advice. Paul had no doubt that Vernon would win the competition. She confided to Vernon that she (Paul) would almost certainly be eliminated. She had very little confidence in her own public speaking ability. Vernon offered what advice she could to the uncertain Paul. In the end, Vernon did win first prize in the event but Paul also made the finals, indicating that she was a much better speaker than she gave herself credit for. Much later Vernon observed that this incident, too, had been characteristic of Alice Paul: she always seemed to downplay her own talents and abilities and believed that others could do things so much better than she.

Paul continued to do well at Swarthmore. However, until her senior year she had no clear idea of her goals for the future. She maintained an excellent academic standing in her biology major, though she still had no real passion for the subject. She had begun to think about teaching after Swarthmore. For women students who wanted to support themselves after college, teaching was the most common goal. Most students did not think in terms of working toward a career or even supporting themselves. The vast majority of students planned on returning home after college. For women students, this meant living with their families until they were married—if they married. For male students, it was usually a matter of going into business with their fathers, whether that meant some form of commerce, farming, or perhaps a profession such as law or medicine. Alice herself might well have graduated with no better idea of where her interests lay were it not for Swarthmore's newest faculty member, Professor of Politics and Economics Robert Clarkson Brooks.

In her senior year Alice took Brooks's courses in political science and economics. For the first time in her college career, she had found something that excited her greatly. Brooks taught his students that the relationship between economy and politics could determine the kind of social changes that would result in a better society. He also explained that political activism did not require holding public office. This gave the Swarthmore coeds something to ponder, as very few women held any kind of public office at the time. A firm advocate of "progressivism," a movement just beginning to effect change across the country, Brooks offered his students the prospect of the better life so integral to Quaker beliefs. This new way of looking at social problems and how to solve them excited Paul immensely. It didn't immediately resolve her indecisiveness about her future, but it did cast a new light on that future.

Paul graduated in 1905. In recognition of accomplishment in an area other than science, she was named the Ivy Poet of her class. The honor required that Paul write an original poem that she would then recite at a Swarthmore traditional ceremony. Each graduating class placed a brick in an edifice constructed for that purpose to commemorate their years at the school. Being named the Ivy Poet terrified Paul for two reasons. First, she had never written a poem before and she didn't think she possessed the proper creativity to pull it off. Second, despite her public speaking efforts, she didn't believe that she could recite the poem in front of the entire college community. She turned once again to Mabel Vernon, requesting that Mabel coach her so that she could get through the ordeal without embarrassing herself, her class, or the college. In the end, her first and only poem turned out to be much better than she thought she was capable of. She also did a very creditable job of reciting it at the ceremony.

Graduation brought another entirely unexpected opportunity. Although Paul had no way of knowing it, taking Professor Brooks's classes gradually but thoroughly changed the direction her life would take. She did so well in his classes that Brooks nominated her for a postgraduate scholarship awarded by the College Settlement Association (CSA). The college settlement movement started by Jane Addams had become very popular by that time. Addams and Ellen Gates Starr founded Hull House in Chicago in 1889. They intended to provide the tools that would allow immigrant populations to assimilate into American life. Their classes, which were taught in English and exposed immigrants to American art and culture as well as to more practical instruction in the labor market and citizenship, brought throngs of would-be Americans to Hull House. Very quickly, Hull House also became a place where social issues were addressed, including education, child labor, occupational and workplace safety, and wages and hours. Before long, Hull House had become the best example of what settlement houses could be. More than five hundred settlement houses were opened across the country, many of them modeled after Hull House. When Paul graduated from Swarthmore, the CSA awarded one-year scholarships to graduates of select colleges who seemed most suited for the field of social work. Paul had never considered social work as a career. She accepted the scholarship as a means of exploring that avenue further. Given the choice of which settlement-house city she wanted to go to, Paul chose New York.

Paul arrived in New York in the fall of 1905. She was assigned to the Rivington Street Settlement House and enrolled in the New York School of Philanthropy, also part of the scholarship award. Founded in 1898, the School of Philanthropy was established to provide a level of professionalism for social workers. It later merged with Columbia University and became the Columbia University School of Social Work. Before social work developed into an academic discipline, charitable giving tended to be haphazard at best. A system in which the needs of clients could be easily matched with organizational outreach programs just did not exist. Indeed, there was no structure even for determining or verifying a client's needs. The founder of the School of Philanthropy was a much-respected figure in charity organization circles. As the first president of the school, he was instrumental in developing much more rigorous training for his students. As a student, Paul attended lectures and went on numerous site visits to various institutions.

In addition to her academic work at the School of Philanthropy, Paul became a Rivington Street associate case worker. Rivington Street was located in a largely Jewish and Italian neighborhood, and Paul's scholarship provided for room and board at the settlement house. She spent her year there working with experienced social workers, mostly observing. They visited several families on an individual basis, and Paul—as the assistant to the case worker—wrote supplemental reports on their status, along with whatever recommendations she believed were in order. In short, it was in-depth training in preparation for becoming a case worker.

Paul graduated in 1906 with a postgraduate degree in social work. Although she worked diligently throughout the year to fulfill the commitment she had made by accepting the scholarship, the most noteworthy aspect of her experience was her attitude toward social work. "I could see that social workers were not doing much good in the world. That's what I thought, anyway." Nearly seven decades later, her opinion had not changed. "I still think so. So to spend all your time doing something that—you knew you couldn't *change* the situation by social work." Her attitude toward social work may have been influenced by the newness of the discipline. She never committed to being a social worker. And, "[b]y the time I had been there awhile, I *knew* I didn't want to be a social worker, whatever else I was."[8]

Even so, she was not dissuaded from accepting another similar job following her graduation from the School of Philanthropy. The Charity Organization Society (COS) invited her to join it for the summer. She was paid a very small stipend and continued to live at Rivington Street. It was a much more hands-on experience than her academic training had been, and one that she seemed to enjoy more—probably because she was now responsible for helping to find actual solutions to her clients' problems. She would meet with individuals, find out what they needed from the COS, and then spend hours upon hours visiting and calling various organizations that might be in a position to provide the sought-after relief. There was no real welfare as such. Solutions came from independent organizations that were generally very specific in the type of assistance or aid they could offer. So the task involved contacting church groups, civic organizations, or medical institutions that offered specific services through the COS. By the end of the summer, Paul had discovered an entirely different New York in her effort to help "the under layer of people who were up against it."[9]

Although she could walk away with the feeling that she had helped to provide some relief to a few families during her social work summer, her primary revelation was that "I didn't know very much. I was thoroughly convinced of that."[10]

At this point, she decided to enroll in the graduate program at the University of Pennsylvania. She knew exactly what she wanted to do. The fire that Professor Brooks had ignited at Swarthmore still burned brightly within Paul. Ever since taking his economics and political science classes, she knew that these were areas she was truly passionate about. In fact, if Brooks had been at Swarthmore for her entire college career and if she'd been exposed to such classes immediately, she would never have been a science major. And giving up the idea of social work required less thought than tying her shoes. She had all the requisite credentials to go into that field. "I *could* have become a social worker, but I am certainly glad I never did *that*."[11]

As a master's degree candidate at UPenn, Paul majored in sociology with minors in political science and economics. The year flew by. Her academic choices excited her as well as her professors. In particular, Professor of Economics Simon Patten had a profound effect on Paul. Patten chaired the Wharton School when Paul was a student. He was one of the first economists to foresee a transition from the economics of scarcity to an economics of abundance. In his view, new technologies had the potential to ensure an abundance of resources that would produce enough wealth to provide everyone in the Western world with a proper diet, basic housing and clothing, and education adequate to meet industries' needs. Achieving these desired goals required only group social action, Patten declared. He envisioned a society that would have as its backbone a segment of the population with the wherewithal to fill the needs of labor, thus ensuring their employability. Many older American cities, such as New York, Boston, and Chicago, had fallen under the sway of corrupt elected officials and party hacks more interested in increasing their own wealth by controlling the voters. People like the notorious Boss Tweed in New York City looked to the so-called Robber Barons—the Rockefellers, Carnegie, J. P. Morgan, and other captains of industry and finance—who seemed to be accumulating enormous wealth at the expense of the workers who were actually building their empires. For the local politicians, corruption was not a vice but a tool to be used for their personal benefit. Patten, like Brooks, believed in progressive reform to eliminate corruption and rein in the disparity of wealth that threatened democracy.

Patten's class and the theories he advocated were another instance of how Paul could not yet know or predict how another individual's ideas would influence her future struggle for women's equality. The seeds, nevertheless, were being steadily planted. In the meantime, she completed the required coursework with flying colors. She also began researching the legal status of women in Pennsylvania and documented her findings in a paper titled "Towards Equality." It was an indictment of how the law defined women in Pennsylvania as second-class citizens without equal protection in comparison to their male counterparts. She would expand upon that research when she returned to the University of Pennsylvania to complete her PhD several years later.

Paul's plans to continue in a doctoral program at UPenn were interrupted by yet another seemingly serendipitous event destined to propel her toward what would eventually become her life's work. Nominated for a coveted fellowship to the central training school for Quakers in Woodbrook, England, Paul jumped at the chance to study in Europe for a year. Woodbrook focused on the academic areas that Paul found so exciting: sociology, economics, and politics. She never knew where the nomination came from, but it didn't really matter. In any event, Paul found herself the recipient of the fellowship. Immediately after the graduation ceremony for her master's degree, she set sail for Europe.

Paul could not have been happier with her Woodbrook experience. Like the New York School of Philanthropy, Woodbrook brought in a variety of speakers and experts in the field, as well as people who lived in the poorer districts and could talk knowledgeably about the issues they faced. And, as in New York, Alice learned a great deal about the city and even more about how poverty affected those who were mired in it. For a brief period of time, she wavered in her determination that social work was something she did not want to do. She had, after all, accepted the Woodbrook fellowship, and felt some obligation to pursue social work as her chosen job. Very quickly, she reverted to her original belief that social workers could not accomplish very much. It wasn't that she thought the needs of the people she met with were not valid or that social workers were not capable and sincere in their efforts. Rather, it was her conviction that, try as they might, social workers could not fix the underlying problems that created poverty. Her sense of moral obligation prevented Paul from ever shirking her responsibilities as a Woodbrook Fellow. But intellectually she had little faith that she was making any difference. It was the wealth of new ideas and experiences that made the year exciting to Paul.

Although it wasn't a requirement, Woodbrook students were encouraged to take additional classes at the University of Birmingham. Alice took as many classes there as she could. Students were also invited to all events that featured guest speakers. At one of these lectures, Alice came face-to-face with the issue that would dominate her life, while also witnessing firsthand the stunning degree of opposition to this issue. The president of Birmingham, Sir Oliver Lodge, had invited Christabel

Pankhurst and two other suffragettes to address his students. No sooner had Pankhurst begun her lecture than the audience broke into rowdy and extremely vocal objections. Neither Paul nor anyone else who wanted to hear what the suffragettes had to say could hear them. This incident was both shocking and revealing to Paul. She was certainly not so naive as to think that women's rights had no opponents, particularly given the subject matter of her MA thesis. But writing about the cultural and legal inequality that affected women's lives, while important, was in many respects an intellectual exercise that could be studied free from emotion. As far back as she could remember, gender equality had been a given. Most of the people she knew believed that women were the equals of men in every respect—and the few who opposed gender equality expressed their disagreement politely and without emotion. Thus hearing the Birmingham students shout down Christabel Pankhurst was an entirely new experience. It not only outraged Paul but also immediately generated in her a complete sympathy for the speakers.

When word of the suffragettes' unruly reception reached Lodge, he too expressed outrage. Lodge was not inclined to dismiss it as simply a matter of students expressing their sentiments. He considered their behavior a disgrace to the University of Birmingham and immediately announced that Christabel Pankhurst and her colleagues would be invited to speak once again. He also demanded of the students their utmost respect and attention. When the suffragettes returned, Lodge apologized to them publicly for the unacceptable behavior at the first lecture. The three speakers then gave a spirited talk explaining what they were trying to accomplish and why they were adopting tactics that many people considered militant. By the end of the lecture, Paul understood exactly what the militant suffragettes were trying to do. "[Christabel] and the other young women who spoke with her—they were all three young girls—they had anyway one heart and soul convert. . . . That was myself."[12] Although the speakers were not yet fully aware, their persuasiveness had hooked Alice Paul.

As the year at Woodbrook wound down, the students heard from a representative from the central charity organization in London. They needed a Birmingham student to help field questions raised by members of the audience. Because Paul had acquitted herself so well, school officials quickly called on her to answer most of the questions. Immediately after the meeting ended, the London people approached her and asked if she would consider working for their charity organization. She would assist Lucy Gardner, the person in charge of the Dalton district—a particularly poor and therefore needy section of the city. The stipend would be small but manageable for living expenses. Paul reveled in the opportunity to spend another year in Europe and agreed immediately. She hadn't changed her mind about the value of social work. She did want to remain in Europe, but she also persuaded herself that she had not yet come to the end of the row and needed to stay the course, as her mother always advised.

Paul arrived in the Dalton district in the fall of 1907, at which point her immediate supervisor asked if she would be willing to spend a month or so in a neighboring district so that she could be trained in the English style of social work. Given her background at the New York School of Philanthropy and the charity organization society in America, as well as her year at Woodbrook and Birmingham, no one doubted that Paul would do very well in London. A quick in-depth immersion in London charity work would be time well spent. Paul happily complied. By sheer chance, her Dalton coworker also happened to be a fervent member of the Women's Social and Political Union (WSPU), founded by the Pankhursts.

After founding the WSPU, Emmeline Pankhurst and her daughters Christabel and Sylvia spent a few years appealing to British politicians to take up the cause of suffrage. By 1905, they were convinced that those who could effect change were not at all inclined to do so. Sylvia, a lawyer, developed the militant strategy that the organization adopted. It consisted of public demonstrations, civil disobedience, and holding the party in power responsible for failure to give women the vote. Paul's coworker told her that the suffragettes were going to hold a massive procession in London very soon and invited her to participate. Paul wanted in. It was the kind of event that she probably wouldn't have known about until it was all over had it not been for her colleague, because the event was not publicized. The procession impressed Alice. It consisted of several thousand marchers divided into sections according to affiliation. She was especially taken with the speech given by Lady Emmeline Pethick-Lawrence, one of the Pankhursts' most loyal and active supporters and a fierce proponent of votes for women. Participating in such an event helped to further fuel Paul's desire to get involved in the suffrage campaign.

As it turned out, Paul's stay as a charity organization worker would be short-lived. Soon after she returned to the Dalton settlement, she was informed that Lucy Gardner was leaving. Gardner recommended to the charity board only one person to take her place: Alice Paul. Paul felt that she could not, in good conscience, take the position because it was her intention to return to America the following year. But she did agree to remain in place until the board found a suitable candidate and to spend whatever time was required to bring the individual up to speed. It took a few months to get everything sorted out. In the meantime, Paul decided to enroll in the London School of Economics. Her aim was not to pursue a degree but, rather, to take the classes she thought would be most informative. Just as she had done in New York and Birmingham and would later do during the suffrage campaign back home, Paul held on to the conviction that she could contribute more to whatever she was involved in if she took advantage of the relevant academic opportunities that existed. The London School of Economics, in her view, presented just such an opportunity. She took courses ranging from "Unemployment in England" to "Cultural Beliefs Regarding Marriage."

By then, Paul had rented a small apartment through the Quakers' headquarters in London. She'd also met more women who worked with the WSPU. One new friend asked her if she would help sell WSPU newspapers to raise money for the organization. So Paul began making the rounds selling newspapers. Before long she had sent in her application for membership in the WSPU, with the requisite fee of twenty-five cents. Over the next year and a half, Paul traveled throughout England and Scotland. She was willing to do whatever was asked of her, from selling newspapers to introducing speakers at rallies; she even gave speeches herself on soapboxes throughout London. Each new assignment was a step further into the heart and soul of the suffrage movement. In the months preceding her return to America, Paul devoted her time almost entirely to working for suffrage. Eventually, she participated in acts of civil disobedience that ended in her being arrested along with other demonstrators.

In the spring of 1909, Paul received a letter from Emmeline Pankhurst asking if she would participate in a demonstration whose target would be England's prime minister, Lord Herbert Asquith. (Sending letter requests was the usual routine whenever volunteers were being solicited.) This letter, like all requests for volunteers at that time, contained the warning that protesters might be arrested and perhaps imprisoned. Paul later recalled being consumed by nervousness, fear, and self-doubt as she paced back and forth in front of the post office for what seemed like hours before finally mailing her response. Prior to the demonstration, Paul attended a preparatory suffrage meeting. Sylvia Pankhurst and Emmeline Pethick-Lawrence presided. They discussed everything down to the smallest detail. "They told us just what to do, where to meet, what to wear, how to act, everything," Paul said.[13] As predicted, as soon as the protesters started asking questions of Asquith regarding woman suffrage, the police moved in and arrested them. They were taken to a local police precinct where no one seemed to know what to do with the prisoners. The police assigned them to wait in the recreation room. It was then that she met fellow-American Lucy Burns, who would become Paul's closest colleague in the American suffrage campaign. From across the room, Paul noticed the American-flag lapel pin worn by Burns. She approached her and they introduced one another. Then, sitting on the only place available—atop a billiard table—they exchanged experiences and their views of both the English and the American suffrage campaigns. They both agreed that, at the moment, English women were waging the battle for women everywhere. From then on, Paul and Burns worked closely together for the WSPU. They were polar opposites in looks, with Burns's striking red hair, piercing blue eyes, robust build, and brash mannerisms contrasting with Paul's quiet demeanor, slight build, and brown hair. Yet the two had much in common. Burns's father, like Alice's, was a banker and a liberal who believed in educating his daughters as well as his sons. Lucy was sent to the prestigious Packer Institute in Brooklyn and then went on to Vassar, graduating in 1902. She had come to Berlin to study German at Baden

University with the intention of pursuing an academic career. And her family, like Alice's, supported her financially from her days as a student in Europe through the American suffrage campaign. Upon visiting England, she was impressed with the battle being waged for woman suffrage and immediately suspended her studies in Berlin to work with the WSPU.

Bail for all of the suffrage prisoners was posted by Pethick-Lawrence's husband. He went to each detainee, telling them he would post bail but only on the condition that they return to court on the appointed day. Paul had already booked her passage home, and her departure date was scheduled before the court date. She readily postponed the trip home in order to fulfill her obligation. Ultimately, all charges against the demonstrators were dismissed.

Shortly after her first arrest, Paul volunteered to participate in another protest in Bermondsey—this time, to take on the chancellor of the exchequer, Lloyd George. (The chancellor of the exchequer is the equivalent of the treasury secretary in American politics.) The Pankhursts asked Paul to be one of the speakers on behalf of suffrage. She had never considered herself a good public speaker but agreed nevertheless to do it. As soon as she rose to speak, the police swooped in and arrested her once again. On this occasion, there was no bail set for the prisoners and she, along with several colleagues, spent two weeks in jail. In August, Paul and Burns agreed to yet another series of demonstrations—this time, in Scotland. They traveled with Emmeline Pankhurst in her car, from London to Scotland, helping to organize demonstrations in Edinburgh, Berwick-on-Tweed, Dundee, and Glasgow. Various members of the British government—including Winston Churchill, still a minor politician at that time—were scheduled to give speeches at those locations. In Edinburgh, Berwick-on-Tweed, and Dundee, the protesters were arrested but no charges were filed against them.

The Glasgow protest was a different story. Paul, Burns, Adela Pankhurst (the youngest of the Pankhurst daughters), and Margaret Smith, who was the niece of the Lord Mayor of Glasgow, were all involved. Burns and Smith were given tickets to the audience section for a featured speech. Paul and Pankhurst were instructed to make their way up to the rooftop of the hall and wait until the government speaker began. At that point, they were to interrupt his speech and start calling out questions. For several hours, they remained in place on the roof, despite a driving rain and periodic searches by the police. Once the meeting was interrupted, police officers swarmed the building, trying to arrest the demonstrators. But the demonstrators who had gathered outside the hall were not inclined to let that happen. Time and again, they helped the women escape the clutches of the police. Nevertheless, Paul, Burns, Pankhurst, and Smith were eventually caught and arrested. Although there was a bail hearing—held behind closed doors so the prisoners were uninformed—and a warrant issued for their detention for failure to pay their bail, the incident closed out without any further legal action.

Back in London, a demonstration against the Lord Mayor of London in November 1909 landed Paul in Holloway Jail for several weeks. Once again, Paul and Burns had been working together. Burns was in the ticketed audience while Paul climbed to the rafters. Disguised as a cleaning woman, she made her way early in the morning into the hall where the Lord Mayor was scheduled to speak. And once again, the police, determined not to let anyone disturb the meeting, searched periodically for intruders. At one point, a police officer came so close to Paul that he unwittingly touched the top of her head. Once she began shouting out questions, she was immediately arrested.

No one took lightly the ordeal of imprisonment, regardless of the circumstances. Suffrage prisoners were routinely placed in solitary confinement. They saw no one; they spoke to no one; they had nothing to occupy their time—not even reading material. Confinement in Holloway Jail was particularly stressful because all of the volunteers had agreed beforehand to go on hunger strikes if arrested and denied political prisoner status. This policy had initially been employed in July 1909, but for Paul, Holloway was her first experience of it. Forced feeding was every bit as invasive and painful as it sounds. Prisoners were held down by several guards so that the victim could not move. A long plastic tube with a funnel on one end was inserted through the prisoner's nostrils and pushed down through the esophagus into the stomach. If the person carrying out the procedure was a doctor or had some medical training, there was a somewhat lower chance that the tube might accidentally be inserted into the lungs or cause damage to the esophagus. In whatever way it was done, the procedure involved considerable pain. A liquid, generally consisting of some combination of milk, raw eggs, and sometime even alcohol, was poured into the funnel. But however dismissive authorities were regarding the dangers of forced feeding, the procedure really constituted little more than a form of torture. It took a horrible toll on everyone who experienced it, including Paul. By the time of her release from Holloway sometime in December 1909, she looked as physically debilitated as she undoubtedly felt. Throughout her WSPU activities, Paul kept her mother informed. But though she wrote pages and pages describing the protests and the prisons, Paul made every effort to shield Tacie from her own dangerous undertakings. She wrote about everything she observed without placing herself in the thick of things. On her release from prison Paul could have returned to her small apartment in Clerkenwell, but she chose instead to accept the invitation of a Jewish family, active in the movement, to stay at their home for as long as she wanted. By now holding both Paul and Burns in the highest regard, Emmeline Pankhurst asked them if they would consider staying on and working with the WSPU as paid organizers—a job that few people were ever offered. Lucy immediately accepted the offer and remained in London. But Paul wanted to return home and in January 1910, after a little more than two years in Europe, she boarded a ship bound for New York.

2

History, Politics, and Strategy

When Alice Paul returned home from England in 1910, she had just turned twenty-five. She had spent two pivotal years in England that forever changed her life. Although she had consistently downplayed the health consequences of imprisonment and forced feeding, friends and family were shocked at her appearance when she returned to Philadelphia. Paul's friend from the Swarthmore days, Mabel Vernon, remembered her as very athletic. To Vernon, the contrast was alarming. Paul appeared wraithlike and on the verge of collapse.

After several months recuperating in Moorestown and Philadelphia, Paul appeared to be on the mend. And though she rarely gave in to family and friends who urged her to take time off for her health's sake, for the rest of her life opportunistic diseases such as colds and flu sapped her energy and sometimes required hospitalization. Nothing could stop her or even slow her down: such was her determination to help achieve woman suffrage through a constitutional amendment.

Although the first women's rights convention held in 1848 in Seneca Falls, New York, had included woman suffrage as a goal, it didn't become a real issue until after the Civil War. In 1869, two suffrage organizations with distinctly different strategic positions were founded. In May of that year, Susan B. Anthony and Elizabeth Cady Stanton—both of whom had long ago established their reputations as women's rights activists—founded the National Woman Suffrage Association (NWSA). Anthony, a Quaker from Rochester, New York, met Stanton in 1851, three years after Stanton and Lucretia Mott organized the Seneca Falls convention. Stanton, a brilliant thinker and writer, wrote volumes on women's rights and religion. Married to a minister and the mother of seven children, she was unable to spend extensive periods of time away from home. But she wrote the speeches and broadsides with which Anthony—with no family ties to keep her bound to Rochester—toured the country, talking to audiences small and large. For more than fifty years, they worked together tirelessly to advance the cause of women. From the start, the NWSA emphasized the necessity to secure an amendment to the United States Constitution that would guarantee to women the right to vote. With Stanton as president of the NWSA and Anthony serving first on the executive committee and then as vice president, 118 women immediately signed on as members. Many of the original signers, such as Lucretia Mott, were noted feminists and veterans of equal rights and the abolitionist movement. As president, Stanton did not mask her radical feminist views, the most controversial of which were her belief in gender equality and her perspective on marriage and religion. Stanton believed passionately that women should maintain their names and their identities and have an equal right on decisions governing children, money, and marital property. As for religion, Stanton didn't have a lot of use for organized religion, even though her husband was a minister. She believed that religious organizations held women back and that they discriminated against women, denying them an equal footing in society. Most of Stanton's views on these issues may seem fairly mild today, but they were clearly not the views of the majority of American women in her day. In general, women fell into one of four groups, ranging from largest to smallest: those who were content to let their fathers, brothers, husbands, and sons determine political and social interests for women; those who believed that women should have voting rights but were not in favor of usurping the male-head-of-household arrangement; those who wanted to see the kind of changes that Stanton advocated; and, finally, those in certain western states who already had state voting rights because their value on the frontier, as it pushed further and further west, could not be ignored or dismissed by men in the states and territories they were helping to build up. To promote the NWSA, Anthony—who had become known far and wide as "Aunt Susan"—undertook a series of cross-country lecture tours, discussions, and rallies. They were held with the intent of igniting the still-fledgling women's rights movement. NWSA chapters soon sprang up, particularly in the eastern and midwestern United States.

A few months later, in Cleveland, Ohio, Lucy Stone founded the American Woman Suffrage Association (AWSA). Stone also was a veteran of the abolitionist movement. But she disagreed with the Stanton and Anthony agenda. Stone believed that their views on gender equality and the pursuit of a constitutional amendment for suffrage were far too radical. By no means could Stone be labeled a conservative. Having fought as long and as hard as she did for the abolition of slavery, she had been painted with the same "radical thinker" brush. Stone's biggest fear was that, by pushing for women's rights, NWSA might be jeopardizing the rights of former slaves as well as universal male suffrage. If NWSA kept pushing for voting rights before universal male suffrage could be ratified, an entirely new can of worms would be opened. Specifically, with both voting rights for women and universal male suffrage on the table, voting rights for former female slaves would also have to be considered. Sorting out the ramifications of all three issues would, in Stone's view, jeopardize universal male suffrage at the very least. The AWSA preferred to defer the woman suffrage issue until after African-American males were enfranchised. Stone and her organization also favored declaring woman suffrage a states' rights issue. It would be up to the states to change their own constitutions if they wanted woman suffrage. Like the NWSA, the AWSA initiated an extensive speaking campaign to attract support. The AWSA claimed to represent the views of the majority of American women, but the hub of their active support remained fixed in New England and consisted primarily of former abolitionists. The NWSA, on the other hand, far outstripped the AWSA in its ability to attract members and money. An insight into what American women really thought, however, could be gleaned from the fate of the two organization's publications. The NWSA's publication, appropriately called *Revolution,* enjoyed a much shorter existence than the AWSA publication, *The Woman's Journal.* The latter attracted a wide audience and became one of the most influential publications of the nineteenth-century women's movement. If the majority of American women were not ready to sign on in support of the AWSA, they were, in a way, voting with their pocketbooks. And if the majority of women favored the states' rights approach, the woman suffrage advocates faced an uphill battle. Southern women especially had a stake in states' rights. Changing state constitutions as a way to keep African-American women from being enfranchised appealed to southerners. A federal constitutional amendment would undoubtedly have to be more inclusive in nature. Southerners feared that would be the case and they didn't like it.

Between 1868 and 1890, several things were happening that discouraged hopes for a federal amendment. For the first time an amendment to the United States Constitution specifically defined representative apportionment to be a function of the number of a state's *male* inhabitants. The Fourteenth Amendment (ratified in 1868) intended to define civil rights to include former male slaves, while the Fifteenth Amendment (ratified in 1870) ensured suffrage rights for former slaves. Within the two amendments there was more than enough wiggle room for the courts to interpret what rights were bestowed by virtue of citizenship status and whether or not citizenship status automatically carried with it the right to suffrage. In 1875, when NWSA officer Virginia Minor sued the registrar of voters, Reese Happersett, in St. Louis, Missouri, for violating her civil rights by denying her the right to register to vote, the Supreme Court dealt yet another crushing blow to women suffragists. In the case of *Minor v. Happersett* (1875), the Court ruled that the United States Constitution did not confer the right of suffrage on anyone. It paid minimal lip service to the letter and intent of the Constitution that dealt with voting rights (Article I and the Fifteenth Amendment). By that feat of gymnastics, the Court could declare that citizenship and suffrage were not automatically linked.

These events met with approval by most people because the Supreme Court had made its ruling. Stanton and Anthony were now quickly losing ground within suffrage circles. They had steadfastly argued that women were entitled to vote by virtue of their citizen status. They argued as well that a federal amendment was the surest and fastest route to woman suffrage. Lucy Stone, despite ratification of the Fifteenth Amendment, continued to advocate for the states' rights approach to granting woman suffrage. The NWSA arguments were being ignored. With voting rights for male former slaves ensured, the more moderate suffragists began to champion women as society's moral balance. If given the opportunity, women would, the argument went, act as the moral balance of power, using the vote to correct societal ills. This argument appealed to women and opened the door to a variety of issues that women had long supported, including temperance, urban reform, and protective legislation for women and children.

Strategically, this shift in the rationale for woman suffrage proved to be beneficial for its moderate advocates. But on principle it was counterproductive to real equality. Once women gave up their claim to suffrage as their constitutional right as full and equal citizens, no more and no less, it was difficult to maintain that men and women were, in fact, equal. At the time, the majority of American women did not take issue with the moderate argument. They forged ahead, secure in the belief that they would indeed create a better society once they could convince state legislatures that they had moral right on their side. Taking the high ground appealed to state legislators and their male constituents as well, particularly since changing state constitutions was neither easy nor— more importantly—desirable. Removing equal rights as the rationale for enabling female suffrage left legislators throughout the country with an obvious excuse for not granting women the vote. Woman suffrage opponents could trot out the old argument that male voters were every bit as invested in correcting the ills of society and would continue to vote in the best interests of all citizens. And so-inclined legislators could claim that they were only following the wishes of their constituents. Years later, this would be exactly the kind of subterfuge that Alice Paul resolved to defeat.

By 1890, the trend toward unification of the two rival suffrage organizations had garnered enough support to proceed. Leaders of the two groups announced the formation of the National American Woman Suffrage Association (NAWSA). The merger had strong credibility because the daughters of the original founders were both in favor of the move. Harriot Stanton Blatch (daughter of Elizabeth Cady Stanton) and Alice Stone Blackwell (daughter of Lucy Stone) both lobbied their constituents to support the merger. The elder Stanton had to be won over to the merger because of her well-founded suspicions that the moderates were not at all committed to a federal suffrage amendment. But the advances made by women in the post–Civil War decades had wrought changes that made a merger desirable for mainstream suffragists.

By 1890, women outnumbered men in high schools and attended the majority of colleges. Nearly one-third of all college students and a full one-third of all professional workers—including doctors, lawyers, and teachers—were women. Women's clubs had sprung up in nearly every sizable community in the country. The clubs were organized for a variety of reasons including civic reform, literary discussion, education, and more locally inspired interests such as gardening and quilting. The women's club movement united under the banner of the General Federation of Women's Clubs and immediately created a national organization that included thousands of members. The Women's Christian Temperance Union also entered its most powerful phase. It had been organized years before and grew steadily, though slowly, over time. Temperance advocates sought to outlaw the public sale and consumption of alcohol because they considered alcohol a detriment to progressive growth and family stability. Suffrage, no longer an isolated vehicle for change, was now part of a larger women's movement.

Stanton and Anthony respectively served as the first and second presidents of the new organization, more out of sentiment than as a reflection of members' willingness to follow their lead. Stanton remained president until 1902, when she resigned and turned to the task of finishing the *Woman's Bible*. The book, a radical critique of organized religion, was an annotated exposition of the standard Bible. Stanton argued that the language and interpretation of the Bible's authors had aided in keeping women oppressed for centuries. As yet another indication of her waning influence, the NAWSA leadership agreed to disassociate the organization from the *Woman's Bible*. The condemnation, spearheaded by Anna Howard Shaw, announced that in NAWSA's view, the *Woman's Bible* was far too radical. Shaw, a physician and the first female Methodist minister in the United States, had always considered Susan B. Anthony her mentor. Anthony succeeded Stanton as president of NAWSA when her longtime friend and suffrage strategist stepped down. But despite Anthony's efforts to dissuade the NAWSA executive committee from condemning Stanton's work, Shaw refused to back down.

In the last years of her presidency of NAWSA (1892–1900), and her life (d.1906), Anthony became increasingly bitter over the direction the suffrage movement was taking. More and more, the rhetoric of the movement was taking on a socially conservative tone. In an effort to attract more southern women to their cause, NAWSA began adopting a more nativist slant in its resolutions and speeches. NAWSA representatives began advocating a toning down of civil rights. They also favored educational requirements for exercising the right to vote and, equally distressing, immigration restrictions. In effect, the national NAWSA organization supported Jim Crow laws enacted in southern states that continued to discriminate against former slaves by enforcing segregation and establishing barriers to their right to vote. The new waves of immigrants also struck a sour note with many women. Male immigrants, they argued, were fast-tracked to voting rights once they became citizens, whereas native-born women still could not vote except in a handful of mostly western states. In both instances—race and immigration—supporting voting legislation intended to be exclusionary fed into NAWSA's nativism.

Nothing seemed more counterproductive to Anthony than NAWSA's willingness to abandon a federal suffrage amendment. To be sure, NAWSA paid lip service to a federal amendment, but almost all of its resources went into the state campaigns. Despite the meager results, the new NAWSA leadership had convinced itself that changing state constitutions, one by one, represented the best way to victory. Even though states sometimes had an impossibly difficult method of bringing about constitutional change, NAWSA was not deterred. For example, some states required that a referendum for a constitutional amendment had to be preceded by a three-quarters legislative margin authorizing voters to vote on the proposed amendment. So even if the legislature agreed to bring the proposal to a vote, and even if legislators voted to allow the referendum on the ballot, yet another campaign had to be undertaken to persuade the male voters to pass the amendment.

Adding to the frustration of hundreds of costly, time-consuming, and almost predictably failed state campaigns, NAWSA leaders came up with yet another ill-advised move. Anthony had to stand by help-lessly as NAWSA's annual conventions were moved out of Washington, DC, in favor of remote locations far removed from the seat of national politics. Almost as bad, NAWSA moved its headquarters from Washington to Warren, Ohio. (The organization's treasurer, a resident of Warren, agreed to remain in office if and only if the NAWSA headquarters was moved to her hometown.) All the indicators pointed to a lack of any real commitment to either a federal amendment or maintenance of pres-sure on politicians to make suffrage a national issue. Aging rapidly and with increasingly less ability to influence events, Anthony finally retired after her eightieth birthday. She was dismayed beyond words at the di-rection in which the women's movement was going. Yet, after having devoted more than fifty years of her life to the cause, in her heart of hearts Anthony believed until the day she died that failure was impos-sible. Sadly for Susan B. Anthony, the one person who could have as-sured her faith in the future— Alice Paul—had not yet made her own appearance on the national stage, dedicated to the federal woman suf-frage amendment that Aunt Susan had given her life to.

Longtime activist Carrie Chapman Catt served as NAWSA's new president from 1900 until 1904, when family illness caused her to with-draw temporarily. Anna Howard Shaw, the minister with fiery oratori-cal skills, succeeded Catt. Both Catt and Shaw were far more moderate in their tactics and goals than either Anthony or Stanton had been. For her part, Shaw became the cheerleader for state-by-state constitutional change, even though four hundred campaigns had yielded only a hand-ful of victories. As late as 1912, there were only nine suffrage states, al-most all in the Far West. These included Wyoming (1890), Colorado (1893), Utah and Idaho (1896), Washington (1910), California (1911), and Oregon, Arizona, and Kansas (1912).

To make matters worse, the NAWSA leadership either did not fully understand or chose to disregard their new advantage in the states where women had won the right to vote. NAWSA leaders could have passed along the winning playbooks from the successful state campaigns. In-stead, they offered little real direction, leaving the logistics and strategy to the in-state suffrage leaders. And, astonishingly, the national organiza-tion never tried to capitalize on the newly enfranchised women voters in states where the campaigns succeeded. Once a state was in the suffrage column, NAWSA moved its focus to the next state campaign. There was no effort to put pressure on elected officials in the suffrage states to benefit the unenfranchised women in the majority of states. As Paul would soon make clear, organizing the voting women to put pressure on politicians in nonsuffrage states by campaigning against them in elections would become an effective strategy to gather support for the federal amendment. Facing their women-voter constituents would leave the politicians with one option: appeal to fellow party members in other states to support suffrage to avoid risking the loss of their seats and possibly political control to the opposition party. At the same time, opposition-party politicians would be only too happy to support woman suffrage in order to get the support of women voters.

More than twenty years after NAWSA organized, and with so few victories, suffragists once again were experiencing frustration. They had been fighting this battle for the vote for over half a century. Most of the original combatants had long since passed on, having never experienced their right to vote. How much longer would it take to win the vote for all women? Most women remained loyal to NAWSA and its strategy, but there were some suffragists who looked toward a more aggressive approach. Many of the early American converts to so-called militant suffragism were women who had spent time in England in the latter part of the nineteenth century and admired the Pankhursts. Witnessing firsthand the activities of the British suffragettes (the term *suffragette* was used exclusively by British women, while Americans preferred *suffragist*) had a profound influence on the Americans. Their views of the Pankhursts were unhampered by the critical filter of the British government and a frequently unsympathetic press.

Among those who would take an active role in the suffrage campaign were Harriot Stanton Blatch, who lived just outside of London for twenty years and worked with the Pankhursts, and historian Mary Ritter Beard, who accompanied her husband Charles Austin Beard to England in 1900. Beard, too, went to work with the Pankhursts. Alva Belmont, who would later become a staunch financial supporter of Alice Paul and the National Woman's Party, readily embraced militant suffragism. Belmont had endured extremely negative press after her divorce from one wealthy socialite and her marriage a year later to another. Belmont came into contact with Emmeline Pankhurst and "her great army." Her admiration for the Pankhursts and public reaction at home to her divorce became the catalysts for transforming Belmont from an insulated society hostess into an ardent feminist. "Yes, I am militant and I glory in it," she boasted to a friend, adding that she felt only pity for those who wanted "the old-fashioned woman you have cowed into a submissive nonentity."[1]

Elizabeth Robins, an American writer and actress, met the Pankhursts and served on the board of the Women's Social and Political Union. In 1907, Robins wrote a popular play titled *Votes for Women* as well as a successful novel, *The Convert.* Both works helped to persuade countless others of the justness of the cause. Like Mary Beard, Robins believed that the concerns and welfare of working-class women were an integral concern of the suffrage movement. Her sister-in-law, Margaret Drier Robins, was head of the Women's Trade Union League back in America.

When journalist and writer Inez Haynes Irwin heard about the Pankhursts and their militant campaign, her reaction was visceral: "When in England, the first militant of Mrs. Pankhurst's forces threw her first stone, my heart went with it. . . . At last the traditions of female patience . . . had gone by the board. Women were using the tactics that, through all the ages, men had used; the only tactics that were sure to bring results: rebellion and violence."[2] College students such as Sara Bard Field eagerly began organizing other college students to join the cause, thus gaining experience that would prove invaluable a short time later. Likewise the Houghton sisters, Katherine Houghton Hepburn of Connecticut (the mother of actress Katherine Hepburn) and Edith Houghton Hooker of Baltimore, Maryland, were quick to express their admiration when they heard Emmeline Pankhurst speak for the first time in Hartford in 1911. For Katherine, the speech became a seminal event, "one of the most remarkable speeches I have ever heard." She pointed to it as the catalyst for her involvement in the suffrage movement and, specifically, her support for militant feminism: "I remember so well [that this was] the first time I even thought of suffrage as something I must work for myself."[3] Although they constituted a small nucleus of activists on behalf of a more aggressive suffrage movement in America, these women and others helped to persuade countless American suffragists who were growing increasingly tired of deferred success and incremental gains. All that was required for the militant nucleus was one person who could step forward with a plan and see that plan through to a successful conclusion. That person would be Alice Paul.

During her last few months in England, Paul did everything she could to shield her mother from the dangerous activities she was involved in. But too many newspaper articles focused on the young American working hand-in-glove with the Pankhursts. The news reports detailed the dangers of being in the thick of the demonstrations and the horrors of prison and forced feeding. An Associated Press correspondent recognized how newsworthy Paul's experiences were and relayed articles back home. The cause itself didn't interest most of the journalists. With stories and newspapers to sell, these journalists focused more on the lurid details of what the suffragette prisoners went through in prison. When Paul left England to return home, she expressed the hope that she would never have to face reporters again—though it is doubtful that she truly wanted this to be the case, since publicity would be such an integral part of getting the suffrage issue fixed in the minds of politicians and the public. In any case, she was hardly off the ship when she gave her first press interview. Asked about her prison ordeal and details of forced feeding, in one of her few public acknowledgments, Paul readily confirmed the details reported in European newspapers. Yes, she was held down by prison officials and sometimes tied down, making the sheer act of breathing extremely difficult. Yes, having tubes inserted through her nostrils, a tortuously painful ordeal, resulted in violent physical reactions, illness, and crying out. Yes, two or more attempts were sometimes required to insert the tubes, making the ordeal infinitely more painful and more dangerous. And, yes, without hesitation she would undergo it again if it ever became necessary. If Mrs. Paul had previously been unaware of what her daughter went through in England, that was no longer the case. But despite the physical dangers involved, Tacie Paul never failed to support Alice.

Following through on her determination to finish her degree, Paul returned to the University of Pennsylvania in the fall of 1910. She spent several months completing her PhD thesis, titled "Towards Equality: The Legal Status of Women in Pennsylvania." She frequently interrupted her work to respond to requests to speak from suffrage organizations in Pennsylvania and nearby states. (The newspaper articles about her experiences with the Pankhursts had made her a name in suffrage circles.) After her speech before the members of NAWSA's Philadelphia branch, the branch president took Paul aside and invited her to serve on their board. She explained quite frankly that they had waited until after her speech to extend the invitation because "we didn't know who you were or what sort of person you were or whether you were wild and fanatical or what you might be."[4] Apparently, Paul passed their test.

Harriot Stanton Blatch invited Paul to speak at New York City's Cooper Union, the free university founded to provide higher education for the city's poor women and children. Blatch and Paul had struck up a friendship of sorts when Alice lived in England. Paul accepted the invitation and spoke to a full house at Cooper Union. Whereas questions from the audience focused on the Pankhursts and their tactics, as well as on the suffrage issue in general, the press once again sought out the details concerning forced feedings. Despite the often graphic descriptions of these ordeals, newspaper sales did quite well because editors continued to accept their reporters' accounts featuring the grisly details. Paul, not one to let herself be intimidated by anyone, least of all the press, used the reporters much more effectively than they thought they were using her. She was quoted—in detail—in news stories regarding her experiences, because she chose to provide the information. Publicity, one of the cornerstones of the tactics she had learned in England, became pure gold for the suffrage cause. Everyone who read the stories knew where Alice Paul stood regarding the Pankhurst campaigns. Emmeline Pankhurst, while on a speaking tour in America in 1909, had included words of praise for "the young American girl" who was doing so much on behalf of suffrage and who, at that very moment, was serving a prison sentence in Holloway Jail in London. Pankhurst challenged her audiences. Paul, Emmeline told them, "is a great object lesson to American women. . . . What are you American women going to do about it?"[5]

Emmeline's challenge did not go unheeded. Though she never lost her anxiety regarding public speaking, Paul proved to be a thoughtful, low-keyed, sincere, and incredibly effective lecturer. Those who attended her lectures formed extremely positive impressions of the slight young Quaker who spoke in such a quiet manner while still conveying the passion she felt for the cause. None could accuse her of being the raving fanatic that much of the British press claimed she was.

Paul defended the Pankhursts and their brand of militancy without hesitation. When questioned by a gathering of Moorestown Quakers who had invited her to discuss her own role in militancy (something most Quakers opposed on principle), she responded honestly and without apology. "I attach no particular sanctity to a twenty-five-cent window pane," she said, adding that she had broken forty-eight windows herself "because it is a means to an end."[6] Far from being defensive about her so-called violent protests, Paul suggested that Quakers, at least in America, had abandoned their traditional democratic foundation—especially, it seemed to her, where women were concerned. "It seems indeed a far cry from the aggressive vigor with which the early Friends challenged the evils of their time."[7] She compared the suffragettes to American abolitionists, a cause that Quakers had actively supported not so long ago. Paul couldn't have asked for any better response to her talks at Cooper Union or to those she addressed to the Quaker groups back home in Moorestown. When NAWSA invited her to speak at the annual convention to be held in Washington in April 1910, she accepted without hesitation.

The issue of militancy would continue to be a negative one for the majority of American suffragists, at least in the short term. And NAWSA would carry their opposition to Paul's tactics throughout the suffrage campaign. By today's standards, militancy in the suffrage campaign would almost certainly not be considered violent or disturbing. For one thing, even the mildly violent action of breaking windows was something Paul had done herself. But she did not advocate that type of action for the American struggle. Militancy consisted primarily of holding peaceful demonstrations, campaigning against political parties, sending organizers to nonsuffrage states, and generating as much publicity for the cause as was possible. Nevertheless, in 1910 these tactics were considered unseemly to most observers. The English suffragettes had been using them for several years, which explained why the Pankhursts were looked upon with suspicion by many Americans. For Paul, who had thoroughly analyzed the American movement, the strategy could work effectively, especially the tactic of holding the party in power responsible for failure to pass a federal amendment.

By the time she arrived in Washington, Paul had become a household name in American suffrage circles. Although she was not considered a main speaker at the convention, the publicity that followed her warranted the invitation because of the widespread interest in what she had to say. People wanted to hear from Alice Paul. For NAWSA's leaders, however, the real excitement surrounding the convention focused on the much-anticipated appearance by President William Howard Taft, who had agreed to speak to the delegates. It would be the first time a sitting president of the United States would do so. Taft did not favor woman suffrage and had made that clear to anyone who asked. But NAWSA president Anna Howard Shaw believed that just his presence at the convention would give the cause a big boost in the eyes of the public. She hoped, as well, that the president's presence would help to quell the frustration many women expressed over the snail's pace that characterized the women's movement. Regardless of what Shaw anticipated or hoped for, Taft's appearance would be a mixed bag at best.

Angry objections from members of his administration inundated Taft prior to the convention. From his secretary of state on down, Taft's men opposed woman suffrage and made every effort to get him to withdraw from the speaking engagement. Appearing would imply that he favored woman suffrage. Taft refused to cancel his speaking commitment, which he considered part of his duties as president of the United States. He assured his advisers that he had no intention of saying anything that could be construed as support for the cause.

After a glowing introduction by Shaw, whose own speech Taft interrupted when he arrived unfashionably late, the president proceeded to address the stunned delegates in both an insulting and condescending fashion. He compared women to Hottentots, noting that while he had once favored woman suffrage in his teen years, he had since realized that the notion that "Hottentots or any other uneducated, altogether unintelligent class fitted for self-government at once or to take part in government is a theory that I wholly dissent from." If that were not clear enough, he went on to say that women in general had to be denied the right to vote because of the possibility that the less desirable among them might actually vote while the more intelligent among them might choose not to vote. The auditorium erupted into almost universal hissing as the delegates digested what Taft was saying. The president then proceeded to chide his audience for their lack of self-control. In his view, the audience reaction simply confirmed for Taft, and presumably any other "right-thinking" individual, why women should not have the right to vote. He then shook hands with Shaw and made his departure from the hall, either unaware of how insulting he had been to the delegates or, more likely, simply not concerned with their response.[8]

Shaw's behavior following the speech may have been as surprising to the delegates as were Taft's insulting words. Shaw took the delegates to task for their show of rudeness to the president. She said nothing about Taft's rudeness to the delegates and their cause. Instead, she instructed the NAWSA secretary to immediately draft a letter of apology to Taft. The letter expressed NAWSA's "great sorrow that anyone present, either a member or an outsider, should have interrupted [Taft's] address by an expression of personal feelings."[9] The letter also contained a NAWSA resolution thanking Taft for his historic appearance. If ever anyone questioned the frustration of women with the suffrage path that American women had taken, they had only to look to Anna Howard Shaw's incredible response to Taft's belittling and insulting speech.

Owing to the good fortune of the speaking schedule, Paul addressed the delegates immediately following the Taft debacle. The audience, still smarting from his inappropriate remarks as well as Shaw's inopportune response—not only calling for an official apology to the President but characterizing the delegates' outburst as one of her "saddest hours"—were ready for Paul. Her main message that day struck a chord as she praised the suffragettes and their activism. They were, she said, "at the storm center of our movement." She went on to say that the English women were fighting the battle for women the world over and were doing so by using new and innovative tactics. "The essence of the campaign of the suffragettes," Paul noted, "is opposition to the government. . . . It is not a war of women against men, for the men are helping loyally, but a war of women and men together against the politicians."[10]

The audience definitely wanted to let the NAWSA leadership know how they felt, especially in light of Shaw's rebuke. At the same time, the desire for more aggressive action was both genuine and obvious. Not all who heard and applauded Paul's remarks were ready to embrace a more militant strategy, but many were now much more sympathetic to the Pankhurst response to government intransigence. Indeed, the delegates gave Paul high marks for her talk. Thanks to the absurdly combined actions of Taft and Shaw, and Paul's far more positive speech, within a short time receptiveness to the message of militancy increased dramatically. "I went to a [suffrage] meeting," Katherine Houghton Hepburn later recalled, "in a theater which seated 1,620 people. There were only about 200 people in the audience. . . . Later on, after they had begun their militant tactics, we had meetings for Mrs. Pankhurst at the same theater—filled the theater and turned away hundreds of people."[11]

Many Americans, and most suffragists, still believed that the American condition was so different from the English one that militancy would not be necessary. Part of the resistance to more aggressive tactics was reflected in the conservatism that accompanied suffrage victories, as infrequent as they were. Moreover, most suffragists still believed that Americans were much more reasonable and willing to enter into good-faith discussions of the merits of the issue. Pro-suffrage males warned suffragists against resorting to militant tactics, which they believed would jeopardize their cause. "The sex," intoned Frederick Sullens, editor of the *Jackson* (Mississippi) *Daily News,* "must show a capacity for self-government. The cause is a great one but it does not require martyrs. . . . While we may cherish a secret admiration for the dauntlessness and the mettle of the woman who declares that she will starve in prison, at the same time clear reason leads us to doubt the logic and effectiveness of such tactics."[12] Sullens probably saw no problem with Taft's Hottentot remarks, but though Paul's Washington audience was overwhelmingly angry over the insult, most Americans still subscribed to the Taft-Sullens philosophy. The idea of militancy may have generated sympathy among audience members who heard Taft and Paul speak, and militancy may have taken an upturn among the more frustrated suffragists, but most American women were decidedly not interested in signing on to that strategy yet.

For Paul, however, the path she would subsequently take became clearer and clearer. Throughout the remainder of 1910 and well into 1911, she continued working on her thesis, still committed to finishing the degree. She chose to spend her nonacademic time helping to organize Pennsylvania on behalf of suffrage. At the same time, she continued to turn down most invitations to work with different suffrage groups. NAWSA's executive committee member from Pennsylvania, besides placing Paul on the state executive board, finally persuaded her to organize a street campaign. The Philadelphia street campaign, hardly a militant one, did mimic in important ways what Paul had learned so well in Britain: holding impromptu street rallies at strategic locations, handing out leaflets to anyone who would take one, and enlisting speakers. At first, Paul and Lucy Burns—who had returned to America during that summer of 1911—did most of the speaking. Passersby who stopped to listen may not immediately have known who Paul and Burns were, but they soon found out and many wanted to hear what the two women had to say. At the same time, Paul knew that others would have to start speaking out lest their cause become basically a limited two-woman show. Her chief lieutenant at that time was Caroline Katzenstein, a member of the Philadelphia NAWSA chapter. Caroline, a great admirer of Paul and an ardent suffragist, had never done anything remotely similar to what Paul and Burns were doing now. In the early days of the street rallies, Caroline feared that they were all going to be arrested by the first policeman to come their way. But she passed out leaflets and did whatever she was asked. When Paul asked her to speak at one of the rallies, a dismayed Caroline objected. She had *never* spoken publicly—unless occasional comments at NAWSA meetings counted. When she told Paul that she couldn't possibly speak, Alice took another page from her Pankhurst training. All Caroline had to do, Paul assured her, was introduce Alice to the crowd. Paul herself had been just as reluctant to speak publicly when the WSPU made its first request. So she wouldn't take "no" for an answer from Caroline. Putting her nervousness aside, Caroline acquiesced. Before long, as Paul intended, she was speaking regularly, helping to spread the suffrage cause.

Paul's most ambitious rally during that period would take place in Independence Square. The location resonated with her. Independence

Square had been dedicated to the Founding Fathers' struggle for independence. In addition to speaking platforms, tableaux commemorating the women's movement and the struggle for suffrage were designed to draw crowds. Suffragist Inez Milholland volunteered to appear at the rally astride her now-trademark white horse. Inez, riding into the arena in costume, never failed to stir the crowd. She had made a name for herself when, as a Vassar student, she was denied permission to stage a rally on campus—and, undaunted, proceeded to jump a low wall that marked the Vassar boundary and held her rally there. Before long she was joined by a host of students who also chose to jump the wall. The Independence Square rally attracted some two thousand people, more than had ever before gathered to hear about woman suffrage in Philadelphia.

Alice Paul had long since proved herself an excellent organizer in England. When she was about to leave for home, Christabel Pankhurst had a long conversation with her, regarding how highly regarded she was by all of the Pankhursts. Christabel also spent a good bit of time trying to persuade her to stay on in England, but as a paid volunteer. Though Paul declined the invitation, her stature among English suffragettes did not diminish. Now, American suffragists were beginning to understand only too well why English suffragettes held Paul in such high esteem: her capacity for planning and execution were flawless.

With Burns back in the United States, and Paul's thesis finally behind her, the two women were ready to tackle the American suffrage movement. They discussed the important elements involved in mobilizing suffragists on behalf of a federal amendment, while also making the movement a national issue in the eyes of politicians and the public. The road ahead would not be an easy one. But it could be considerably more effective and faster than the current state-by-state approach. Their main strategy was to hold the party in power responsible for the fate of a federal woman suffrage amendment—a tactic they firmly believed would make even more sense in America, given the political structure there, than it did in England. With six full suffrage states and 2 million women voters, there already existed a ready-made voting bloc with the potential for influencing state and national elections. One initial objection concerned the effectiveness of blaming all members of the party currently in power for failure to enact a federal amendment. Critics feared that pro-suffrage politicians from the full-suffrage states might be alienated from the cause if they were members of the majority party. Paul never considered this a real impediment to their strategy, but she *did* have to answer the critics. Quite simply, she pointed out that—by virtue of having been elected—all elected members of Congress, as well as the governors from the suffrage states, *had* to be pro-suffrage. Whatever their private views on the issue might be, their public stance *had* to be pro-suffrage. Campaigning as an anti-suffrage candidate in a state where women could vote would be nothing less than political suicide.

In her discussion with Burns, Paul noted another extremely important element of the strategy as well. Under the existing method, there was absolutely no incentive that compelled elected officials to use their influence to persuade their anti-suffrage, apathetic, or even neutral fellow party members from other states to change their views and their votes. By making the whole party accountable for failure to pass a suffrage amendment and by mobilizing women voters to vote accordingly, suffrage state politicians would have ample reason to exert pressure on recalcitrant party members. If not for the party's sake, they would certainly do it for the sake of retaining their own seats. The validity of Paul's argument would be difficult, if not impossible, to deny.

An additional element of the strategy came under the heading of *publicity:* speaking tours, organizing women voters and nonvoters, pageants and parades, publications, and meetings with national officials, including members of Congress, administration figures, and even the president. All of these elements would be necessary in order to make suffrage a national issue and not just a local states' rights issue.

Finally, there would be no violence in the American movement. Violence of the sort engaged in by the English suffragettes had no place in Paul's strategy. Indeed, the movement on behalf of a federal suffrage amendment would be nonviolent in all respects.

As their first step, Paul and Burns submitted a proposal to the NAWSA board outlining their strategy for pursuing a federal amendment and offering to spearhead that effort. Both were willing, they emphasized, to work as unpaid volunteers. The NAWSA convention, held in Philadelphia in November 1912, followed a meeting between Paul and Burns with NAWSA secretary Mary Ware Dennett. Dennett heard their proposal. She conveyed her opinion that a federal amendment campaign did not impress her. She characterized such an attempt as foolish at best. And she was extremely suspicious regarding the intentions of Paul and Burns. Dennett was certain they were intent on a militant campaign. NAWSA wanted nothing to do with a strategy of holding the party in power responsible for a suffrage amendment. Woodrow Wilson, the Democrat from New Jersey, the well-known and well-regarded president of Princeton University, had only just been elected as president of the United States. The idea of initiating an anti–Democratic Party campaign, in the eyes of the NAWSA leaders, could not be more ludicrous. They would not approve such a proposal and Dennett dismissed it out of hand.

The NAWSA executive board quickly discovered that neither Paul nor Burns was easily dissuaded. Paul sought out Harriot Stanton Blatch for help. Blatch, busy with her own organization in New York, pointed to another person who might be in a position to assist them: Jane Addams. Addams, already in the midst of a controversy with the NAWSA executive board for having politically endorsed Progressive Party candidate Theodore Roosevelt for president, decided to meet with Paul and Burns. Everyone knew that NAWSA policy was opposed to endorsing political candidates. Having crossed that line, Addams nevertheless remained the one figure at the convention who commanded respect from nearly all delegates. Addams listened to the proposal put forth by Paul and Burns and, perhaps because her own career was such a monument to the unorthodox, agreed to champion their cause before the committee at the proper time. But she strongly advised the two young women to tone down their proposal. They couldn't afford to alienate the faint of heart among the committeewomen who would be considering it. Paul and Burns quickly reviewed the proposal and pared it down to the one element that would conceivably gain the greatest amount of publicity for their cause: they asked to be appointed to the Congressional Committee and to be allowed to organize a suffrage parade in Washington the following March. True to her word, Jane Addams interceded on their behalf. NAWSA appointed Alice Paul the new chairman of the Congressional Committee. She would replace Elizabeth Kent, who had let it be known that she wished to step down. (Elizabeth was the wife of

Congressman William Kent.) Lucy Burns was appointed vice-chairman of the committee.

In addition to chairing the Congressional Committee, Paul had a free hand in choosing other committee members and in implementing all preparations for the parade scheduled to coincide with Wilson's inauguration. NAWSA also agreed to allow them to use some NAWSA resources in the work of the committee. Paul had to agree to one major stipulation made by NAWSA: under *no* circumstances would NAWSA fund any part of the parade or the committee's work. The Congressional Committee would have to raise its own operating funds through its own efforts. Paul not only readily agreed to this condition but reiterated that she would be working as an unpaid volunteer and would ask nothing from the NAWSA treasury.

The negotiations between Paul and NAWSA did not bode well for a good working relationship. NAWSA made it clear that the organization wasn't going to abandon its current strategy. And though it may have felt compelled to accede to Jane Addams's intervention on behalf of Paul and Burns, its refusal to fund any committee work demonstrated what little interest it had in pursuing a federal amendment. By accepting only a severely modified proposal from Paul, NAWSA also made it clear that it rejected a more aggressive—or militant—approach as strongly as it embraced the more conservative state-by-state approach. Yet Paul and Burns got what they asked for. Though they made clear at every step that they wanted to work with NAWSA to achieve their mutual goals, they were careful not to fritter away a real opportunity to inject new life into the suffrage movement. They couldn't have been happier or more excited about the prospect that lay ahead of them.

Paul lost little time in gathering her new committee. Burns reached out to one of her Vassar classmates, the dynamic Crystal Eastman. A complete feminist, pacifist, and self-proclaimed socialist, Eastman had earned a master's degree in sociology from Columbia after graduating from Vassar, as well as a law degree from New York University. She had also worked for Paul Kellogg on the famous "Pittsburgh Survey," the first in-depth study of the effects of industrialization on the lives of blue-collar workers. As a consequence of her work with Kellogg, New York Governor Charles Evans Hughes appointed Crystal to the New York

State Employers Liability Commission. From this post, she launched a successful drive to persuade the state legislature to enact a workmen's compensation law in New York. Among her friends, Eastman was known for her unyielding commitment to feminism and gender equality, even after her marriage. She had been encouraged from childhood to strive to overcome socially imposed inequality. And she recognized all too well the dilemma that society posed for the modern woman, who, Eastman believed, could no longer find satisfaction in traditional domesticity: "She wants money of her own. She wants work of her own. She wants some means of self-expression, perhaps some way of satisfying her personal ambitions. But she wants a husband, home and children, too. How to reconcile these two desires in real life, that is the question."[13] That question continued to haunt women throughout the twentieth century. By 1912, Eastman knew two things for sure: her own marriage was over and she had to return to the mainstream of social activism. When Burns contacted her, Eastman couldn't wait to move back to the East Coast.

Mary Ritter Beard also responded to the call. Returning from England, she enrolled in Columbia University's graduate program. Her career as a graduate student was short-lived, both because of what she considered the narrowness of academic life and because of the pressure of parenting. Following the birth of her second child and no longer encumbered with academic demands, Beard rekindled her interest in the condition of working-class women—an interest that had been ignited when she was in England. She joined the Women's Trade Union League (WTUL) and became a key organizer of the shirtwaist makers' strike in 1909. Beard also belonged to the Women Suffrage Party of New York and edited its publication, *Votes for Women*. When the call came, Mary Beard—like Crystal Eastman—needed little persuasion to join forces with Paul and Burns as a member of the Congressional Committee.

At Alice Paul's request, the fifth committee member was Dora Kelley Lewis of Philadelphia. She married Lawrence Lewis, Jr., in 1883. Both the Kelley and the Lewis families were prominent in Philadelphia society. Lawrence Lewis, a promising young attorney, fell under the wheels of a train and died at the age of thirty-two. Thus, in 1890, still in her late twenties, Dora Lewis had three young children to raise on her own. Paul met Lewis when both women were members of the Philadelphia Equal Franchise Society. By that time, Lewis had successfully navigated the shoals of widowhood. Her son Robert had already established himself as a respected Philadelphia physician, and Shippen Lewis was just beginning to earn what would become a national reputation as an expert in constitutional law. (Shippen later helped to represent the National Woman's Party during its ratification campaign.) Dora Lewis's entrée into Philadelphia society made her invaluable as a fund-raiser. It was to Lewis that Paul turned immediately after the NAWSA convention.

With her committee in place, Paul prepared to establish its credentials as a vehicle for a federal suffrage amendment. The tasks that had to be tackled immediately included finding appropriate headquarters, enlisting whoever they could persuade to do volunteer work, fund-raising, and preparing for what they hoped would be a massive and hugely successful suffrage parade. The logistics of all these necessities might have been too daunting for the less committed. Now Paul and Burns had to follow through on the promises they had made to the NAWSA board and to their supporters. Could they do so in the short period of time remaining before Wilson's inauguration? They had only three months to accomplish an enormous undertaking. This would be the task that would test Alice Paul's mettle and validate her leadership.

3

Where Are All the People?

On Monday, March 3, 1913, the newly elected president, Woodrow Wilson, arrived in the nation's capital. To his puzzlement, there was no crowd gathered to greet him. When a member of the new president's party asked, "Where are the people?" the answer came, "Over on the Avenue watching the suffrage parade."[1] That parade was the work of Alice Paul.

By the spring of 1913, Alice Paul was finally on her own, and she knew exactly what she wanted to accomplish. NAWSA had handed over the Congressional Committee to her and had okayed a suffrage parade to take place in Washington, DC. Now she had to put to work everything she had learned over the past four years. Just one of the details to be worked out was how she was going to raise the money necessary to organize the kind of parade she envisioned. She knew when she wanted the parade to take place—the day before Wilson's inauguration. And she knew where she wanted it to take place—Pennsylvania Avenue, the only thoroughfare in the city that would ensure that she got both the crowds and the publicity she sought. Any other route would diminish the impact of the parade, resulting in less publicity for the cause. A little over three months earlier, immediately following the NAWSA convention, Paul moved to Washington and began putting her plan into motion. She arrived in the nation's capital on December 7 and moved into a third-floor room in a Quaker boarding house. Her starting point for organizing both her committee and the parade was a list of names supplied to her by NAWSA. It was the only tangible help the organization provided for the benefit of the new committee members. Paul immediately began tracking down members whose names were on the list, looking for donations, volunteers, and any other form of help that might be forthcoming. Very quickly two things became evident: first, that most of the people whose names were on the list had moved out of the DC area and, second, that most of those who hadn't moved had long since died. With three important exceptions, the list was useless.

As she went through the NAWSA list, the first useful name she came across was that of Emma Gillette. Paul later recalled that "Miss Gillette was the first person I met who was interested and friendly and still living."[2] Gillette, a lawyer and cofounder of the Washington College of Law, had a basement office in a building not far from the Willard Hotel. She was enthusiastic both about the prospects of renewing the campaign for a federal amendment and about Paul's plan to organize a parade the following March. Gillette recommended to Paul that she take the vacant office next to her own office and set up the Congressional Committee headquarters there. Gillette was sure the landlord would reduce the rental asking price. Though offered the space for $60 a month, Paul had to be sure she could raise enough money to pay the rent each month. In the meantime, Gillette agreed to become the treasurer for the Congressional Committee's parade.

The second useful name was that of journalist Helen Gardener. Like Gillette, Gardener was older than Paul. But whereas Gillette exhibited enthusiasm for Paul's task, Gardener was initially somewhat standoffish. She was a bit cool to Paul at their first meeting, perhaps because she thought Paul was too inexperienced or too young but, more likely, because Gardener thought NAWSA should have appointed her chairman of the Congressional Committee. Speaking of NAWSA, Gardener told Paul, "Well, they don't have much sense about who they put in charge. . . . [A]ll these undertakings require great experience."[3] It was the first and last time that Gardener would question Paul's abilities throughout the suffrage campaign. Even so, Paul quickly realized that with her journalism background Gardener could be a valuable asset and persuaded her to become the new press chairman, despite the older woman's initial resistance. Throughout her life, Paul's charismatic appeal made converts to her wishes seem effortless.

The third name that proved valuable was that of Elizabeth Kent, the previous chairman of the Congressional Committee. As far as Paul knew, Kent wanted to withdraw entirely from committee work. NAWSA had always made it clear that it expected very little from the committee under Kent's leadership. "No busier woman could have been selected and beyond making excellent arrangements for the hearings [before Congress], the committee was not active."[4] Indeed, it was well known that NAWSA allowed Kent an annual budget of $10 for committee work and that Kent had returned the unused portion of that money each year. When Paul called on Kent, the former chairman immediately invited her for Christmas dinner at her home. Paul accepted and spent an enjoyable and informative day with the Kents. Perceptions to the contrary, Elizabeth Kent was far from lukewarm on the federal-amendment subject. She had always been an ardent supporter of pursuing a federal amendment, and it was only NAWSA's insistence on ignoring what was surely the most efficient way of securing the vote for women that prompted her to resign at the 1912 convention. She was thrilled to hear about Paul's plans for highlighting suffrage as a major issue—one that no politician could ignore. Kent was more than willing to do whatever she could to advance the cause. This included pledging $5 a month toward payment of the rent. Kent's commitment encouraged Paul to sign the lease and move into the new office.

By the time the committee held its first meeting at the new headquarters, it had grown to twice its original size. It now included Paul, Burns, Eastman, Beard, Lewis, Gillette, Gardener, Kent, Elsie Hill (the daughter of a Connecticut congressman), two female federal employees, and feminist and activist Belva Lockwood. Lockwood, then in her eighties, was a retired lawyer who had run for president of the United States in 1884. While her age prevented her from becoming an active participant, she wanted to sit in on the meeting to encourage the younger women present.

Paul explained what she wanted and why. She wanted Congress to pass a federal amendment and she wanted the states to ratify it. And, most importantly, she wanted to persuade the president of the United States to support their efforts. Theodore Roosevelt had changed the concept of the office dramatically with his much-publicized view of the presidency as a "bully pulpit" that could provide strong moral leadership of both party and nation. This view gave the executive branch new significance. Paul was one of the first suffrage activists to recognize the importance of this development. She was convinced that lobbying for national political reforms was futile if the president could not be persuaded to support those reforms. Win the president's support and you win the battle. This is why Paul believed getting the parade when and where she wanted was not just desirable but essential. Moreover, if the parade was a success, it would attract thousands of visitors in the city for Wilson's inauguration. If the crowds were large enough, newspaper coverage and publicity would follow.

Additionally, Woodrow Wilson would be on notice from day one of his tenure in office that the suffrage issue was not going to go away. Suffragists would be a force to be reckoned with. Their intent was to deal directly with the president and the Congress. They were moving the battle out of the front parlors of Boise and Sacramento and away from the street corners of Philadelphia and Boston. From now on, their arena would be Washington, DC—specifically, the White House and the halls of Congress.

The response to the call for the first national suffrage parade came swiftly and forcefully. Although the committee had barely two months to organize and finance the parade, the results were spectacular. A letter-writing campaign raised much-needed funds and helped publicize the parade. But to keep costs down, Paul and Gillette worked out a plan for individual groups to sponsor their own participation in the parade. In short, everyone who wanted to march had to pay their own travel and lodging expenses as well as the cost of their parade floats and any associated costumes that they required. By the time the parade took place, the committee had begun to forge a national support network.

The number of participants continued to grow even though the route and date were still uncertain. For other events, including the gathering in Independence Plaza in Philadelphia, Paul hadn't asked for permission or permits. As she explained to Caroline Katzenstein, if she didn't ask permission to hold an event, she couldn't get no for an answer—and if the event went smoothly, future requests for similar events would be hard to refuse. But a national parade was another matter altogether. Paul knew that the committee needed the proper permits to proceed. The man who could provide those permits was Richard Sylvester, the superintendent of police of the District of Columbia. Paul and various committee members met with Sylvester several times in December and January. They wanted nothing less than Pennsylvania Avenue, but Sylvester kept trying to persuade them to take another route. At one point he suggested 16th Avenue, explaining that it was half again as wide as Pennsylvania Avenue. Time and again, Paul rejected the alternate route. Toward the end of the negotiations, when it seemed that Sylvester would never give in, every committee member except Paul agreed to take another route. Paul was the only holdout, but she had the final say. Finally, Sylvester relented and issued the permit for Pennsylvania Avenue. Paul also got permission to use the visitor bleachers that had earlier been set up for the inauguration. She even struck a deal with the ticket sellers in charge of the bleacher seats, bringing in much-needed money to the committee. All that was left in the few remaining weeks was to organize the parade's participants.

By mid January, Paul had established a routine. For most of the day, every day, Paul stayed in her small office at the headquarters, unless she had appointments elsewhere. Those who caught a glimpse of her when her office door opened were likely to see her typing one of the hundreds of letters she sent out across the country. Paul was petite in stature, with compelling eyes, delicate features, and long dark hair caught up in a soft bun at the nape of her neck. Her usual attire was a simple but elegant dress in muted tones, mostly purples and lavenders. She almost always wore a hat. Often she could be seen with a shawl wrapped tightly about her, as she still suffered from a severe sensitivity to the cold. Those who knew little about her, upon meeting her for the first time, probably underestimated her by a considerable margin. How could this young girl with such a quiet demeanor accomplish anything so spectacular as organizing a massive parade, let alone persuade people to do what was necessary to secure a federal amendment? They quickly discovered, beneath her surface appearance, an individual with an indomitable will, a passion for her cause, and a powerful charisma. People who stopped by the headquarters just to see what all the fuss was about were quickly—and inevitably—persuaded by Paul that they could not leave without doing something for suffrage. A young lawyer making an impromptu stop suddenly found himself addressing envelopes. An elderly matron painstakingly typed a letter—undoubtedly something she'd never before done—because "Alice Paul told me to." As one journalist concluded in an article she wrote about Paul, "There is no Alice Paul. There is suffrage. She leads by being . . . her cause."[5]

The journalist's observation had a ring of truth to it: Paul refused to reveal anything about her private life that she thought would be a distraction. Her brief correspondence with a young Wall Street broker who liked Paul and wanted to spend time with her in New York never went beyond an exchange of letters. And she gave up one of her most pleasurable pastimes—reading, especially mystery novels. She went out of her way to avoid walking past her favorite bookstores, and despite her painful aversion to cold, damp weather, she purposefully kept her small room uncomfortably cool lest she be tempted to indulge in the latest novel. She had never been one for small talk; conversations with her were always to the point and almost always about suffrage. Whether she consciously developed an air of mystery is uncertain, but many volunteers were somewhat unnerved by it. One volunteer vividly recalled her first meeting with Paul. The volunteer had been assigned tasks at the headquarters but was never told specifically what job she was being trained for or what was expected of her. Unknown to her, however, Paul had been receiving reports from her lieutenants about the volunteer's progress, performance, and potential. "And then Miss Paul sent for you. I will never forget that first interview. Miss Paul sat at a desk in a room seemingly completely dark except for a small desk lamp. . . . I felt she deliberately created the atmosphere of the tough executive. There was no subtlety about her. Direct, blunt, she asked why I wanted to do this, she wanted to probe sufficiently without wasting time, to discover if I had any weaknesses and to what extent she and the movement could depend upon me." Yet this volunteer left the meeting with a deep sense of commitment both to the suffrage organization and to Paul herself.

Paul always applied her abilities to the task at hand, whatever it was. She rarely revealed an introspective side to colleagues. Her intellectualism and purposefulness made her seem cold, aloof, and abrupt, sometimes to the point of insensitivity and rudeness. It was far from an accurate perception. What appeared to be insensitivity was often just an absent-mindedness when it came to social amenities. She did not, for example, consider it a necessity to thank volunteers for what they were doing. One woman left abruptly and angrily, and when Paul asked why, she was told it was because the woman felt she had not been properly thanked for her work. This astonished Paul. "But she didn't do it for me. She did it for suffrage." Thereafter, however, she made it a point to try to remember to thank people for their contributions and even, on occasion, apologized for transgressions she had not committed in order to avoid discontent.[6]

Paul was not immune to criticisms and attacks on herself and her organization. Indeed, she never forgot an incident that occurred in 1914, just after she had initiated the first anti–Democratic Party campaign. She had gone to Mississippi to attend a conference with NAWSA and other suffrage groups. Because of her unyielding commitment to holding the party in power responsible for the fate of a federal amendment, many people there treated her like a pariah. They were convinced that her chosen path would do irreparable harm to suffrage. The profound sense of isolation she experienced at that time remained with her sixty years later. "I remember going down in the morning for breakfast and here were all these people from all different states in the Union, and I remember that not one human being spoke to me. I just felt *such* an outcast, and for a long time we were regarded in that way."[7]

Lucy Burns, who had joined Paul in Washington that January, spent her days mostly outside the office, on street corners and in places where people gathered, speaking extemporaneously about suffrage and the necessity for a federal amendment. When she and Paul returned to their rooms after each long day's work, they would talk far into the night about what had transpired that day, where they were in terms of their objectives, and what needed to be done the following day. Whether or not they saw it themselves, they could easily have been compared to Stanton and Anthony. Like Stanton, Paul formulated the strategy, developed the arguments, and directed the attack. And Burns, like Anthony, took her cues from her friend, internalized her arguments, traveled the countryside speaking on behalf of the federal amendment, and carried out the attack. With her distinctive red hair, sturdy build, quick wit, and ready sense of humor, Lucy Burns was hard to ignore.

Opposite in temperament and appearance, the two women admired one another. Burns was impressed with Paul's "extraordinary mind, extraordinary courage and remarkable executive ability." Yet, very early in their relationship, Burns was convinced that Paul had two serious disabilities that would hamper her effectiveness in a grueling political campaign. The first was her apparent ill-health and the second was her "lack of knowledge about human behavior." It didn't take long for Burns to acknowledge that "I was wrong on both counts."[8] For her part, Paul insisted that Burns was far more courageous than she. She pointed out on several occasions that Lucy never hesitated to run the risk of possible arrest and imprisonment as a consequence of picketing activity, despite her phobia-like fear of the rats and other creatures that inevitably found their way into prison cells.

Paul and Burns worked so well together that many observers ascribed a single mind and spirit to them. One suffragist, when asked to describe the differences between the two, found more similarities than disparities in their beliefs. But she had no problem defining the differences in their temperaments. "Both saw the situation exactly as it was, but they went at the problems with different methods. Alice Paul had a more acute sense of justice. Lucy Burns a more bitter sense of injustice. Lucy Burns would become angry because the President or the people did not do this or that. Alice Paul never expected anything of them."[9]

As the two women worked together to organize the parade, every day seemed to bring its own successes. The more publicity the suffrage committee received, the greater the numbers of new volunteers who showed up on a daily basis. And the more well-known or connected the volunteers, the more publicity they generated. Paul and Gardener saw to it that no relevant detail went unnoticed. Every politician's wife, daughter, sister, mother, or other relative who joined the forces of the Congressional Committee was fodder for the daily papers. Elizabeth Kent had long been associated with suffrage, but when she and socially connected Elizabeth Seldin Rogers began appearing on Washington streets speaking out on behalf of a federal amendment, it was big news. When Elsie Hill joined the committee and Hazel Mackaye, the sister of playwright Percy Mackaye, agreed to direct the tableau on the steps of the Treasury Building, it was even bigger news. And when Paul announced that they had finally succeeded in getting permission to march down Pennsylvania Avenue, it was the biggest news of all. As more and more contingents from other states signed on as participants, their hometown papers picked up the story as well. Nothing, it seemed, was too mundane or too insignificant to send reporters scrambling to file their stories for publication. The committee's headquarters became a daily stop for several journalists whose regular beat was Washington. And so it went, with more and more news coverage generating more and more interest in the parade—and in the suffrage issue itself.

Yet crises also cropped up with regularity. Paul had to be concerned with fund-raising to cover parade expenses, including some costumes. (Paul chose what each contingent would wear, but not everyone could afford that additional expense.) The logistics of housing participants, even though they were paying for their own lodgings, had to be worked out. Permits had to be obtained. And not least, every NAWSA request or order had to be tended to. When NAWSA leaders realized that the colors Paul had selected for official banners and printed materials matched those of the English suffragettes' colors, they objected. Anna Howard Shaw and Mary Ware Dennett, in particular, insisted that Paul change the colors. Paul did so, choosing what would become her organization's official colors: purple, gold, and white. When NAWSA leaders also made it clear that they intended to lead the parade, Paul again quietly acceded. In truth, she *preferred* to march with the college contingent.

Two critical issues became increasingly relevant to the success of the parade as the event approached. The first was racial in nature. In January 1913, an African-American woman asked if "colored women" would be allowed to march in the parade. Just as Quakers had always advocated female equality and the right to vote, they were supporters of equality for African-Americans. Indeed, Quakers were prominent in the abolition movement in the years leading up to the Civil War. So Paul saw no problem with black women in the line of march. But when word got out about their inclusion, the issue became particularly divisive. White contingents from southern states threatened to withdraw if African-American women were allowed to march. The potentially devastating situation grew worse when a contingent of women from Howard University asked to participate. Elsie Hill told Paul that several white women's groups were again threatening to withdraw. Mary Ware Dennett insisted that black women be included. Paul turned to Mary Beard to help find a solution. Beard met with the group of women from Howard and suggested that they could march with the New York City Woman Suffrage Party. But some of the Howard women resisted, arguing that southern whites were acting as spoilers and bigots. Beard reported to Paul that she had not found a solution. At that point, when Ida Wells-Barnett, a high-profile and prominent anti-lynching activist, petitioned to participate, Paul knew she had to find a solution— and quickly.[10]

In 1913, virulent racism, both overt and covert, prevailed throughout the land. Even Teddy Roosevelt, the Progressive candidate for president in 1912, had conducted a "Lily White" campaign in order to curry favor among southern voters. And as the country soon discovered, the newly elected Woodrow Wilson would embark on a program of institutionalized segregation among federal employees that had not existed before. Like the politicians, most suffrage leaders tried to avoid alienating white legislators, voters, and current and potential suffrage supporters. The social climate that encouraged and fostered bigotry in general also encouraged suffrage leaders to exclude African-Americans from speaking at or attending suffrage meetings in most sections of the country. Paul could have given in to the prevailing sensibilities on race issues, despite Mary Ware Dennett's instructions to include African-Americans. She did not. She rejected an obvious solution in favor of finding an acceptable solution. In the end, she worked out an agreement with the male marchers to act as a protective wedge for the Howard women in the event that parade participants gave in to their prejudices. Southern whites who threatened to withdraw from the parade could pretend that the African-American women were sufficiently isolated. Though not entirely happy with Paul's solution, both sides accepted it.

The African-American issue was a perfect example of Paul's refusal to allow any other issue to compete with suffrage as a focus and goal. At her core she believed that women had to participate fully in the democratic process if they were to be considered equals in a so-called democratic society and achieve true equality as human beings. But in order to achieve those ends, she made judgment calls that not everyone supported. For example, working women and labor union members were included among the marchers, but they had to downplay or eliminate altogether their support for issues that were important to them, including protective legislation and improvements in wages and hours. The fact that Paul's actions were often seen as autocratic, elitist, and racist left a stain on her reputation. For years after the suffrage parade, she had to contend with periodic accusations that she had relegated African-American women to second-class status by insisting that they march as part of a male delegation. But it bothered her even more that people were willing to interject distractions rather than focus solely on suffrage.

The second serious problem that arose involved the safety of the parade participants. Several days before the parade, Superintendent Sylvester tried once again to persuade Paul either to change the intended route or to change the date. He was concerned, he said, that the crowds might prove to be too unruly to ensure the safety of the participants. This was a new worry for Paul, but one that she should have anticipated. Before Sylvester's dire warning, she had not thought about crowd control or potential danger to the participants. But just as British students had behaved in a rowdy fashion when the suffragettes dared to address them in Birmingham, Americans, too, were not yet comfortable with women speaking out, especially on behalf of political issues. Public speaking for women was far more acceptable when the subjects dealt with their perceived traditional interests. Challenging the government did not fall into that category.

Paul's repeated requests to Sylvester for more police protection along the parade route were routinely rejected. Sylvester sincerely believed that his force could provide adequate protection. But he was either having second thoughts about letting the women march on Pennsylvania Avenue or getting flack from other sources who did not appreciate his decision. He did, however, enlist the assistance of Boy Scouts just in case the rumor that college students intended to let loose hundreds of mice in the line of march proved to be more than just a rumor.

On March 1, 1913, Congress passed a special resolution ordering Sylvester to prohibit all ordinary traffic along the parade route and "to prevent any interference with the suffrage marchers." Yet Sylvester remained intransigent in the face of Paul's numerous requests, despite having raised the initial concern regarding safety. Sylvester insisted, in any case, that responsibility really lay with the Department of the Army and not the DC police. With waning confidence in the superintendent's ability—much less commitment—to ensure marcher safety, Paul made one last effort to secure more help.

Paul asked Elizabeth Seldin Rogers to go with her and appeal to Rogers's brother-in-law, Henry Stimson, to provide protection for the marchers, should it become necessary. While Stimson expressed sympathy for their plight, he said his hands were tied. He could not, by law, order army personnel to guard the women. Paul and Rogers were disappointed, but not surprised. It was, after all, a last-ditch effort. Stimson did take some precautionary measures after the two women left. He ordered the Fifteenth Cavalry from Fort Myer, Maryland, to bivouac on the western perimeter of Washington, with instructions to be prepared to move into the city on a moment's notice should trouble develop.

Paul had done everything she could to make sure the parade proceeded without incident. After a short delay on the day of the parade, Inez Milholland nudged her horse out onto the avenue and the parade was on. It was a spectacular event by any measure. Almost eight thousand marchers participated. Interspersed with the marchers on foot were twenty-six floats, ten bands and six chariots. Marching units were divided into six sections: women from other nations; a colorfully garbed section representing the progress made by women since the 1848 Women's Rights Convention; women in a variety of occupations and professions; the local, state, and national governments' contingent; unaffiliated volunteer marchers and male supporters of suffrage, including the women from Howard University; and, lastly, the state delegates' contingents. The parade went up Pennsylvania Avenue, past the Treasury Building, where the "allegorical tableau" was presented. The tableau was written especially for the occasion to show "those ideals toward which both men and women have been struggling through the ages and toward which, in co-operation and equality, they will continue to strive." Beginning with the commanding figure of Columbia dressed in national colors, who emerged from the great columns at the top of the Treasury Building steps and was joined by figures representing Charity, Liberty, Peace, and Hope, all in flowing robes and colorful scarves, with trumpets sounding, the pageant continued on past the White House to the Ellipse. The *New York Times* described it as "one of the most impressively beautiful spectacles ever staged in this country."[11] Over half a million people lined the parade route; they all stood to watch the oncoming procession. "As far as the eye could see, Pennsylvania Avenue, from building line to building line, was packed. No such crowd had been seen there in sixteen years."[12] But things began to unravel for the parade participants very quickly. Spectators started hurling insults at the marchers. The police seemed to be indifferent to the crowd's increasing boldness. Encouraged that no one was going to stop them, the crowd began to push out into the line of march. In a flash it became impossible to distinguish marchers from observers. A near-riot had erupted.

The police continued to stand idly by, leaving the marchers to defend themselves. The wife of a congressman appealed to a nearby police officer for help. Instead of responding to her pleas, the officer said: "If my wife were where you are, I'd break her head."[13] A senator who participated in the march later testified that he personally took the badge numbers of twenty-two officers, including two sergeants, who failed to lift a finger to restore order. Testifying before Congress, Paul asserted that the Boy Scouts of Philadelphia were the only ones who did any effective police work. Her anger was evident when she testified that one youngster, heroically trying to hold back the crowds, was thumped on the head and sent sprawling, instead of receiving assistance from nearby police officers. The disturbance continued and order was not restored until the Fifteenth Cavalry, summoned from their bivouac on the western perimeter, rode into the city. One hundred and seventy-five calls went out for ambulances and more than two hundred people were treated— mostly for minor injuries—at local hospitals.

The special investigating committee of the Senate convened on March 6 to hear testimony that lasted nearly two weeks. An editorial in the *Washington Post* said the public had simply overreacted and dismissed the so-called riot as just an "occasional isolated piece of rudeness." The Senate committee, however, found a good deal to criticize about the lackluster behavior of the officials concerned. But while many politicians may have strongly suspected that Major Sylvester let it be known that the police should do nothing to assist the suffragists, the Senate report indicated that there was not enough evidence to attribute blame to any individual or individuals. The police, they concluded, acted on their own and not in a predetermined manner. Ultimately, the unprofessional behavior of the police officers who failed to do their jobs properly cost Major Sylvester his job. But for the moment he was safe and continued to serve as superintendent of police.

When the dust had settled, Paul and Burns could surely congratulate one another. In a little over two months, they had succeeded in organizing a massive parade that drew over half a million spectators. Despite the near-riot, there were no serious injuries to the marchers. They had accomplished what they set out to do: make suffrage a front-page story in the nation's newspapers and ignite enthusiasm among suffragists for a federal amendment. Even though they had legitimately feared rough treatment by unruly spectators, they took full advantage of the outcome. Paul stirred public sentiment against the authorities even more when she asserted in a newspaper interview that top police and public officials had conspired to promote trouble for the suffragists: "There is no question that the police had the tip from some power higher up to let the rough characters . . . try to break up our parade."[14] Whether or not there was merit to her accusation, people paid attention to it, including the members of the Senate investigating committee. When Sylvester testified before the Senate committee, many of the questions asked of him had to do with the extent to which the police turned a blind eye to a situation they knew to be dangerously unstable.

NAWSA leaders were not entirely happy with the way things played out, but the immediate benefits for the suffrage movement held them back from criticizing the young upstarts. Contributions to the Congressional Committee increased markedly and included a gift of $1,000 from the editor of the *Washington Post.* Funds including ticket sales to parade-related activities were supplemented by unsolicited donations in the days following the parade. The parade expenses totaled $13,750 and were paid in full. Alva Belmont was one among many who contacted Paul to offer her assistance to the committee. Writing from Atlanta, Georgia, a woman praised Paul's work: "I stand in readiness to . . . render any assistance possible to the cause so dear to my heart. . . . At present we are only a struggling band of women, but we see victory already crowning our efforts."[15]

The South, nevertheless, remained a bastion of opposition to woman suffrage. In an editorial following the parade, the *Jackson* (Mississippi) *Daily News* played down the whole event, stating that "walking is splendid exercise, but it has nothing to do with a woman's ability to determine whether a law is wise or unwise."[16] Other critics chose to interpret the disturbance as a reflection on the suffragists and not on the spectators who started it. Senator William A. Clark, a Democrat from Montana, when asked to support a subsequent suffrage parade, tersely refused. The March 3rd parade, he said, "amply demonstrated that they [the American suffragists] are unworthy of enjoying any greater rights than they now possess."[17] This was exactly the kind of criticism, even when unjustified, that the NAWSA leaders feared—but they still felt constrained from taking any steps against Paul and her committee, at least for the moment.

Woodrow Wilson, of course, had nothing to do with either the parade or the ensuing commotion. Still, there were valuable lessons to be learned, not only from the near-riot itself but also from the fact that a small group of women were able to organize such a massive parade in a few short weeks. At a minimum, this outcome provided clear evidence that suffrage was an issue that women responded to in great numbers. On March 17, 1913, just days after the parade, Paul organized a delegation to meet with the new president at the White House. Paul hoped to persuade Wilson to at least consider including suffrage in his agenda. Wilson, a southerner himself, decided to use the meeting as an opportunity to school the delegates. Somewhat to their chagrin, the delegates were seated in a semicircle facing the president. But they were downright dismayed when Wilson chose to lie, saying that woman suffrage was an issue that had never been brought to his attention and that he would have to learn more about it before he could offer an opinion. As for adding it to the agenda of issues he intended to deal with, Wilson claimed that his hands were tied. He was bound, he insisted, by the desires of the Democratic party, and suffrage was not an issue the party expressed any interest in at the present time. The meeting was brief; Wilson thanked the women for their visit and then dismissed them.

In the early months of his administration, Wilson continued to respond in standard political fashion to questions regarding suffrage. With the possible exceptions of Paul and Burns, no one could foresee the dimensions that the suffrage issue would assume during his term as president. For the time being, suffrage remained for Wilson a minor but irritating nonproblem that would be "handled" with as little disruption as possible. The administration's attitude regarding women's right to vote—despite the opinions of hundreds of thousands of women— prompted little more than superficial responses at best. Such responses were intended to pacify and not inform. It was clear to Paul's delegation and to the Congressional Committee that much would have to be done to move suffrage from its low-priority status among politicians to one of paramount concern that could not be ignored. *The Suffragist*, the newspaper that Paul started and for which she wrote virtually all the editorials and articles for the first few months, argued that the urgency of a federal amendment could not be overstated: "Until women vote, every piece of legislation undertaken by the Administration is an act of injustice to them. All laws affect the interests of women and should not be enacted and put into execution without the cooperation and consent of women."[18]

4

A Splendid Year and a Growing Rivalry

Immediately on the heels of the suffrage parade, Paul began to put in place plans that she and Burns had talked about since they met in England. They would continue to build on the gains made as a consequence of the parade. Suffragists who had participated in the parade were more fired up than they had been for a decade. They clearly had a window of opportunity as long as NAWSA did not want to appear jealous or dictatorial after their stunning success. Paul knew that they had to take advantage of the situation if they really intended to secure a federal amendment in her lifetime. Anything less than that would be unacceptable.

In all likelihood, this would be the best chance of going forward without fear of interference from the national organization. The Congressional Committee had never been set up within the NAWSA framework as a standing committee. Because of that, it could at any time be terminated by NAWSA leaders. They needed a national organization that would work solely for a federal amendment. As a first order of business, Paul had to persuade NAWSA that a new—and separate—congressional committee should be organized as a standing committee. It would work closely with NAWSA, but it would be dedicated solely to pursuing the federal amendment. In addition to the risk that the current committee would be discontinued, raising money for a federal campaign would be difficult if donations intended for the committee landed in NAWSA's treasury instead. Indeed, once donations intended for Paul's committee were received by the national treasury, even in cases where donors specified where they wanted their money to go, the donations would never find their way to Paul's committee. And if the committee members couldn't count on the funds that they raised, they had little hope of being able to organize and implement a federal campaign. A standing committee would make it much easier to collect donations directly instead of through the national organization.

In March 1913, Paul asked Dora Lewis to go with her to New York to meet with Anna Howard Shaw and Mary Ware Dennett. Dennett had always been somewhat standoffish, if not hostile, when it came to proposals from Paul. An open-arms welcome didn't seem likely under the circumstances. Paul hoped that Lewis's demeanor might have a more calming effect on Dennett. She outlined her plan to the two NAWSA leaders, and much to her surprise, both Shaw and Dennett thought it was a good idea. They "approved heartily" of the plan, and Dennett even suggested that the new committee be named the Congressional Union of NAWSA. More than likely, the hearty approval had more to do with timing than with any real commitment to a federal amendment. When Shaw, a short time later, informed Paul that the new committee could not use NAWSA in its name, she may simply have been referring to an oversight that had to be cleared up. But no one believed the relationship between NAWSA and the CU would be a smooth one. Whatever the NAWSA leaders' reasoning, the new Congressional Union for Woman Suffrage was formed in April 1913 as a permanent NAWSA committee.

When the CU launched its first membership drive, it sought quality of commitment rather than quantity of members. Certainly the number of NAWSA's members was impressive. But the vast majority of these members were content to count themselves as inactive suffrage supporters. They could not or would not participate actively in NAWSA's suffrage campaigns. Paul, on the other hand, selectively sought out women who were committed to a federal amendment and who were willing to work actively toward that end. She also believed wholeheartedly that the unifying characteristic that drew a variety of women to the CU—

and to the federal-amendment strategy—was their belief in feminism. Paul defined *feminism* as gender equality in all respects. Her choice of members to serve on the original Congressional Committee—Burns, Beard, Eastman, and Lewis—certainly emphasized their feminist convictions. Three influential and powerful additions to the new CU— Dorr, Belmont, and Havemeyer—were recruited in the same vein.

As noted, Paul had previously decided to publish a newspaper, *The Suffragist*. As soon as she negotiated with NAWSA to establish the new committee, Paul began looking for exactly the right individual to edit the paper. She sought out respected journalist Rheta Childe Dorr. Few women could have matched either Dorr's background or her credentials as a journalist. At the age of twelve, Dorr defied her parents to go and hear Anthony and Stanton speak; such was her commitment to women's rights even as a child. Her brief marriage to conservative businessman John Pixley Dorr ended when Rheta took her son Julian and moved to New York City, where she intended to pursue a writing career. Before long, she had a regular column in the *New York Evening Post*, which brought her into contact with influential movers and shakers of the day. Her commitment to suffrage—and to elimination of the double standard—compelled Dorr to champion the rights of working women and children in particular. That, in turn, led to her appointment as chairwoman of the General Federation of Women's Clubs' Committee on the Industrial Conditions of Women and Children. In concert with the Women's Trade Union League and the Association of Social Settlements, Dorr helped to persuade Congress to initiate the first official investigation of the status of working women.

In 1906, Dorr resigned from the *Evening Post* in order to travel in Europe as a freelance writer. During that period she met the Pankhursts and became a committed militant suffragist. Back in the United States, Dorr was approached by Paul and accepted her invitation to become editor of *The Suffragist*. Under Dorr's leadership, the publication quickly became financially self-sufficient.

From the start, *The Suffragist* was intended to be a news publication and not a propaganda vehicle. Suffrage had long since passed the stage where propaganda was required in order to bring people up to speed on why it was necessary and what was at stake. Published weekly, it kept

readers informed about the status of the federal amendment and suffrage activity throughout the country. As noted, editorials and articles
were initially written by Paul, with occasional pieces by Burns. The most
important purpose of the magazine was to keep the suffrage issue before
the public and Congress. Dorr's experience and expertise as a news journalist went a long way toward accomplishing that end. One tactic she
employed was to hold press conferences during which she would raise
provocative questions that reporters ought to be asking of President Wilson and other public officials and politicians. Reporters present at her
press conferences frequently did raise the questions in their own newspapers, so the tactic was successful. In this way, even though Dorr's paid
subscribers numbered only about 1,200, the paper's message went out
to a far greater audience.

Another ongoing preoccupation for Paul and the CU was to make
sure that the organization was fully funded. In addition to the money
raised in membership dues, Paul initiated a program of monthly pledges
similar to that promised by Elizabeth Kent. Because men controlled
most of the household finances in homes throughout the country, this
was not an easy task. More than one pro-suffrage woman confessed to
not seeing five dollars in cash from one month to the next. In order to
funnel money to the CU, women had to persuade their husbands to
sign a donation check. While some men supported suffrage, the vast
majority did not believe in it or disapproved of the manner in which it
was being pursued or did not care enough even to think about it, let
alone spend money supporting it. Some women became quite creative
in securing funds from the family budget. Many of them made an
arrangement with local vendors whereby—for a small fee—the vendors
would issue bills of sale for nonexistent purchases, perhaps for an article of clothing or gas for the family car. When the husband paid the
bill, the vendor would give cash back to the wife, who could then make
her suffrage donation. By staying within the family budget and remaining willing to do without, she succeeded in this ploy more often
than not.

Economic reality and creative bookkeeping notwithstanding, Paul
knew she had to attract key donors to keep things going. Alva Belmont
was one such benefactor. Belmont considered herself a feminist and

proudly advocated militant suffragism. She had no qualms about singing the praises of the Pankhursts and quickly came to admire Alice Paul. Since she controlled her own purse strings, she could and did support Paul's efforts to the tune of thousands of dollars. Her liberal spending habits and her willingness to open up her two homes to suffragists were both newsworthy and capable of making politicians sit up and take notice in ways that normal fund-raising could not.

Social status was another important factor in the solicitation of funds. Louisine Havemeyer, the widow of the former head of the American Sugar Refining Company, had vast sums of money at her disposal. She also had the kind of social respectability that Belmont had lost as a consequence of her messy divorce and remarriage. In addition to her support of suffrage, Havemeyer involved herself in a variety of philanthropic endeavors. A patron of the arts, she met the Impressionist painter Mary Cassatt in Europe. Havemeyer became an instant enthusiast of Impressionism and was introduced by Cassatt to her circle of artist friends, including Courbet, Degas, and Monet. In turn, Havemeyer became instrumental in introducing Impressionism to America. Over the years, she was able to acquire a modern-art collection, including several Cassatts, valued in the millions of dollars. When she died, she left her collection to the Metropolitan Museum in New York, an act that transformed the Met into the foremost museum of modern art in the country.

Like Paul, Havemeyer had been interested in suffrage since childhood, when she became aware of her mother's support of and friendship with the pioneers of the movement. As a young woman, Havemeyer lived in Paris and attended boarding school with the granddaughter of Lucretia Mott. Havemeyer's marriage was fortuitous for many reasons, not the least being her husband's own attitude toward suffrage. He told her that if women did not know how to vote, they had better get busy and learn. Havemeyer's social prominence, name, and reputation for "salty speech" made her a popular favorite with suffrage audiences. She donated generously to the CU, and the only time she consented to a public showing of her art collection, she did so for the benefit of Paul and the Congressional Union. By cultivating the support of people like Dorr, Belmont, and Havemeyer, along with assistance from her network of small donors, Paul succeeded in raising the kind of money necessary to support the work of the organization. And she did so without compromising either goals or strategy.

At the same time, however, she had to respond to critics who believed that suffrage was harmed by her tactics—holding the Democrats responsible for failure to enact a federal amendment, for example. Though she never felt obligated to justify her strategy, she always insisted that, while she would welcome the support of these critics, they might be better off working with a suffrage organization more in line with their sensibilities. In short, Paul found it much more productive to remain polite and positive. If critics were going to leave the CU, she wanted them to leave without rancor. And more than once she had to advise people working for the CU to avoid expressing negative opinions about the probability of seeing a federal suffrage amendment enacted. CU member and journalist Doris Stevens, writing to the president of NAWSA's Ohio branch, tried to convince her that the CU was not destructive in its policies. In Stevens' opinion, it made perfect sense to insist that the Democratically ruled Congress vote on a federal amendment, even though the CU knew the vote would fail. Upon reviewing the letter—as she did with almost all correspondence going out from headquarters—Paul went immediately to Stevens. Don't ever express such a negative opinion again, she told Stevens, and never put it in writing. "You see, we *can* get it this session if enough women care sufficiently to demand it now. . . . Success can be ours if suffragists stand shoulder to shoulder behind the federal amendment."[1] Carrie Chapman Catt once asserted that she considered her work on behalf of securing woman suffrage to be a lifelong job. To Paul, this was defeatist. As noted, she believed in the psychological advantage gained in always remaining optimistic. It was, she believed, another edge in making the possible a reality. This attention to individual recruitment and to the smallest of details informed Paul's actions and set an example of what she expected from everyone working for suffrage.

Given their differences in philosophy and strategy, the relationship between NAWSA and the CU was problematic at best. Although Paul and Burns seemingly ignored the undercurrent of unease that had existed ever since their plan was so roundly rejected in 1912, in reality it must have informed every decision they made. Even so, the strained relationship might have been minimized if NAWSA was willing to allow the CU to work the federal amendment side of the street without undercutting their efforts. Shortly after the formation of the CU, Paul applied to NAWSA for auxiliary status. This was routine for every group that wanted an affiliation with NAWSA and ought to have been quickly accomplished. Because of the difference of opinion regarding Paul's support of a federal amendment, the situation dragged on for months.

If anyone thought that she would slow down her agenda while the membership question was being batted back and forth amongst NAWSA leaders, they didn't know Alice Paul. By the end of 1913, the Congressional Committee (CC) and the Congressional Union—whose boards were identical—had accomplished a remarkable record of successes. Ironically, NAWSA held its annual meeting in Washington, DC, that year and the host organization was the Congressional Union. Most of the financial burden of putting on the meeting had to be absorbed by the CU. When it came time to deliver her report to the membership, Paul quite frankly admitted that it was impossible to divide the work of the Congressional Committee and the Congressional Union. Her report, therefore, was presented as a joint report.

The CC/CU, Paul noted, concentrated much of its time and effort on legislative work with Congress. On April 7, Senate Joint Resolution I called for passage of the federal amendment. The Resolution went to the Senate Woman Suffrage Committee, a standing committee since 1877. On May 14, the Senate Woman Suffrage Committee reported favorably on the bill to the Senate, and July 13 was set aside for full discussion on the floor. Twenty-three senators spoke in favor of the amendment; only three opposed it. In September, the senator from Arizona announced that he would press for a vote on the issue at the earliest possible moment. In the House, meanwhile, three different resolutions urging creation of a House Woman Suffrage Committee had been introduced and were under consideration.

Even though Congress did nothing more than consider and discuss a federal woman suffrage amendment, suffrage advocates characterized this as a major success. Woman suffrage had last been discussed in Congress in 1878—seven years before Alice Paul was born. And never had it been discussed in both houses at the same time. Thanks to Paul, more congressional attention was now being directed to the possibility of a suffrage amendment than had taken place in the preceding quarter-century. Once the Senate scheduled the topic of woman suffrage for full discussion on the floor, Paul wanted to show Congress how much support the amendment had. Delegations from throughout the country began to head east with petitions signed by thousands of women along the way. They arrived in Washington on July 31 and were met by a CU escort who accompanied them throughout the streets of the city to the Capitol building. The lead car was filled with pro-suffrage senators. Once they reached the Capitol, the petitions, containing 250,000 names, were presented to the Senate.

Paul organized delegations to lobby the president as well. The College Equal Suffrage League met with Wilson in April; the National Council of Women Voters saw the president in June; and in November, seventy-five women from Wilson's own state of New Jersey asked him to take up suffrage during the upcoming session of Congress. Wilson told the New Jersey women that, just the day before, he had spoken with several members of Congress about a House woman suffrage committee. When Anna Howard Shaw led a delegation in December, Wilson offered the noncommittal observation that a woman suffrage committee would be a good thing. Shaw and her NAWSA delegation left the White House buoyed by the comment while failing to take into account Wilson's refusal to commit himself on the issue one way or another.

At that point, Paul reported to the NAWSA convention that the first issue of *The Suffragist* had been published in November. She also reported that several organizing campaigns were under way in New Jersey, Long Island, Rhode Island, Delaware, Maryland, and North Carolina.

Another initiative that Paul began but did not report on, because it was just being organized, was a card index file. All CU members who met with any politician, from the president on down and including state officials, were required to write up details of the meeting on index cards that would be kept at the CU headquarters. In this way, anyone scheduled to meet with a politician, even months down the road, could consult the card file and know whether the politician had been spoken to before, what the dates and places of the meetings were, who attended, and whether any significant statements or commitments were made. The card file became a valuable tool for keeping track of officeholders and their stance regarding woman suffrage.

Finally, Paul reported on income and expenditures, including both the cost of the suffrage parade and the cost of hosting the annual convention. With one thousand dues-paying members by the end of 1913—and thanks to the pledges from people like Belmont, Havemeyer, and Elizabeth Kent—the CU was able to do what the NAWSA leaders had demanded of it when they put Paul and Burns in charge. The CU leaders raised enough to cover all of their operating expenses for the year: $25,343.88. Overall, Paul's glowing report provided ample evidence of her success as a strategist and leader. The audience responded enthusiastically, applauding frequently and cheering to show their approval of what had been accomplished. Clearly, the report that Paul delivered to the NAWSA convention had conveyed both a new sense of urgency and a renewed commitment to the pursuit of a federal amendment.

If any of the hardworking committee members expected praise from the NAWSA leadership, however, they were surely disappointed. Almost before the cheering stopped, it became apparent that trouble was brewing. At least two CU members—Paul and Mary Beard—were not terribly surprised. Before the convention, they had discussed in detail how the NAWSA leadership would likely respond, and why. NAWSA knew, before handing over the CC to Paul, that she was committed to renewing the campaign for a federal amendment. Nevertheless, they appointed Paul and Burns as chair and vice-chair. It was no secret that many of the older board members believed that these two younger women didn't have the experience or wisdom to succeed where their predecessors, including Anthony and Stanton, had failed. Yet, despite their criticisms, they weren't opposed to giving Paul as much rope as she wanted. After all, another failure by proponents of a federal amendment would be in NAWSA's best interest. Defeat in pursuance of a federal amendment would reinforce the wisdom of NAWSA's state-by-state strategy. This clash of political ideologies—pitting the federal amendment supporters against the states' rights advocates—would not likely be resolved to everyone's satisfaction. Paul and Beard agreed that NAWSA would not give an inch, regardless of the success or failure of the CU. Paul also knew that the CU could not back down from its position; thus she chose to make the federal amendment as much a focal point as possible during the meeting. Toward this end, she placed a conspicuously large sign behind the speaker's podium that read: "We Demand an Amendment to the Constitution of the United States Enfranchising Women."

Almost immediately after Paul delivered her year-end report to the audience, the NAWSA leaders began to reveal the depth of their displeasure with Paul's committee. In particular, Carrie Chapman Catt, the former NAWSA president, seemed intent on ascribing nefarious motives to the CU. Even the sign behind the speaker's podium was open to question. To Catt, it represented nothing less than a dark conspiracy to capture NAWSA for the "militant" enterprise. In truth, Catt was partially right about the sign—though not about the degree to which Paul meant it as indicative of a "coup." Catt had to persuade those who had just given Paul a standing ovation that efforts to secure a federal amendment were really nothing more than an attempt to take over the NAWSA in order to wage a militant campaign. Certainly Paul had never tried to conceal the fact that her main intention was to promote a federal amendment. And the activities of the CC/CU could hardly be characterized as "militant" by any standard. Dark conspiracies resided only in the minds of NAWSA leaders who did not trust Paul because of her association with the militant Pankhursts. Many of them truly believed that Paul wanted to take over NAWSA. Catt continued her attack by asking "What has become of the National American Woman Suffrage Association? It seems to me," she went on, "that there is something called the Congressional Union which is running the whole campaign on Congress."[2] It was a disingenuous question at best, since NAWSA had long ago given up on pursuing a federal amendment.

Catt forged ahead. The next barrage of questions dealt with finances. Carrie Chapman Catt was nobody's fool. She would never have initiated this line of questioning if she didn't have all the details already. She had to know that Dennett and Shaw not only agreed, at Paul's request, to form the new standing committee but also expressed their "hearty approval" of that request. And she also had to know about the restraints imposed on Paul regarding paying her own way for the suffrage parade. But Catt's inquiry made it sound as though Paul had acted solely on her own initiative in organizing the CU. Why, Catt asked, did the CU not have a budget allowance from NAWSA? What was the purpose of organizing the CU? By whose authority did the CU raise over $25,000 and not forward one penny to the national treasury when sharing fund-raising receipts with the national treasury was standard operating procedure for all affiliates? Didn't the CU misrepresent itself when it used NAWSA stationary for its fund-raising efforts?

By now, the entire audience was so quiet that a dropped pin would have echoed throughout the hall. Catt's questions came faster and faster and the audience grew quieter and quieter as the drama unfolded before them. When NAWSA's national treasurer, Katherine Dexter McCormick of Boston, joined the fray, she succeeded in inserting even more rancor into the discussion. McCormick made no bones about her dislike of Paul and her committee colleagues. Catt was not attempting to cast her doubts in a politic or subtle fashion. McCormick was even less subtle: she adamantly insisted that NAWSA could not—and should not—tolerate the state of affairs that, in her view, bordered on insubordination.

If Catt and McCormick seriously did not know about the controversy surrounding the appointment of Paul and Burns, there was at least one woman in the audience who could speak to the issues. This was Jane Addams, who reminded the NAWSA board that NAWSA had *insisted* that the CC raise its own operating funds. Addams also testified that NAWSA had made it clear that not one dime would be forthcoming from the national treasury. Reviewing her role in the negotiations between NAWSA and Paul and Burns, she noted that as far as she could determine, both the CC and the CU had been entirely aboveboard in their fund-raising and were scrupulous to the penny in their collection and disbursement of funds. And, finally, she pointed out that the NAWSA leaders had been well aware that the CC, under Paul's direction, would focus on a federal amendment.

A review of the financial records of the CC/CU confirmed that Paul had indeed been meticulous in terms of both fund-raising and expenditures. Pennies were as important to Paul as dollars. In addition, she demanded—and received—fiscal responsibility from her volunteers. All financial records were open to the NAWSA leaders and board members. From the tenor of the discussion following Paul's report, it may have seemed that Addams was the only person who had examined the records. But Catt and McCormick almost certainly looked at them, too. If they were intent on discrediting Paul, it would have been foolish to overlook a potential source of misconduct. Pursuing a line of questioning unsupported by the evidence was surely a tactical choice. Pretending not to know what was in the financial report allowed them to ask leading questions that they hoped would plant some seeds of doubt regarding the honesty of Paul and her colleagues. In addition, they wanted the audience to believe that the CC/CU had overstepped its bounds and needed to be brought back into line. Although members of the audience were clearly confused about what was going on, their overwhelming support of Paul just moments earlier made it difficult to criticize her successes. Impugning Paul's integrity was thus Catt's best bet.

The question still remains as to why Catt exhibited such a visceral dislike of Alice Paul. In many ways, she and Paul were similar. Both were astute tacticians and strategists, and both were fundamentally dedicated to achieving woman suffrage. Their means certainly differed, but with a little effort they could have worked together with effective results. The biggest disparity between them concerned the best way to get the vote for all women. Paul believed the only effective route was a federal amendment and was unwilling to compromise or postpone that strategy for even a moment. And Catt was committed to a state-by-state strategy and was not willing to acquiesce to a federal campaign as long as she believed the timing was wrong.

NAWSA had to be careful, as well, not to antagonize southern supporters. To southerners, states' rights were a paramount issue. They had no intention of approving any campaign that included subjugating states' rights to federal imperatives. After the Civil War, southern states began passing a series of laws that became known as Jim Crow laws. These were intended to effectively deny former slaves the rights they had gained with ratification of the Fourteenth and Fifteenth Amendments. One such law required that state citizens pass a literacy test in order to vote—a test that most former slaves would fail. But preventing African-Americans from voting would be more difficult—even with Jim Crow laws—if a federal suffrage amendment were passed and ratified.

As noted, many NAWSA members also believed and feared that Paul had imported too much militancy into the suffrage movement. Parades, demonstrations, deputations, and petitions were all fine. But the possibility that Paul might engage in an anti–Democratic Party campaign, holding the party responsible for failure to enact a federal amendment, would be going too far. These fears were heightened by the December 6th issue of *The Suffragist*. An editorial by Lucy Burns pointed out that the current Democratic Party was extremely powerful. "Those who hold power are responsible not only for what they do but for what they do not do," Burns wrote. "Inaction establishes just as clear a record as does a policy of open hostility."[3] If Paul and Burns went down that path of holding the Democrats responsible for not taking action because they were the party in power, the fear was that the Democrats who did support suffrage would be lost to the cause.

Catt's antipathy toward Paul, on the other hand, may have been triggered by an incident that occurred years earlier. At that time, Catt had "organized a committee, undertaken to raise funds, and made it the rejuvenating force of the Association, just as this young woman was doing now."[4] Catt's success brought out jealousies in her superiors who feared being seen as ineffective. When confronted with this dilemma, Catt chose to avoid open conflict. Instead, she gave in to the demands of the older women and disbanded her committee. Confronted now with a situation in which she represented the status quo and Paul represented the forces of change, Catt likely wanted to validate her own decision, twenty years earlier, to back down and disband her committee when pressured by NAWSA. And at present, as a staunch advocate of a strong, centralized authority within NAWSA, Catt had little patience for anyone she thought was overstepping. From that point on, there was an undercurrent of suspicion in Catt's dealings with and opinions of Paul. Catt was, Paul later said, one of the few suffragists "who seemed to have in her heart any real animosity."[5]

Despite the NAWSA members' admiration for what Paul had accomplished, on the one hand, and their confusion about her intentions, on the other, the lines had been clearly drawn at the annual convention. Paul, keeping her eye on the prize, refused to be flustered over Catt's insinuations. Most of the NAWSA members would ultimately choose to back the national organization, but a significant minority of motivated activists followed Paul and embraced her vision of how to get the vote. Their support became crystal clear in 1914, when Paul and Burns launched the first anti–Democratic Party campaign in the off-year elections.

As the New Year approached, one thing became particularly apparent: Paul and her Washington colleagues would soon be either brought to heel by NAWSA or expelled altogether. Shaw, Dennett, McCormick, and other NAWSA leaders were increasingly agitated by virtually everything that Paul did. They continued to define the Paul/Burns strategy as "militancy." To the NAWSA leadership, such a strategy would result in nothing less than a scorched-earth policy, which in turn would only retard the progress made since 1890. NAWSA insisted that any support that Paul and Burns showed for the Pankhursts in England, however minor, was evidence of militant intentions for the American campaign.

When Emmeline Pankhurst, the head of the British suffrage movement, announced that she intended to come to America on a speaking tour in order to raise funds, Shaw and Dennett were angry, to say the least. They feared that any funds raised by Pankhurst would take away from donations that would otherwise go to NAWSA. The two NAWSA leaders had continued to be publicly laudatory toward both younger suffragists in the wake of the successful parade. Neither Shaw nor Dennett wanted to appear critical. Indeed, Dennett, despite her earlier disapproval of Paul's plans for the CC, was almost effusive whenever Paul's name came up. All of that ended abruptly at the 1913 convention. Shaw and Dennett were now more openly critical. They disapproved of Pankhurst's tactics, especially after learning that Paul and Burns were helping Pankhurst organize her tour as well as researching the legal rights of their guest should she be arrested in the United States. The NAWSA leaders also learned that Rheta Childe Dorr would be accompanying Emmeline on her passage to the United States. All of this helped to convince Shaw and Dennett, among others, that Alice Paul was preparing to adopt militant tactics similar to those advocated by Emmeline Pankhurst.

Leaping to this conclusion was somewhat justified. Paul had long since made it clear that she intended to take the Democrats to task. But she refused to turn her back on Emmeline Pankhurst, whom she continued to admire for doing the hard work that other woman suffragists refused to do. In Paul's eyes, the Pankhursts were still fighting the good fight for women worldwide. However, at no time did Paul ever suggest that adopting violent tactics would be appropriate for the American movement. In her view, it was not in the American tradition to bomb buildings. Admittedly, Paul did not consider breaking windows a violation of her core beliefs. But from the very first she and, more reluctantly, Burns agreed that violence would not become part of their strategy for America. Shaw was convinced otherwise.

By early 1914, the conflict between NAWSA and the CU had gone public. Newspapers, including the *New York Times,* were featuring stories about the accusations that the CU had solicited funds under false pretenses. Quoting sources that could only be attributed to NAWSA personnel, one paper reported that the "liberal financial support" that had poured into CU coffers was purposefully solicited in such a way as to confuse donors who thought they were supporting the work of the national organization.[6] These accusations were geared to cast doubt on Paul's integrity. Moreover, they were reaching a wide audience. NAWSA leaders, as Carrie Chapman Catt later recounted in her own version of events, didn't really believe that Paul was misappropriating funds or using underhanded solicitation methods. Nevertheless, they refused to deny the newspaper accounts publicly.[7] What they did do was publicly insist that Paul and the CU deserved the bad publicity they were getting.

Paul quickly came to the conclusion that NAWSA's behavior, not to mention its imperious demands, constituted too great a price to pay for continued association with the national organization. She made it clear that the CU would not be dictated to by NAWSA—that it would not surrender its rights to decide how lobbyists, the organization, or its press bureau would operate. On January 12, 1914, in a forceful message that

NAWSA could not ignore, the CU demonstrated its support for Paul and her leadership. Elizabeth Kent opened her home to more than four hundred suffragists, who were unanimous in their insistence that the work of the CU should continue. Assisted by several high-profile volunteers, Kent raised $10,000 for the CU. If Paul had any doubts about what her volunteers thought of her leadership abilities, this gathering certainly put them to rest. In addition to the money raised, CU members presented Paul with an engraved silver cup in recognition of her successful year. No one had expected Paul to slow down or rethink her strategy in the wake of the NAWSA criticisms. It came as no surprise, therefore, when she announced that she intended to proceed as scheduled. The Congressional Union, Paul said, "will make a vigorous campaign against the Democratic candidates for Congress in close districts as the responsibility for the failure of the legislation should be placed on the Democratic Party."[8] This was the very strategy that NAWSA feared would be most harmful to the suffrage movement.

Despite all of her disagreements with NAWSA, Paul was reluctant to make a final break. She did not particularly want to start an independent and rival suffrage organization. At the same time, Paul was not about to let NAWSA call the shots regarding the pursuit of a federal amendment. The only real question that remained was how long it would take for the two groups to sever all relations. The answer came very quickly. Anna Howard Shaw had previously approved the formation of the CU and favored inclusion of the group as a NAWSA auxiliary. Now her tune changed. She let it be known that she agreed with other NAWSA leaders that the CU posed a threat not only to NAWSA but perhaps to the entire suffrage movement. As Shaw pointed out, the consequences of admitting the CU as a NAWSA auxiliary could be dire. A memo went out to all NAWSA members urging them to support the decision not to admit the CU. The Executive Committee backed Shaw's repudiation of the CU and voted 54 to 24 to deny auxiliary status.

Even so, Alice Paul asked for yet another face-to-face meeting with NAWSA leaders. On February 12, NAWSA met with her. Paul opened the discussion with a summary of plans that included another suffrage parade to be held in May. She hoped, in this way, to defuse some of the rancor that existed between the two groups, but it quickly became apparent that there were serious impediments to any real efforts at co-operation. The meeting soon broke down over the most pressing issue that continued to separate them: when and how to pursue a federal suffrage amendment. No agreement could be reached on this most pivotal issue. NAWSA believed that the CU would not be able to survive as an independent organization. Paul, for her part, was confident that a split with NAWSA would all but ensure a vigorous pursuit of a federal amendment because the CU would no longer have to spend time and energy trying to placate NAWSA. NAWSA informed Paul and her colleagues that they were no longer included within the NAWSA family of organizations. The fate of a federal amendment for woman suffrage now lay entirely with Paul.

There were real issues that had to be addressed before the CU could move on. Not the least of these were the persistent complaints from a small minority of CU members regarding how the organization was being run. Paul was accused of exercising authoritarian leadership without regard for any input from CU members. Paul and Burns knew the matter had to be settled. And since a new CU operating constitution had to be drawn up, this was the appropriate time and place to address the complaints. The dissenters argued that the process for choosing CU leaders was undemocratic, leaving them adrift from decision-making. Neither Paul nor Burns wanted to change how things were being done, and the overwhelming majority of members felt the same way. In Paul's opinion, the biggest impediment to an effectively responsive organization would be to run it like a big debating society. Perhaps her experiences as a social worker influenced her attitude toward this issue. More often than not, having to reach a consensus before any real action could be taken left everything up in the air. Getting a federal amendment in that environment could add years to the task. While equality for women continued to be Paul's goal, she accepted the fact that centralized leadership and authority created a more effective organization. In her mind, the responsibility for advocating equality in a democratic society and supporting the unilateral authority that would best achieve that goal lay entirely with the leadership. The Executive Committee had to ensure that everyone understood the necessity of maintaining a small centralized leadership that could make and implement policy without waiting for consensus from the rank and file. Their continued success, Paul believed, should amply demonstrate that necessity.

While some of her critics may have objected to this "ends justifying the means" approach, there was no confusion in Paul's mind. Getting equality and having equality were, in her view, two very different things. If she and Burns could not take the steps necessary to achieve equality, even if they were considered authoritarian by some, they would not have the luxury of defining and acting upon what having equality meant in a democratic society. Having equality would mean different things to different people, to be sure. But Paul's job, as she saw it, was to get that equality in the quickest and most straightforward way. She remarked more than once that when women did have equality under the law, many of them would do things she would never endorse. But she could not—and would not—attempt to define equality for all women. Until women had legal equality, she would continue to insist on centralized authority within her organization. If critics insisted on labeling her as authoritarian, she would live with that if doing so meant success.

At the same time, Paul realized that she could generate goodwill by asking the critics for their advice and suggestions. "We would be most grateful," she implored them more than once, "for any constructive plan which you can lay before us."[9] Edith Houghton Hooker offered a somewhat flawed solution that the CU adopted. She proposed a National Advisory Committee that, in turn, would elect the Executive Committee and provide for the election by the rank and file of state chairpersons who would have voting privileges at CU conventions. The national council would ultimately be appointed by the Executive Committee— the flaw in the plan. This solution did serve to placate the critics, however. And it retained the integrity of the leadership, thus guaranteeing the effective functioning of the organization. The new constitution also provided for state committees that would elect their own state chairpersons with voting rights at conventions. The Executive Committee chose a chairperson and appointed a National Advisory Council composed of prominent and influential women who held no other official position in the CU. The real power of the CU remained solely in the hands of the Executive Committee.

Hooker's proposal had other potential benefits as well. Establishing a National Advisory Council would provide an opportunity to enlist the visible support of nationally recognized women in a variety of fields who were immediately identifiable to other potential supporters. It could also engage wealthy women who were attracted to the work of the CU but did not necessarily want to take an active day-to-day role in the organization. These considerations contradicted Paul's insistence that she wanted members willing to work for suffrage rather than just putting their names on a membership list. But, as NAWSA had long understood, every organization needed members who were willing to invest their money to keep the organization afloat as well as members who were willing to invest their time and effort to accomplish the goals of the organization.

By the end of the first year, the CU had put together a stellar Advisory Council. It was not a group accustomed to rubber-stamping decisions, even Alice Paul's. However, even this group could not allay the persistent criticisms of authoritarianism, most of which were directed at Paul. One member who resigned from the Advisory Council made it clear that she was doing so because "the Congressional Union is an autocratic organization with its controls entirely in the hands of one woman."[10] Nevertheless, Paul refused to enter into any agreement that would compromise the Executive Committee so long as she and it were making progress toward the goal of securing a federal amendment. In the end it was easier to send a polite note to critics, acknowledging their complaints. "I do not see how you can possibly belong to an organization with whose policy you are not in sympathy,"[11] she wrote to one critic. Perhaps, she suggested, the woman might wish to consider resigning in favor of another organization—one where she would find more congenial circumstances.

In the meantime, NAWSA kept up its own criticisms of Paul and the CU. Neither side was able to stop the wild rumors that began first as ripples following the 1913 annual convention and quickly grew to tsunami proportions. Shaw seemed unable to refrain from publicly taking Paul and the CU to task as rumors reached her desk. Paul, on the other hand, refused to comment on any of the rumors circulating, believing that answering the criticisms leveled against her would only needlessly prolong the discussion. In the long run, Shaw's public responses helped to produce the very situation she most feared: the defection of NAWSA members in favor of the CU. Even some previously longtime members of NAWSA were attracted to the new activism inspired by Paul. Shaw's criticisms struck them as petty and vindictive.

A number of suffragists were torn between loyalty to NAWSA and a desire to be part of the new movement. But holding membership in both organizations became increasingly difficult as time went on. When Shaw and Ruth Hanna McCormick aired their displeasure over NAWSA members belonging to both organizations, the possibility for cooperation became even more problematic. At one point, a delegation of NAWSA members appealed to Shaw to "unite us on a platform broad enough to hold all suffragists" so that they could work together and accomplish their goal. Still, Paul was not going to abandon her focus on the federal amendment. Shaw and other NAWSA leaders and members who had been working diligently in state campaigns felt just as strongly that their strategy would be more effective. It would be unfair to fault Shaw for her loyalty to the cause as she saw it. Yet her inability or unwillingness to let rumors die a quick death was needlessly divisive. Moreover, some of the residual suspicions generated by Shaw's public criticisms further convinced Paul that NAWSA, whatever it might have indicated in the past, was not interested in doing anything constructive to promote a federal amendment. At the same time, Paul had no interest in promoting state-by-state campaigns to change constitutions. Both sides were going to continue pursuing their own goals.

In March 1914, Paul decided to go home to Mooretown for a brief rest. Having worked nonstop for the year prior to the NAWSA convention in December 1913, she needed time to rejuvenate. She planned to spend a few weeks surrounded by family, away from the stress of the rumor mill, just relaxing and catching up on her much-missed reading. Tacie Paul was more than happy to have her oldest daughter at home for any length of time. In her opinion, Alice looked too thin and too tired since her return from England. Almost before she had a chance to settle in at the family home, Alice received an urgent note from Lucy Burns. Burns reported that Ruth Hanna McCormick, who was now chairperson of NAWSA's Congressional Committee, had, without notice or warning, endorsed a new suffrage amendment on NAWSA's behalf. The Shafroth-Palmer legislation, popularly known as the Shafroth Amendment, had been introduced in Congress early in March. The Shafroth Amendment weighed in on the side of suffrage as a states' rights issue rather than a federal issue. Shafroth stated that suffrage could be placed on the ballot in any state if 8 percent of the voters who had voted in a previous election requested such a referendum. The official request would be in the form of a petition signed by the requisite number of voters. For reasons that are hard to fathom, since Shafroth had added yet another layer to the process of getting suffrage onto a state's ballot as a referendum item, NAWSA went along with McCormicks' endorsement of the amendment. Shafroth would, of course, appeal to states' rights advocates, especially in the South. It would also appeal to members of Congress outside of the South who did not favor a federal amendment. But none of those reasons would actually ensure that suffrage would receive any real benefit from the Shafroth Amendment.

Paul recognized Shafroth for the red herring that it was. All Shafroth did was to require any woman suffrage action to begin at the state level rather than at the federal level. There was nothing in the legislation as written that made securing constitutional changes in the states any easier than the way women had been pursuing it for the last three decades, with little to show for their efforts. Paul immediately cut short her vacation and returned to Washington, DC. She also requested a meeting with NAWSA to discuss the new situation. Knowing full well that NAWSA remained committed to state-by-state campaigns, Paul nevertheless hoped that logic would persuade them to denounce the Shafroth Amendment. The alternative she recommended—the Anthony Amendment, named for Susan B. Anthony—was a straightforward piece of legislation containing no ambiguity or subterfuge: "The right of citizens of the United States to vote shall not be denied or abridged by the United States or by any State on account of sex. Congress shall have power to enforce this article by appropriate legislation." Anyone comparing the two proposed amendments would, she believed, have to recognize that the Anthony Amendment was the most direct path to woman suffrage.

Shaw, Dennett, Jane Addams, and Katherine Dexter McCormick met with Paul, Burns, Mary Beard, Dora Lewis, and Elizabeth Kent. Over a two-day period, the two sides debated the potential repercussions of the proposed legislation and NAWSA's support of it. In the course of the discussion, it became apparent that Ruth Hanna McCormick had acted upon the advice of her father's political cronies. Mark Hanna was a powerful influence within the Democratic Party, and he opposed the idea of a federal woman suffrage amendment. He and his political colleagues had convinced Ruth Hanna McCormick that Congress would never approve the Anthony Amendment—and that the states would never ratify it if it did somehow become law. What also became painfully clear is that McCormick acted on her own without first consulting with the NAWSA Board.

The NAWSA representatives knew they were in a position of weakness but insisted that they would follow the advice of Mark Hanna. As *The Suffragist* reported, "Mrs. McCormick has all these positions and friends in Congress who know so much about it all and think it is the best thing to do, and have already introduced it." Paul and her colleagues tried to reason with the NAWSA leaders, but they continued to assert that they were acting on well-informed advice. Even the sympathetic Jane Addams could not change their minds. The leaders' stubborn insistence that any suggestions emanating from the CU had to be an effort to discredit them forced NAWSA to support McCormick, even though members of their own board questioned the value of the Shafroth Amendment. Try as they might, the CU delegates probably knew they were fighting an uphill—if not futile—battle. At the very beginning of their talks with NAWSA, Katherine Dexter McCormick turned her chair around and for the entire two days sat with her back toward the CU.

Now that NAWSA's leaders had made it clear that they were committed to the Shafroth Amendment, Paul had no choice but to ensure that the CU would do everything in its power to continue fighting for a federal amendment. In truth, there was never a question that any other avenue would be investigated by the CU. The Anthony Amendment not only had to be kept alive; it had to be at the forefront of the struggle for woman suffrage. Rheta Childe Dorr immediately put the issue on the front page of *The Suffragist*. Dorr detailed the CU's objections to the Shafroth Amendment. She also pointed out the irony of NAWSA's insistence that the CU leadership was autocratic: "The action of the National American Association in introducing the new amendment without consultation with the body of the Association savors a bit of autocracy."

In one of the few instances that Paul responded publicly to accusations coming from NAWSA, she managed to dismiss both the Shafroth Amendment and NAWSA in one stroke. This was a moment in which it was imperative, Paul believed, to make her position absolutely clear—because the issue struck so close to matters critical to the movement. "We are not antagonistic to the new resolution at all," she stated, "and think that if some initiative and referendum society were to press it, it might be a helpful thing. We feel, however, that we must concentrate upon one amendment or another as otherwise one will be used by congressmen against the other."[12]

Many of NAWSA's rank and file were confused and angry at this new turn of events. In March 1914, attendees of the Mississippi Valley Conference talked about almost nothing else. Conference members circulated a petition, to be sent to NAWSA headquarters, that endorsed the Anthony Amendment and pointed out the impediments contained in the Shafroth Amendment. The petition was signed by almost all of the conference delegates. The few exceptions were those who feared they might lose the support of NAWSA if they put their names on the document.

In reaction to the uproar that resulted from the Shafroth Amendment controversy, Shaw felt compelled to issue a long, detailed response to the rank and file. She immediately denied any conflict between supporting the Shafroth Amendment and supporting the Anthony Amendment. The two amendments, she argued, were not inconsistent. The CU was to blame for spreading false information, thus creating the internal dispute. Shaw also supported Ruth Hanna McCormick's endorsement of Shafroth, even though McCormick had consulted no one except her father's anti-suffrage political cronies. She ended with an appeal for loyalty from NAWSA members and one final slap at Alice Paul and the CU: "If the Union would stop trying to create false impressions . . . there would be less difficulty. . . . [The] main purpose of the Congressional Union is to create a disturbance. . . . To cooperate with an organization that is outside the National Association . . . seems to me lacking in that sort of loyalty which gives courage and strength to an organization."[13]

The fault for driving a wedge between Shaw and NAWSA, on the one hand, and Paul and the CU, on the other, did not lie solely with either organization. The Democratic Party had consistently chosen to reject a federal amendment in favor of states' rights. From President Wilson on down, the party refused to consider any substantive proposal for securing woman suffrage. Even worse, Wilson continued to insist that he was not free to express his support of woman suffrage unless and until his party endorsed it. Even when it was pointed out that Wilson had chosen to act on the tariff issue without the endorsement of the Democratic Party, he continued to hide behind his party's inaction. The time had come to hold the Democrats responsible for failure to enact a woman suffrage amendment.

5

Taking on the Democrats

Despite the dire predictions from political analysts who warned that any dissension in the suffrage ranks would do irreparable harm to the women's movement, Paul initiated her long-contemplated anti–Democratic Party campaign. While some may have doubted she would do so—and others hoped she would not—the campaign had never been just an idle threat. The electoral successes of the Democratic Party in 1912 ironically made her task easier than it might otherwise have been. Because of the split in the Republican Party, with Teddy Roosevelt campaigning as the third-party Bull Moose candidate, the Democrats won not only the presidency but substantial margins in both houses as well. For the first time since before the Civil War, the Democrats were in a position to call their own legislative shots. Paul could argue credibly that the Democrats should be held responsible for failing to do anything on behalf of woman suffrage.

In the summer of 1914, the so-called militants met at the home of Alva Belmont to map out their strategy. Belmont's monument to her reentry into New York Society—Marble House, a $2 million "cottage" built in the 1890s on the shores of Newport, Rhode Island—stood among a row of ostentatiously magnificent mansions on the Atlantic coast. Their extravagance mirrored the wealth of their illustrious owners, who spent little more than two or three months in residence each summer. Now, in the summer heat of August 1914, CU Advisory Council members gathered in Newport at the mansion. Only one CU member—Mary Ritter Beard—refused to attend the meeting. Although totally in accord with the purpose of the conference, Beard could not bring herself to participate in a meeting held at such a bastion of wealth and privilege. She refused, she said, to do "the Newport stunt." As she confided to Alice Paul, "I shall probably be the only one who, for labor attachments, feels that participation in the Newport plans is inadvisable." Paul tried her best to persuade Beard, whose political savvy she greatly valued, to put aside her qualms and come to Newport.

Beard may have refused to attend, but she did not discount the political spin that Paul could put on the conference. "Newport and money stand in the popular mind for one and the same thing," Beard noted, "and you might just as well play them up together in the press reports of the conference and get all the help possible from the combination. There is no advantage in having Congressmen against whom we propose to wage war to get an impression that we went into Newport and ate in Child's restaurant and brought away no money. Let them think we invaded the seats of the mighty and brought away a war chest." Ever gracious and committed to the cause, Beard also refused to criticize or condemn her colleagues who did go to Newport, even if she would not: "I just don't feel like making that play, invaluable to success as it is, especially since so many of you are brave enough to do it well alone. I think I am a pure coward in this."[1]

Paul and Burns already knew what they were going to propose. Now they had only to convince their Advisory Council that their strategy was the only path open. To be sure, regardless of whether she was able to persuade the majority of her members that they had to take on the Democrats, Paul would not let anything deter her. Time and again, the Democrats had demonstrated their allegiance to states' rights. And Paul was convinced that much of the states' rights argument was little more than a way to avoid publicly coming out against woman suffrage altogether, while at the same time solidifying Democrats' solid southern support. In the Far West, where several states already had equal suffrage, the story was much different. Democrats in those states were politically compelled to be pro-suffrage, including advocating a federal amendment. Indeed, although some elected officials supported suffrage on principle, the reality was that the issue rested more on politics. This held true for Republicans as well. As long as suffragists like Paul were willing to hold the party in power responsible for failure to enact a federal amendment, Republicans were more than willing to support that stand without much fear of being targeted by their constituents. Equal suffrage had not yet reached the point where a majority of voters favored it. But the voters were no less susceptible to the politics involved than were their elected officials.

Even in the midst of the conflict with NAWSA, Paul had continued to organize delegations among the Democrats. Deputations and demonstrations continued with regularity. In February 1914, four hundred working women met with President Wilson. They were led by women from the National Women's Trade Union League and the New York Women's Trade Union League as well as by textile and laundry workers from Pennsylvania. In choosing the delegates' leaders, Paul knew exactly what she was doing. Two leaders of large labor organizations along with two women workers sent a clear message that among working women, leaders and rank and file all supported suffrage. It was another example of Paul's political acumen. Wilson chose to fall back on his now-standard excuse for not engaging in any meaningful efforts to promote woman suffrage, announcing that "[u]ntil this party, as such, has considered a matter of this very supreme importance and taken its position, I am not at liberty to speak for it." In this instance, Wilson did not have to wait long for his party to make its views known. The next day, February 3, the Democratic House Caucus met to announce its stand on woman suffrage. A California congressman proposed to his colleagues that they establish a House Woman Suffrage Committee. But J. Thomas Heflin of Alabama, a powerful member of the party, proposed a substitute resolution declaring suffrage a states' rights issue. Heflin's power within the party was apparent when, by a vote of 123 to 57, the caucus voted in favor of his states' rights proposal. To ensure that everyone understood exactly where the party stood, Heflin's fellow Alabamian and equally powerful party member, Oscar Underwood, clarified things further: "I not only said I was opposed to it, but I said the party on this side of the chamber was opposed to it, and the party that has control of legislation in Congress certainly has the right openly and above board to say that it will not support a measure if it is not in accordance with its principles."[2]

Not surprisingly, NAWSA responded by aiming its guns at the CU instead of at the Democrats. In particular, it took Paul and the CU to task for insisting on an early vote by the Democratic caucus. "Five years of good suffrage work has been undone by this action," a NAWSA leader claimed. Paul refused to be undone by the attack. She pointed out that suffrage would benefit regardless of how the caucus voted. If the Democrats voted favorably, suffrage would be advanced. And if the Democrats voted against supporting a federal suffrage amendment (as they did), the Democrats, who held all the political power, would have to be held accountable. It was far easier, Paul noted, to curry support for women once a party showed a weak hand on suffrage instead of hiding its opposition behind a wall of silence.[3]

Paul planned a nationwide series of demonstrations to be held on May 2. She had been working on the demonstrations for several months. NAWSA, aware of the upcoming event, now demanded that the Senate also bring the issue to an early vote. Paul asked NAWSA to withdraw its request for an early Senate vote until after May 2. Even without the scheduled demonstrations, NAWSA would have been wise to get a postponement of a Senate vote. Anna Howard Shaw had specifically been told that if the Senate voted quickly on the suffrage issue, the measure would meet defeat just as it had in the House. Despite the best efforts of the CU, NAWSA succeeded in getting the vote scheduled for March 19. For the first time in twenty-seven years, the Senate voted on a woman suffrage bill. As predicted, it was defeated—by a margin of one vote. The majority of votes against the measure came from southern Democrats. NAWSA may have hoped that Democrats would support the bill, particularly since Democrats had been the ones who pushed for an early vote. Their hope was misplaced. But Paul expected nothing more. The vote in the Senate merely reinforced her long-held conviction that expecting any opponent to do the right thing would lead to disappointment—and distraction. In her view, this outcome was just another instance in which the Democrats failed to support something after misleading the public regarding their intentions. As she explained earlier, through their vote they demonstrated once again their opposition to suffrage.

Women rallied in cities and towns across the nation on May 2. CU organizers had gone to almost every state to coordinate the event, drawing together nearly every suffrage organization in the country. As her chief organizer Paul chose her old Swarthmore friend, Mabel Vernon. Paul had always been impressed with Mabel's ability to mesmerize audiences. Stylish, if not a natural beauty, Mabel always wore a trademark white suit, coordinated blouse, sheer white stockings, and white shoes. She also sported a fashionable hat. Paul had contacted Mabel in the spring of 1913, imploring her to join their campaign for woman suffrage. Mabel hesitated for two very good reasons: she had a secure job teaching high school, and she depended on her salary since—unlike Paul and Lucy Burns—she had no independent means of support. But once again Paul would not take "no" for an answer. Typical of her somewhat brash pronouncements from time to time, she pointed out that "anyone" could teach high school students. If Mabel didn't know Paul as well as she did, she might have been offended by this thoughtless dismissal of her chosen career. But she had long since learned that Paul didn't always edit her conversation, especially with old friends. In the end, because Mabel's fund-raising skills were truly formidable, Paul asked her how much she needed to support herself, in the event that she quit her teaching job. Mabel thus became one of a handful of organizers who received a small stipend.

The demonstrations and rallies exceeded expectations. Even the leaders of NAWSA agreed to participate as long as it was understood that they were not endorsing the CU. The rallies were intended to show support for the Anthony Amendment. NAWSA still professed not to see any conflict in its dual support of the Anthony Amendment and the Shafroth Amendment, but Paul unhesitatingly admitted that without NAWSA's participation and ability to turn out great numbers of suffragists, the rallies would have been less successful than they were. Indeed, this positive outcome ought to have been a convincing example of the value of cooperation. But, unfortunately, Paul and Shaw still refused to cooperate in finding a way to pursue both of their goals. Paul remained relentless in her pursuit of a federal amendment. And Shaw continued to view Paul more as an enemy than as a potential ally. In these circumstances, neither woman felt compelled to cross the lines they had drawn in the sand.

Whether or not Congress intended to do so, it seemed to acknowledge the pressure brought to bear by the demonstrable success of the May 2 rallies. On May 5, the House Judiciary Committee reported out the Mondell Resolution (Anthony Amendment). The Rules Committee couldn't bring itself to do anything other than report out the resolution without recommendation. Even so, this result was significant because it was the first time that a suffrage measure had been out of committee in the House. Ordinarily, the Rules Committee would meet to allocate a specific date on which to discuss a resolution and vote on it. However, its May 5th action notwithstanding, the committee chose instead to stall. Paul and Burns immediately began organizing delegations to members of Congress in an effort to schedule the hearings. After pressing the issue, they were finally able to extract a promise from Democrats to convene on July 1. Paul would have preferred an earlier date, but the delay gave her an opportunity to organize yet another delegation to President Wilson. Led by Rheta Childe Dorr, a delegation of members from the General Federation of Women's Clubs (GFWC) met with Wilson in the East Room on June 30. Dorr presented Wilson with a resolution passed by the GFWC several weeks earlier, urging him to use his influence to ensure prompt action by the Rules Committee. Once again, Wilson told the women that he was bound by his party's platform. This time, however, he went further, telling the delegation that he believed suffrage was a states' rights issue and ought to be decided by the states and not by the federal government.

July 1 came and went with no action taken by the Rules Committee. In an effort to placate the suffragists who had gathered in Washington for the hearings, the committee assured them that its members would meet without fail in one month. August 1 also came and went without any action. Then, on August 28, one day before the Marble House meeting was to convene, the Rules Committee finally met. The members voted to report favorably on legislation providing greater self-government for the Philippines. At that point, having completed its work for the day, the committee promptly adjourned. No one in the CU had waited around for this latest bit of Democratic hostility toward suffrage to play itself out. Even as the Rules Committee was meeting, CU Advisory Council members were either on their way to Newport or already at Marble House. As word of the Rules Committee's actions on behalf of Philippine self-government reached members of the CU, their resolve to deal boldly with the Democrats made Paul's task that much easier.

Lucy Burns opened the August 29th proceedings by outlining the work of the past several months. Then, setting the stage for Paul, Burns offered an analysis of how Congress worked. When Paul took the podium, she initially requested that all members of the press withdraw. She then pledged everyone present to secrecy, explaining that attendees should not tip their hand prematurely. By that she meant that the secrecy pledge should remain in effect until every phase of the plan was ready to be implemented. For the benefit of those who might have been less informed, Paul also explained the function of political parties in American politics. The CU's goal in the weeks to come would be to "convince the dominant party, and all other parties, that opposition to suffrage is inexpedient." Paul then submitted, for the delegates' approval, the Executive Committee's plan to wage political war against the Democrats in the nine western states where women already had the vote. Pausing briefly to give weight to her words, Paul declared: "[T]he time has come when we can really go into *national* politics and use the nearly four million votes we have to win the vote for the rest of the women in the country." Looking at each member of the Advisory Council, Paul concluded: "Our fight is a political one. . . . The question is whether we are good enough politicians to take four million votes and organize them and use them." It was a rhetorical question. As far as Paul was concerned, the only answer was "YES!"[4]

Paul had delivered a masterful speech. The soft-spoken little general flawlessly built her case. This was no casual off-the-cuff talk. She had anticipated every objection that could be raised against the plan. And, in the course of her talk, she had answered each one, including all of the accusations raised by NAWSA—not the least of which was the charge of partisanship. "This policy is absolutely non-partisan," she declared. About this issue, she was unequivocal: "It calls upon women to lay aside all party affiliations and put suffrage before party." To those who accused her of doing "irreparable harm" by opposing pro-suffrage Democrats, Paul was equally clear. She pointed out that all congressional candidates in full-suffrage states were, by definition, pro-suffrage. Could a candidate in a suffrage state, whether a Republican, a Progressive, or an Independent, go before the electorate and tell voters that he opposed their right to vote? Campaigning against Democratic candidates could only serve to assure voters that non-Democratic candidates were absolutely in favor of woman suffrage. The CU's anti–Democratic Party campaign would have a predictable effect, Paul asserted. "When once the political parties are made to realize that opposition to suffrage means their defeat, when once it is shown that suffragists can actually affect the results of a national election, our fight will be won." Finally, Paul addressed the militancy issue. To those who accused her of fomenting militancy, Paul answered: "It is militant only in the sense that it is strong, positive and energetic."[5]

The members of the Advisory Council needed no further convincing. They overwhelmingly approved Paul's strategy. Katherine Houghton Hepburn later confided to Paul that "the way you and Lucy Burns with your program swept us all completely into the movement is something I was very much impressed with." Florence Kelley of the National Consumers League spoke for many of her Advisory Council colleagues when she noted, "I do not see how there could possibly be a more statesmanlike proposal than that which has been made this afternoon."[6]

The Marble House plan marked a new departure in the history of woman suffrage in America. The states' rights advocates, despite their small successes, had never attempted to enlist women voters in suffrage states to help their sisters in nonsuffrage states. NAWSA's *modus operandi* in state campaigns left the details to each state's resident suffragists: state leaders ran the campaigns, decided on methodology, raised most of the money to support the campaign, and composed and distributed their argument for state constitutional change in favor of allowing women to vote. When they failed, as they most often did, they frequently had to wait two or more years before they could mount another campaign. There were three reasons for this. First, state constitutions often required a specified amount of time before citizens could revisit the issue electorally. Second, raising new funding for another campaign was always harder the second time around. And, third, those who ran the campaign found the defeat both exhausting and demoralizing. They were in no hurry to begin the fight all over again. In the few instances where the campaigns ended in success, NAWSA considered its work done in those particular states. There was no consideration of how to use the potential power of the newly enfranchised women voters. Paul intended to change that dynamic.

Paul and Burns knew that they had to mount a reasonably credible anti–Democratic Party campaign. Although never publicly suggested, the year 1914 would be a warm-up for the main event—the national election in 1916. The major goals in 1914 would be to convince politicians of all parties that woman voters could be mobilized as a voting bloc, that by solidarity they could further the interests of all women, and that the parties or individuals who opposed a suffrage amendment did so at their own peril. The candidates in 1916 would be much less certain of their ground if the CU demonstrably succeeded in laying the foundation for a potentially powerful special-interest group. Toward that end, the 1914 campaign had to be waged with commitment and vigor by all concerned. Again, without announcing their expectations, Paul and Burns proceeded with the knowledge that publicity and perception would be crucial in 1914.

The CU press department immediately swung into action, and the media did its intended part by reporting that the Marble House meeting marked an important departure for women. The *New York Tribune* declared unequivocally that Marble House "marked the entrance of women into the arena of practical politics. . . . At Newport for the first time was launched a national movement of women armed to fight with political weapons for their rights."[7] Though the CU press department was careful to divulge only what Paul wanted revealed at the moment, other newspapers ran similar versions of the story. Indeed, publicity and perception were already being generated before the delegates had left Marble House.

Within two weeks, Paul began to implement her plan. Whatever drawbacks she encountered elicited quick modifications of the original plan. For example, she wanted two organizers dispatched to each of the nine suffrage states. But persuading members to drop everything and head west proved to be a difficult proposition. It wasn't that the CU rank and file disagreed with her strategy. Rather, not many members had the time and the means to travel west and spend several weeks organizing women voters. Moreover, they had to raise their own expenses to the extent possible. And they had to accomplish all this while figuring out how to reach women voters who were isolated in small towns miles and miles from populated centers. Moreover, CU members had to be prepared for weather ranging from oppressive heat to blizzard-like conditions, the antipathy of Democrats who would surely do their best to discourage the organizers, accommodations that would try their resolve, and grueling drives by one means or another through uncharted territory. Overall, it would take courage, determination, and spunk to survive these two months of campaigning.

With "no" not in her vocabulary, Paul eventually found her hand-picked team of organizers. They had to have the right combination of independence, motivation, managerial skills, and public-speaking talent with style and flair. And, to remain in the field, they had to be politically astute, creative, tactful, and hard as nails. Ideally, one woman would take charge of opening and operating a state headquarters—attending to the press, distributing literature, arranging speaking tours—and the remaining state organizer would stump the state, speaking on behalf of the federal amendment and the CU and urging women to vote against the Democratic candidates in their districts as a matter of honor on behalf of women not yet enfranchised.

Paul sent Lucy Burns and Rose Winslow, a fiery and riveting speaker for both the suffrage and the labor cause, to California. In Denver, Doris Stevens, a young woman with journalistic experience and ample reserves of sheer nerve, noted in suffrage circles for both her radical views and her stunning appearance, teamed with Ruth Noyes, whose demeanor was much quieter but who possessed unflagging energy. Josephine Casey, a labor organizer with a reputation as a no-holds-barred speaker, signed on to organize Arizona with Jane Pincus, an effective fund-raiser. Lola Trax and Edna Latimer, both organizers of Maryland's Just Government League, were sent to Kansas. The CU press secretary, Jessie Hardy Stubbs, went to Oregon with Virginia

Arnold, whose mild-mannered personality masked a single-minded persistence. In Washington State, Margaret Faye Whittemore and Anne McCue, both of Philadelphia, were on hand. Gertrude Hunter, the founder of the Wage Earner's League of Minneapolis, was the sole organizer in Cheyenne, Wyoming, and lone organizer Elsie Lancaster, a seemingly placid soul with a spine of steel, headed to Utah. In Idaho, Helena Hill Weed took a six-week furlough from home and children to open headquarters in Boise. Finally, the ever-reliable and effective Mabel Vernon was sent to Nevada at the request of NAWSA—and with Paul's approval—to assist Anne Martin in the then-ongoing referendum in that state. Mabel would spend just a couple of weeks in Nevada, mostly fund-raising, before heading for one of the understaffed states.

Most of the field organizers were unmarried. Those with families, such as Helena Hill Weed, found a way to spend extensive periods away from home. But for all involved, the work required sacrifices. Rose Winslow and Josephine Casey, despite having no family financial support, gave up their jobs. As a rule, organizers were not paid salaries, though the CU did pick up their expenses when necessary. In extreme cases, like that of Weed, a widow with small children and staggering debts incurred by her spendthrift husband, a small remuneration was paid. In many cases the living accommodations were even more primitive than anticipated and remained largely unchanged from 1914 to 1916. Sara Bard Field, who was enlisted in 1916 to organize in Nevada, found herself stranded in a small town in the same run-down hotel that the 1914 organizers had to deal with. She later described it as "one big spittoon with all the cooking odors in the state for two generations collected within its walls."[8]

States varied in their reception to the organizers, but virtually all of them had to endure the antipathy of Democratic politicians and the pro-Democrat press. Anti-Democrat publications were similarly effusive. The *Republican Herald* of Salt Lake City, Utah, reported that "the Democratic generalissimo [W. R. Wallace] and his gang of political manikins" threatened "to advertise Miss Lancaster the country over by means of the Associated Press as being in league with 'sinister' influences in Utah."[9] And the *Seattle Sunday Times,* a Democrat newspaper, reported that the Democratic candidate for the Senate showed up at the union headquarters in Seattle to express "his fatherly concern for the two young women suffrage leaders. He suggested that they should go on home . . . and let the Democratic congressional candidates alone."[10]

Less predictable were the responses of voters. Jane Pincus was initially frustrated by the intransigence of Arizona's women. In mid-October, however, she reported that "the one woman in Phoenix and almost in the state, who has to take the initial step before the rest do anything, came down to our office." Pincus's entire effort in the state seemed to revolve around attracting this one individual. In contrast, Lucy Burns reported that California women came "in droves" to the headquarters, located just around the corner from a major San Francisco thoroughfare, Market Street. When Edna Latimer was told that local residents who were holding a political meeting "out on the prairie" had requested that she come and speak to them, she headed out to find the meeting. She didn't get there until eleven o'clock at night and fully expected that everyone would have gone home. To her utter amazement, three hundred Kansans were patiently waiting to hear what she had to say about suffrage. The next morning, at the train station, a man approached her saying, "My wife was at your meeting yesterday . . . and I thought I would tell you that I have voted the Democratic ticket for forty years, but I have voted it for the last time."[11]

But whether greeted as friend or foe, the CU organizers reported a similar experience overall, describing the time they spent in the western states as grueling, exhausting, sometimes frightening, and occasionally exhilarating. Paul, as it turned out, had chosen her organizers wisely. Though they all could tell tales of having driven aimlessly on unmarked roads through back country, sometimes in the wee hours of the morning, putting up with rainstorms, snowstorms, desert heat, and bone-chilling cold and grateful for even the most rudimentary accommodations, they accomplished more than perhaps anyone—with the exception of Paul—could have anticipated. The postelection analysis was more than encouraging. Newspapers across the country tended to support the CU's claims, thus helping to favorably shape readers' perceptions regarding the effectiveness of the campaign. In one instance, an article syndicated by the Newspaper Enterprise Association stated that the Democrats were only just beginning to take seriously the importance of the CU campaign. The article pointed out that in Colorado, where the power of women's influence was generally acknowledged, the Democrats were obliged to devote their last campaign circulars, issued on the eve of the election, entirely to the women's campaign. Similarly, in Oregon, while arguing for the reelection of Senator George Chamberlain, state Democrats made a plea for the support of women voters: "The importance of the situation will be more fully realized by the Democratic pols when they understand that this wonderful fight which the women made this time was the result of a very short campaign, by only two women organizers in each state, with very little money. . . . [W]ith two years more, the women can absolutely assure a Democratic defeat."[12]

This was no dismal failure, contrary to what the anti-suffragists and even NAWSA claimed. One organizer remarked wryly but with great satisfaction that "every candidate who was running, even for state or county offices, felt it necessary to declare that he had always believed in woman suffrage, that his mother had believed in woman suffrage and that his grandmother believed in it."[13] In the field of candidates in the suffrage states, the CU campaigned against forty-three Democrats running for House, Senate, and governors' seats. Of those, twenty were elected to office. Paul wisely refrained from making extravagant claims regarding the CU's role in the twenty-three defeats. Many of these candidates may well have lost in any case. In the 1912 elections, the Progressive Party acted as a spoiler for Republicans, thereby benefiting Democrats. But in 1914, there was no credible third party to upset the apple cart. This fact, along with the traditional losses incurred by incumbents in off-year elections, undoubtedly accounted for the substantial losses suffered by the Democrats nationwide. But the CU could, and did, make the modest claim that their efforts helped to contribute to Democrat losses. They could also point to several Democrat losses that they took full credit for. In Kansas, Colorado, Utah, Oregon, Washington, and Idaho, Democratic Party incumbents in both the House and Senate who were, by all accounts, assured of reelection lost their seats. In each of these elections, the voters, the press, and sometimes even the candidates themselves acknowledged that they went down to defeat because of the CU buzz-saw.

A very gratified Alice Paul confided to Mary Beard that the Congressional Union had succeeded beyond her "fondest hopes."[14] The campaign had begun with a burst of energy that was quickly becoming an Alice Paul trademark—specifically, with organizers departing Washington on a "suffrage train" resplendent in purple, white, and gold banners. And it had ended with the organizers returning home exhausted but victorious. Indeed, the CU itself had succeeded in one of its major goals. By the time Election Day had come and gone, the topic of woman suffrage was on everyone's lips; it was played out in daily newspapers across the country and debated on the floors of state and national legislatures and by voters and nonvoters alike. Regardless of whether the CU was being praised or vilified, people in all walks of life were talking about suffrage. It was a national political issue. In addition, during the course of the campaign the CU had grown markedly in terms of membership, money, and importance—not just within the suffrage movement but in the women's movement overall. Suffrage was discussed at the Heterodoxy club's weekly Greenwich Village luncheons attended by New York's most radical and influential feminists, as well as at social gatherings attended by farm women in Kansas, working women in eastern manufacturing towns, and housewives in just about every state. Regardless of which side of the questions they came down on, women were talking about it in ways that they hadn't before. Even male voters were talking about woman suffrage.

If Alice Paul needed any further confirmation that she was on the right track, the news brought back from a delegation to the chairman of the House Rules Committee erased any lingering doubts. Elizabeth Kent and Helen Hamilton Gardner called on Chairman Robert Henry right after the election. Wasting little time, he assured the suffragists that the Rules Committee would report favorably on House Resolution 514, which would set aside time on the House calendar to debate the issue and vote on the amendment. As for the Rules Committee's previous inability to get a report out, Henry attributed this to vague "sinister" influences. Alice Paul could not have cared less about unidentified sinister influences. On the heels of CU's stunning success, she was already moving toward her next challenge.

6

A New Plan, a New
Party, an Old Fight

The word *exhausted* described everyone involved in the campaign, including Alice Paul. Although she had not traveled to the western states, she spent every day from early morning to the late hours of the night writing directives, contacting people, evaluating reports, fund-raising, tracking down members of Congress, keeping abreast of the press coverage, changing procedures that seemed not to be working, and ensuring that her state organizers knew how much suffrage depended on their efforts and how grateful were the women back home. Paul allowed herself no downtime. She knew what her state organizers were going through and, for their sake, believed she could do no less. So for Paul there were no weekends off, no lazy Sundays, no trips to Moorestown. There was only work; there was only the suffrage campaign.

Returning from their weeks on the campaign trail, CU organizers were probably looking forward to well-deserved rest and relaxation. As committed as they were to their suffrage work, imagine their dismay when Paul announced that the Advisory Council would meet on March 31, 1915. She planned to announce the next phase in the plan to secure a federal amendment. Beginning immediately, Paul told the Advisory Committee, the CU would now organize in those states where they did not yet have an active branch. They were not organizing, Paul made clear, in order to undertake state campaigns. NAWSA had already waged more than four hundred state campaigns with very little success. That was not the route that Paul wanted the CU to take, nor did she wish to repeat anything that NAWSA was already doing.

The purpose of organizing in states where they lacked representation was to continue what the 1914 campaign had begun: to make suffrage a national issue and to create a nationwide demand for a federal amendment. The CU would have to mobilize quickly. Paul planned to cap off the campaign by holding the first national convention of women voters at the Panama Pacific Exposition, scheduled to take place in San Francisco in September 1915—only five months away. "We want to make woman suffrage the dominant political issue from the moment Congress reconvenes. We want to have Congress open in the middle of a veritable suffrage cyclone."[1] The Advisory Committee unanimously consented.

NAWSA leaders continued to oppose Paul. At their annual convention, they reiterated their support of the Shafroth Amendment. They either did not realize or did not care that most of the NAWSA rank and file were opposed to the Shafroth Amendment and hoped desperately for a return to support for the Anthony Amendment. The dissension over Shafroth had become so bitter that Jane Addams refused to continue to serve as vice-president of NAWSA and further refused to accept the title of honorary vice-president. Even with the discontent over Shafroth, delegates would not take the next step. Once again they voted for Shaw as president, thus assenting to support of Shafroth.[2] Shaw's antipathy toward Paul and the CU had caused problems in Nevada in 1914. After Mabel Vernon arrived in Nevada, at the request of NAWSA, Shaw accused Anne Martin of being a dupe of the CU—even though she'd had nothing but praise for Martin prior to the Nevada referendum. When the Nevada referendum campaign ended in success, there were no apologies regarding Anne Martin's judgment forthcoming from Shaw, who preferred, apparently, to just forgive and forget. For better or worse, it was this unrelenting attitude that remained a hallmark of NAWSA leaders.

To complicate matters, Carrie Chapman Catt, then the head of NAWSA's New York organization, tried to set up Alice Paul. Catt asked Paul to put off organizing on behalf of the CU in New York State until after the referendum. At that point, win or lose, Paul should have felt free to establish CU representation in the state. With apparent goodwill, Catt suggested that Paul concentrate on those states where there were no ongoing referendum campaigns. Paul was receptive to the suggestion. She preferred not to be in conflict with NAWSA and welcomed a potential way of overcoming its disputes. Paul assured Catt that the CU would not be doing any organizing work in referendum states. Within a week of this cordial exchange, which Catt had initiated, Catt took the president of the Ohio Woman Suffrage Association to task for inviting both NAWSA and the CU to set up offices in that state. The Ohio Association, said Catt, "had lost its senses." She stated that the rank and file would be incapable of deciding the merits of the two organizations. Catt issued this diatribe despite the fact that there was no referendum campaign under way in Ohio in 1915.

A month later, Catt initiated another attack. She claimed that Alice had reneged on her pledge not to organize in referendum states, citing the fact that Paul had spoken to New York state legislators as evidence. The charges were a clear effort to undermine Paul's integrity. Paul sent Catt copies of their previous correspondence in which Alice had told Catt exactly what she intended to do in New York. The papers included Catt's agreeable responses. "You may not have had these letters accessible," Paul told the irate Catt.[3] Whatever discomfort Catt may have experienced when confronted with her own duplicity, she managed to hide it.

The vast majority of NAWSA rank-and-file members still refrained from bolting from the national organization. But the continued assaults upon the CU, including accepting as true certain rumors that NAWSA leaders knew to be untrue, were beginning to take their toll. NAWSA loyalists across the country began to make their feelings known, including expressions of support for the CU. The South remained the section of the country that proved least troublesome for NAWSA. For southerners especially, the race question intertwined with the suffrage issue. In the South, racial tensions far eclipsed the difficulties that suffragists in other regions had to deal with, including anti-suffragists, special-interest groups, and the Roman Catholic Church. For the CU, organizing in the South remained a truly formidable task. But even in this stronghold of conservatism and racism, the CU heard from an occasional supporter willing to put all else aside for the sake of suffrage. As one woman put it: "The Congressional Union to me means the freeing of eight million women of my sunny South who would never be freed if we have to wait for the vote by way of the states."[4] Such expressions of support were relatively rare, however. Southern women were no less immune than men to the social and cultural mores that were an ingrained part of their daily lives.

At the same time that she was overseeing the organizing work in the states, Paul was going to extraordinary lengths to put together a spectacular event sure to attract national attention. This event was to be part of the Panama-Pacific International Exposition, a world's fair commemorating the completion of the Panama Canal that would be held in San Francisco in 1915. San Franciscans also saw the fair as an opportunity to showcase the city's recovery from the devastating 1906 earthquake. For both reasons, everyone associated with the fair wanted it to succeed beyond expectations. The site of the Exposition would be the Presidio, a military compound overlooking San Francisco Bay. The cluster of colorful and architecturally dazzling exhibit buildings appropriately became known as the "Jewel City." Thousands of daily visitors—eager to be entertained, educated, and dazzled by the wonders of the modern world—took advantage of everything the Exposition had to offer. Before long, attendees began to keep an eye out for the activities scheduled by woman suffragists, for Paul had staged some breathtaking exhibitions. For example, she persuaded Hazel Hunkins, a young Californian, to fly in an airplane above the Bay and drop thousands of leaflets advertising suffrage. For most of the spectators lucky enough to catch her act, it was the first time they had seen a real airplane. And for Hazel, it was her first airplane ride. Though a daring soul, Hazel later indicated that were it not for Paul urging her on, she probably would have declined the opportunity to fly. Fortunately, the pilot and his trusty biplane were up to the challenge, and it became one of those "Did you see? . . ." questions that everyone who witnessed it asked of everyone they talked to.[5]

Paul also managed to secure a hard-to-come-by booth in the Education Building. Visitors were asked to sign a pro–federal amendment petition that would be taken cross-country to Washington and presented to Congress. For three days during the Exposition, the women voters' convention met and discussed plans for enfranchised women to use their voting power on behalf of a federal amendment. On the final day of the convention, which Paul persuaded Exposition officials to declare "Congressional Union for Woman Suffrage Day," the public had an opportunity to hear several illustrious speakers, at the otherwise members-only convention. Paul's roster of guest speakers included Helen Keller and her teacher, Annie Sullivan Macey; evangelist Billy Sunday; former president Theodore Roosevelt; popular actress Mabel Talliaferro; and Italian educator Maria Montessori. In short, there were speakers appropriate to everyone's interest. Conventioneers and fairgoers alike were nothing less than effusive about the speakers, most of whom they'd never before seen or heard in person.

As soon as the convention adjourned, and amid much fanfare, Paul dispatched Sara Bard Field to Washington with the great petition supposedly in hand. Sara did not want to make the cross-country trip and intended to decline Paul's request. In fact, she had been warned about Paul by Mabel Vernon. "She's no bigger than a wisp of hay," Mabel said, "but she has the most deep and beautiful violet-blue eyes, and when they look at you and ask you to do something, you could no more refuse."[6] Mabel, it turned out, was right. As Sara rode off in a touring car, accompanied by two Swedish women, one of whom was the driver, the crowd seeing them off was told that the petition contained an impressive 500,000 names.

The long drive across country proved to be perilous at times. Field's two Swedish companions often seemed not to know where they were going, but went anyway. On one particularly hazardous night, the Swedes—who rarely spoke English—drove the car into a muddy roadway. In a flash, the car was stalled and sinking in the muddy water, requiring the hapless Sara to jump out of the car, slog through hip-deep mud, and make her way to the closest farmhouse in order to get help. They were still hundreds of miles away from Chicago when she discovered that she didn't even have the petition with her. Frantic phone calls to Paul ensued. Finally, Paul assured Sara that the petition would be waiting for her at the train station in Chicago. They also discussed the fact that the number of signatures probably fell far short of 500,000. No one seemed to know who had floated that number, but in any case Paul instructed Sara to gather more signatures at stops along the way.

The CU press department kept suffragists informed of Sara's progress and the enthusiastic receptions given her in cities along the way, including Reno, Salt Lake, Denver, Chicago, Detroit, Cleveland, and Boston. While the public generally greeted Sara warmly, some city officials were less than thrilled. In Boston, the mayor had much to say about women, Sara related. "He said that woman was a Muse that soared, that she was the poetry of our existence, and something about the sun, the moon and the stars. And then he added," Sara told her audience, pausing with perfect timing, "that he didn't think women ought to be allowed to vote."[7] Sara's ability to turn negative remarks into humorous anecdotes won over her audiences and made her especially popular with the public.

As 1915 drew to a close, events sometimes seemed to move at warp speed. President Wilson accepted the petition from the suffrage delegates entrusted to deliver it. Though he still fell back on the excuse of having to follow his party's lead on the issue, Wilson had recently and without warning announced that he would vote for suffrage in New Jersey. It wasn't the sea change that Alice Paul was looking for, but it represented some movement on Wilson's part. Two factors, in particular, influenced his decision. His daughters, Jessie and Margaret, were both suffragists and Jessie had participated in several CU events. And Wilson would soon announce that he and Edith Bolling Galt intended to marry. Wilson's first wife, Ellen, had succumbed to illness shortly after he began his first term and while there was nothing improper about his relationship with Edith, several members of the administration feared a backlash from women—especially western voters, who could actually do some damage to his reelection campaign. To add more support to Wilson's announcement, several members of his cabinet, as well as his secretary, Joseph Tumulty, had either already voted or declared their intention to vote in their home-state referendums.

At the 1915 NAWSA convention in December, Anna Howard Shaw announced her decision to step down as president. Had the choice of her successor been different, her resignation might have been an opportunity for NAWSA and the CU to start fresh in their suffrage work. But Shaw's chosen successor, Carrie Chapman Catt, had already established her dislike of Paul. Her election as NAWSA's president didn't alter that one bit. But Catt outshone Shaw's political abilities by far. One of her first acts after the election was to maneuver behind the scenes to drop the Shafroth Amendment with as little fanfare as possible. She still insisted that state campaigns were the surest route to full suffrage, but for the first time, both suffrage factions were now making Woodrow Wilson the focus of their efforts. Paul intended to force Wilson to support a federal amendment with the continued threat of electoral reprisals. Catt hoped to educate him. "Educating" the president of the United States, however, would not be an easy task, despite his decision to vote for suffrage in New Jersey. Wilson, in his long career as an educator and as president of his alma mater, Princeton University, never exhibited any evidence that he thought women had anything to teach him. Even when he taught at Bryn Mawr, whose students were intellectually equal to any Ivy League male student, Wilson frequently expressed his dismay at having to teach women. He considered his summons from Princeton to be a rescue from a stalled career. Nevertheless, educating Wilson was part of Catt's strategy.

Because of Catt's plan, some of NAWSA's younger members thought it was time for a reconciliation to take place. Zona Gale, an author, playwright, and poet who would go on to win a Pulitzer Prize, initiated the reconciliation attempt. Gale was president of the Wisconsin Woman Suffrage Association, a NAWSA affiliate, but also a staunch friend of Alice Paul and the CU. She approached Paul about setting up a meeting with NAWSA members, which Paul was very much in favor of. Gale then spoke to the Executive Committee at NAWSA's convention. Arrangements were made for the two groups to meet at the Willard Hotel on December 17, 1915. Two days earlier, on December 15 and 16, both the CU and NAWSA testified before the Senate Committee on Woman Suffrage and the House Judiciary Committee. The Senate hearings were uneventful, but not so the House hearings. This was the first opportunity, since the 1914 elections, that members of Congress were able to question the notorious Alice Paul. Their primary concern was what Paul intended to do in 1916. Did she intend to repeat her campaign against Democrats? Again and again, this question or a variation of it was fired at Paul. For her part, Paul remained calm and composed each time it was put to her. When asked if it were true that the Republican Party had sought out the CU's help for the 1916 campaign, Alice replied that it was not true but "We are greatly gratified for this tribute to our value." Congressman Joseph Taggert of Kansas insisted to Paul that she had not succeeded in defeating a single Democrat in 1914. Paul inquired politely, "Why, then, are you so stirred up by our campaign?" Paul was accused of maintaining a blacklist of Democratic targets. It wasn't true but this accusation, in the eyes of some congressmen, went beyond the pale. "It is cheap politics," one of them declared finally, "and I have gotten awfully tired listening to it." Failing to rattle Paul with their questions, the House Judiciary Committee seemed content to let this parting shot end its inquisition.

Paul expected similar hostility at the Willard Hotel meeting but hoped for a more positive outcome. NAWSA sent Catt, Ruth Hannah McCormick, Katherine Dexter McCormick, and Antoinette Funk to meet with Paul, Lucy Burns, Dora Lewis, and Anne Martin. The NAWSA leaders wasted little time with niceties, preferring to cut to the chase. They invited the CU to become a NAWSA affiliate, but the price for doing so would be to renounce any more anti–Democratic Party campaigns, to stay out of any political campaigns in the future, and to stay out of all the states where NAWSA already had an affiliate. In short, NAWSA wanted everything but gave nothing. The meeting ended abruptly when Catt stood up and, looking squarely at Alice Paul, declared: "All I wish to say is that I will fight you to the last ditch." It was the last time the two organizations attempted reconciliation and the last time that Catt and Paul confronted each other directly.[8] Within a year of becoming president of NAWSA, Catt announced her "Winning Plan." Remarkably, its major elements were fairly similar to the strategy Paul had been following since her arrival in Washington. They included lobbying the president and Congress on behalf of a federal suffrage amendment, and enlisting women voters in the West to help win the campaign.

In January 1916, Alice celebrated her thirty-first birthday. She had been working nonstop since her return from England, mostly for the suffrage cause. Overseeing the western campaign, dealing with an often-hostile press, keeping her volunteers motivated, raising money to support their efforts, lobbying the president and Congress, organizing spectacular events, and making every effort she could to deflect NAWSA's constant stream of attacks on both her and the CU—each of these concerns, alone, was stressful and exhausting to deal with. Trying to keep everything under control and moving forward proved to be a monumental task, even for Paul. Given her often fragile health, she might have been wise to take a breather before moving on to each subsequent challenge. But she demanded as much of herself as she did of the people she asked to work on behalf of suffrage. She could not, in good conscience, insist that her volunteers do what she asked of them and then proceed to take even a few days off from her work, regardless of how she felt physically. Besides, in addition to the 1916 national election, Paul had already decided on an interim next step.

In January, the CU moved into its new headquarters, Cameron House; generally referred to as the "Little White House," it was located directly across Pennsylvania Avenue from the real White House. Paul directed the Executive Committee to organize a meeting of the Advisory Council, along with state and national officers, on April 8 and 9. Many of those gathered expected to hear plans for the election campaign, but at the moment Paul had other fish to fry. She announced her intention, with the consent of the Advisory Council, to organize a woman's political party intended to serve as the balance of power in the national election. In her usual persuasive fashion, Paul had done her homework and put forth a compelling argument. "The state of Nevada was won by only forty votes in the last Senatorial election," she pointed out. Moreover, Nevada was not unique. Over the last twenty years, a change of only 9 percent of the total vote in the presidential elections would have been enough to throw the election to the other party. Thus November 1916 was an opportunity to exert electoral power that would not come for another four years. The time had come to seize the day. The CU delegates needed little convincing—other than that coming from Alice Paul—to give their blessing.[9] Paul immediately called for a convention of women voters to be held in Chicago in early June for the purpose of organizing a National Woman's Party (NWP).

Membership in the NWP would be confined to enfranchised women. Its sole purpose would be to promote a federal amendment. Paul stressed this when she spoke about organizing the political party. She knew that if the party's platform included any other issues, regardless of how important they might be to women, it would have the effect of diluting the power of an enfranchised women's voting bloc. In preparation for the Chicago meeting, Paul, along with her hand-picked team of organizers, headed west to drum up as much support as possible among women voters. Though it might have seemed impromptu, organizing a political party wasn't a last-minute decision on Paul's part. She had been planning the western swing for several weeks. A train, dubbed the *Suffrage Special,* departed Washington on April 9. For the next month, the emissaries from the East lived and worked on the train. It was crowded and cramped—a beehive of activity. The publicists on board did their level-best to make sure that stories of their reception, in cities and small towns alike, reached state headquarters, the national press, and their own publication, *The Suffragist.* In addition to the objections from western Democrats. Alice anticipated that NAWSA would follow through with the usual opposition. It almost went without saying that NAWSA would not do otherwise.

On June 6, thanks to the success of the western swing, more than 1,500 women delegates from suffrage states presented themselves at Chicago's Blackstone Theatre, eager to participate in the historic event. Armed with the knowledge that reversing previous electoral results could take as little as a 9 percent change in the 1916 vote, they were energized by the prospect that success might actually be within their grasp. The NWP organized along the same lines as the CU, including the leadership structure, but with the obvious requirement that members had to be voters from suffrage states. In the only exception to that rule, Paul would serve as one of two vice-chairwomen. The new party chose Nevada's Anne Martin as chairwoman. Alice Paul succeeded in organizing the NWP as a single-issue political party, a crucial aspect if they were to have any success in the 1916 election.

In her usual thorough fashion, Paul chose Chicago as the convention city for two reasons. First, both the Republicans and the Progressives were going to hold their conventions in Chicago. And, second, the national press would be there in full force. Because of this, the women were deluged by reporters anxious to file stories on the new political party—and they received maximum news coverage. Having become masters of the art of press capitalization, the delegates were only too happy to provide detailed information of the proceedings. Paul also extended invitations to every major party to come and address the convention. Even this gesture served as grist for the media mill. Ida Tarbell, the famous muckraking journalist, covered election politics in Chicago for the *New York World*. She reported the situation to her readers with great amusement:

> We do not ask you here to tell us what we can do for your Parties, Miss Martin told the speakers in a tone of exultant sweetness. . . . Another thing the gentlemen must have noticed—used as they are to the same game—and that was that no amount of eloquence made the faintest scratch on the rock-ribbed determination of the women. The one and only thing they wanted to know . . . was whether or not they proposed to support the amendment. . . . Was it yes or no?[10]

Charles Beard later described the purpose and function of a third party in a two-party system. Third parties, he said, used marginal votes in close campaigns to force the gradual acceptance of their leading doctrines by one or the other of the great parties. Through their inevitable competition, the two major parties would educate the whole nation into accepting ideas that were once abhorrent.

The CU's two main Washington lobbyists, Anne Martin and Maud Younger, had also been working nonstop since January to persuade the House Judiciary Committee to vote out the suffrage amendment. As usual, the Democrats stalled, until the committee chairman finally told them that he would schedule a meeting if the lobbyists could assemble a majority of the committee members. When Martin and Younger reported that they had the majority consent, as requested, the chairman had little choice but to schedule a meeting of the Judiciary Committee. Actually, it mattered little at that point because the Democrats had their strategy in place. As soon as the closed-door meeting convened, a proposal was made to shelve *all* constitutional-amendment proposals for an indefinite period of time. What this meant was that committee members would have to either accept or reject a wide range of pending amendments on issues including marriage, divorce, and the ever-popular prohibition of alcohol. Regardless of their support for or opposition to any specific proposed amendment, committee members would have to consider all of them as a combined entity. The anti-suffrage Democrats had no qualms about tying everything up in order to avoid dealing with suffrage. Their efforts toward this end threw the meeting into chaos, and angry members finally adjourned without taking any action after two hours of argument. Pro-suffrage congressmen had been blindsided, and the Democrats once again demonstrated their contempt for the issue of suffrage.

Not many of those attending the Chicago convention objected to another anti–Democratic Party campaign in the 1916 election. Anything that would advance the goal of securing a federal amendment was considered in a positive light. Even those who may have held out hope for greater state referendum successes were ready to abandon that avenue. While it was true that the Nevada and Montana referenda in 1914 were successful, the big eastern states that suffragists had hoped to win over—New York, Pennsylvania, Massachusetts, and New Jersey—all failed to win the necessary votes. As a consequence, even Harriot Stanton Blatch, who had been critical of Alice Paul for opening an office in New York, now threw her support fully behind a federal amendment. Nevertheless, the arrogant actions of the Democrats who controlled the House Judiciary Committee represented the last straw for many suffragists.

As their 1916 campaign unfolded, the NWP became almost a textbook case of Beard's definition of a third party. The NWP appeared before the resolutions committees of each political party in an effort to persuade them to support a federal amendment. For the first time, the Republicans and the Democrats included suffrage planks in their platforms, though neither endorsed a federal amendment. The Progressive, Socialist, and Prohibition parties unequivocally endorsed a federal suffrage amendment. While NAWSA continued to throw barbs at the NWP, a *New York Times* analysis concluded that Paul's party was running the suffrage show. "Whatever the more conservative suffragists think or say . . . the radical wing which calls itself the Woman's Party . . . offered facts and figures to prove that they have an organized vote which can be swung in any direction they want. . . . Whether the hand that ruled the Democratic Convention today rocks the cradle in its hours of recreation . . . it can certainly add up a column of figures in a convincing manner."[11]

Though the NWP's election campaign of 1916 resembled the 1914 campaign in many ways, there were significant differences. For one thing, just one month into the campaign, organizers were suffering from health problems. When Paul heard that nearly ten organizers were unable to campaign because of illness, she confided to Dora Lewis that she feared the whole enterprise might collapse around them. (In Colorado, for instance, the organizers had to leave for less mountainous terrain. They had trouble functioning in the high altitude.) As things seemed to progress from bad to worse, even Paul was unable to maintain her calm. Complaining telegrams arriving daily on her desk finally caused Paul to wire back that the organizers had to figure out how to handle things on the spot without expecting her to solve their problems. Paul's frustrations mounted even higher as she sought to make sure that organizers had proper transportation so they could fulfill their commitments. One organizer told Paul she was beginning to feel like an inmate in an insane asylum. At Cameron House, where Paul and other Washington-based NWP volunteers lived during the campaign, inter personal tensions began to take their toll as well. Anne Martin and Maud Younger worked together but didn't get along very well and created an atmosphere that seemed to affect everyone. In addition, Lucy Burns decided to go back to Brooklyn for an indefinite period of time. No one, including Paul, knew if she would return at all.

Having to deal with the endless logistics and details of the campaign took its own toll on Paul, who became short-tempered and sometimes demanding. Things finally reached a breaking point when Paul's health gave out. Her physician ordered her admitted to a Washington hospital so she could undergo tests that would determine the cause. The first diagnosis proved to be devastating. Doctors treating her thought Paul had Bright's disease. Ironically, Bright's was the same illness that proved fatal to Woodrow Wilson's first wife, Ellen, shortly after his first term began.

Doctors broke the news to Paul that she was looking at a month to perhaps as long as a year. They couldn't promise any more than that. The diagnosis and outlook sent shockwaves throughout her organization. Yet, for her part, Paul was already regaining strength and feeling better. After consulting with her doctors, she was transferred to Johns Hopkins in Baltimore, where more tests would be done. At Hopkins, she received the best possible news. She did not have Bright's disease after all. There had been some kind of mix-up in her previous tests, resulting in a wrong diagnosis. Within a short period of time, Paul returned to Cameron House and resumed full activities. Everyone breathed a sigh of relief. Without Paul at the helm, their chances for success would have been marginal at best.

The one major issue that made all the difference in 1916 was war in Europe. Because World War I was still raging there, American voters in that year greatly feared that a political misstep might involve the United States in the war. The Wilson slogan—"He Kept Us Out of War"—resonated with voters overall but especially with women. They had no intention of watching their husbands and sons go off to fight a war in Europe. Even some of the CU/NWP's longtime supporters, such as Jane Addams and Crystal Eastman, were compelled to place peace before suffrage.

The national campaign between the two major candidates, Woodrow Wilson and Republican Charles Evans Hughes, played itself out around the motif of peace versus preparedness. For most voters, Hughes's advocacy for preparedness came far too close to an advocacy for US entry into the war. Even Hughes's announcement of his support of a suffrage amendment in the course of the campaign failed to prevent Wilson from emerging victorious, although just barely. The electoral vote count was 277 for Wilson and 254 for Hughes. In one of the ironies of the campaign, Wilson's narrow victory was attributed to women voters—because of the peace issue. The *New York Times* noted that California had voted disproportionately for Wilson. William Allen White noted that if women in Kansas had not voted for Wilson, "Kansas would have gone for Hughes." And analysts in Arizona, Idaho, Utah, and Washington all concluded that it was the combined votes of women that had swung the election in favor of the Democrats.[12]

Although many NWP supporters were dismayed and discouraged by the election results, Paul believed the campaign was far from a failure. She had consistently stressed the importance of maintaining, in the minds of the public, their active campaign against the Democrats. The response of both major parties demonstrated the success of this strategy. The Republicans tried to capitalize on the NWP campaign; the Democrats tried to put a damper on it. Both parties made unprecedented efforts to win over women voters. As far as the press was concerned, whoever won the election, the NWP did not lose. As the *Wichita Eagle* observed, "When the Congress next meets, no matter whether Wilson or Hughes is elected, the women of the nation are going to have a powerful argument for national woman suffrage." The *Ventura Free Press* (California) noted that "the universal opinion of political leaders of all parties is that no new political party ever before made such a remarkable showing in a presidential campaign as had the National Woman's Party." The *New Republic*, a national news magazine, said that the Democrats owed their victory to women voters: "Yet but for women suffrage, to which he tepidly assents, Mr. Wilson would not have been continued in the White House. The balance of power, so far as Congress is concerned, and so far as rival parties are concerned, is conceivably in women's hands." And the *San Francisco Examiner* reinforced what Alice Paul had no intention of letting Democrats forget: that suffrage had ceased to be "a western vagary. Nothing that has 2,000,000 votes is ever vague to the politicians."[13]

7

The War Against Women

On January 10, 1917, Alice Paul launched the next phase of her well-thought-out campaign to secure a federal amendment. Following the anti–Democratic Party campaign of 1916, Paul huddled with several of her lieutenants, including Lucy Burns, Harriot Stanton Blatch, Mabel Vernon, Mary Beard, and Dora Lewis. She proposed to start a picket line outside of the White House gates. The biggest problem she had to deal with before implementing the plan was ensuring there were enough volunteers to do the job properly. It would not do to begin a picketing campaign and watch it fizzle out for lack of volunteers. If that happened, the NWP would appear to have lost the momentum for support of a federal amendment. Initially, Paul wanted members of both the NWP and the CU to go on the picket line. But Blatch, whose New York organization had already picketed the state capital building in Albany, suggested that picketing ought to be something that was left to the unenfranchised women of the East. In other words, the NWP membership should continue to lobby in their states but picketing should be the contribution made by women who could not yet vote. Taking this step, Blatch believed, would provide a focus for women not yet sure of how they could personally participate in the cause. Blatch's argument persuaded Paul. The decision was made that if there was to be a picketing campaign, volunteers would be sought from the CU membership. Paul chose Blatch to present the case for a picketing campaign to the National Executive Committee. "We can't organize bigger and more influential deputations," Blatch reasoned. "We can't organize bigger processions. We can't, women, do anything more in that line. We have got to take a new departure."[1]

No one disagreed with Blatch's proposal regarding the makeup of the picket lines. But some women were ambivalent about undertaking a picketing campaign at all. Not only Paul but many NWP members had received complaints related to the anti–Democratic Party campaigns waged in 1914 and 1916. And a number of pro-NAWSA suffragists, Democratic Party voters, and family members continued to express severe doubts about the wisdom of campaigning against Democratic politicians who favored woman suffrage. Then, too, a great many suffragists did not approve of what they considered a militant strategy. Under the circumstances, it was not at all certain that, if they initiated a picketing campaign, there would be sufficient support to carry it through as long as necessary. Even Paul's mother asked Alice to reconsider her new tactic because it seemed so undignified. Fortunately for Paul, President Wilson himself tipped the scales in favor of the new campaign.

On January 9, 1917, three hundred women met with Wilson in order to present him with a resolution passed on Christmas Day 1916, at a memorial service for Inez Milholland. Inez had been a highly effective speaker on behalf of suffrage. She was able to draw crowds whenever her name appeared on the speakers' list at rallies. Inez astride her white horse had become an iconic figure for suffragists ever since she rode at the head of the 1913 suffrage parade in Washington. But she suffered from health problems, including severe anemia, a condition she refused to allow to prevent her from participating in the suffrage movement. When she collapsed on stage at a rally in Los Angeles in 1916, she had just spoken to hundreds of people. She was hospitalized for several days, but there was nothing the doctors could do to reverse the illness. Her death sent shockwaves through suffrage circles. When the delegation met with Wilson on January 9, they expected that he would accept the resolution without necessarily commenting on it. Although he refrained from his usual states' rights position, what he did say outraged his audience. He advised the delegates that political change could come only through the instrumentality of parties, and that women had to stir sufficient public opinion in order to spur action. With his words, Wilson had effectively dismissed the participation of woman suffragists in the previous two elections. It was as though the NWP did not exist and that the death of a popular suffrage figure warranted no acknowledgment. Heading back to Cameron House, the delegates were clearly angry. They could not believe that the president had refused to acknowledge their efforts, even if he did not agree with their tactics. There was no reason now to object to a picketing campaign. As Harriot Blatch told them, they must now "stand beside the gateway where he [Wilson] must pass in and out, so that he can never fail to realize that there is a tremendous earnestness and insistence back of this measure."[2]

The very next morning the first picketers left Cameron House with purple, white, and gold banners, crossed Pennsylvania Avenue, and took up their vigil at the White House gate. Passersby were somewhat bewildered by the Silent Sentinels, as they quickly became known, letting their banners speak for them: "Mr. President, What Will You Do for Woman Suffrage?" To coordinate the picketing campaign, Paul turned once again to Mabel Vernon. Mabel had done an exemplary job of organizing during the 1916 campaign. Now, she took on the task of ensuring that enough picketers were on duty each day, beginning with the very first day. Mabel quickly sent out a call for volunteers. An unexpectedly tremendous response surprised and pleased Paul and everyone else concerned. During the eighteen months of picketing in 1917 and 1918, thousands of women volunteered to take their turn on the picket line. Whether they could volunteer for only an hour, or for several days, made no difference. Everyone who volunteered was called upon to do so. Equally gratifying were the thousands of letters received from women who, for one reason or another, could not volunteer but wanted to make known their solidarity with the picketers. "I approve every act of the brave women who promote the cause of their sisters," wrote one supporter. "There are thousands of women scattered over the country who are watching your achievements with pride and gratitude," said another. And a mother with a young child wrote: "If it were not for the fact that I have a young daughter . . . and no one to leave her with, I would be there with you. *I feel ashamed to have other women suffering for my cause,* and not to be there to help them."[3]

Some financial donors, though not entirely sure of the effectiveness of the picketing campaign, trusted Paul's judgment enough to continue their support. An example was Josephine DuPont, of the Delaware DuPonts, who made no bones about opposing the picketing. She believed it was "sensational and undignified. . . . [M]y confidence in you [Paul] leads one to hope for better results than are apparent to the mere on-looker." Nevertheless, DuPont enclosed a check for $1,000 with her letter. Another donor noted that "it no doubt seems necessary to you but it is so unlovely that I could not feel that I want to support *that* effort." She, too, sent a check—for $250—along with a pledge for another $250 "for the congressional work and the federal amendment . . . which I heartily support." That kind of trust in Paul was not uncommon, even among volunteers who didn't particularly like the way she did things. As one volunteer said years later, it wasn't that she disliked Alice Paul; she just didn't like her. Not all donors continued to send money. In response to Paul's handwritten request for a donation, a few women sent back terse messages. One wrote to say that she did not "sympathize with your conduct."[4]

The press seemed not to know what to think about the pickets. After some deliberation, the *New York Times* characterized the campaign as "silly" and "monstrous." An editorial in that newspaper declared that it was a female thing to do. "That the female mind is inferior to the male need not be assumed. . . . [T]here is something about it that is essentially different and . . . that this difference is of a kind and degree that votes for women would constitute a political danger . . . ought to be plain to everybody." Most periodicals, however, did not immediately find the picketing to be offensive, nor did they hold it up as evidence that women were inherently inferior.[5]

In the early weeks of the campaign President Wilson seemed relatively unaffected by the pickets. Often, as he passed through the gates, he would tip his hat to the picketers. On one particularly bitter winter day, he extended an invitation to the sentinels to come inside and warm up. "If they come, see that they have some hot tea and coffee." The Head Usher quickly returned, saying: "Excuse me, Mr. President, but they indignantly refused."[6] Members of the president's family were less sanguine. Wilson's cousin Helen Woodrow Bones was contemptuous of the suffragists' efforts. And Edith Bolling Wilson found their behavior reprehensible. Their constant presence outside of the White House elicited only angry words from her.

As the campaign continued, Paul instructed Mabel Vernon to organize special days. She wanted to impress upon the president, Congress, and the press just how diverse was the support for the picketing campaign. On Maryland Day, the picket line was composed entirely of residents of Maryland. This was followed by Pennsylvania Day, New York Day, Virginia Day, and New Jersey Day. On College Day, thirteen colleges were represented. Teachers Day was one of several professional days. And theme days included Patriotic Day, Lincoln Day, and Labor Day. As Paul anticipated, the series of "Days" provided a constant source of press attention, which kept the issue before the nation.

The public initially responded to the picketers with apparent sympathy. People passing by often stopped to offer words of encouragement. Material comforts, such as mittens and hot bricks to stand on, were offered. The Washington winter weather prompted some out-of-state members to send warm coats and galoshes, in hopes the picketers would be able to keep their feet dry and stay warm. Even the White House guards looked upon them as comrades. When the pickets arrived five minutes late one day, a guard told them, "I was kind of worried. We thought perhaps you weren't coming and we would have to hold down this place alone." Everything changed once Congress declared war on Germany.

The war in Europe had been raging since 1914. Throughout his first term in office, Wilson managed to maintain a neutral stance among the belligerents. He saw himself as an arbiter who could bring about a peace agreement that would be acceptable to all sides. He was also beginning to develop the idea of establishing an organization of nations that would act as the mediator in future disputes. The primary function of such an organization would be to circumvent war as a means of settling disputes—and maintaining a neutral stance would arm the United States with the moral authority to negotiate a peace.

However, within a few short months of his reelection, on January 31, 1917, Germany made a game-changing decision. The German ambassador hand-delivered a message from his government announcing that, beginning immediately, Germany intended to undertake a campaign of unrestricted submarine warfare against all ships at sea, whether belligerents or neutrals. For four days, Wilson consulted nonstop with his advisers, Congress, and members of his cabinet in an effort to resolve the situation without jeopardizing American neutrality. It soon became clear, however, that nothing Wilson did would deter the German government from pursuing its policy. Wilson concluded reluctantly that he had no choice but to sever all diplomatic relations with Germany. On February 3, 1917, Wilson took precisely that step. In the eyes of many observers, it was now just a matter of time before war would be declared. The triggering event undoubtedly would be the first time a German submarine opened fire on an American ship. The consequence of the unexpected turn of events forced everyone to confront the possibility, if not the likelihood, that the United States would soon be engaged in a world war. All US citizens had to determine what their response should be. The nation's suffragists were no exception.

Having sent out a convention call to state chairwomen of the NWP and the CU, Paul began to map out her strategy—one she hoped would become the consensus of the convention. Deciding on how the organization would respond to the United States entry into the war was an instance where a majority vote, if not consensus, would be valuable. Paul believed that, unlike day-to-day decision-making and strategizing, how one chose to deal with the question of war was absolutely a personal decision. Her hope was that members would agree that the NWP should continue its suffrage activism regardless of how they felt about the war. The two options being discussed by NWP and CU members attending the convention were either to forgo all suffrage activity in order to get behind the war effort or to transform their organizations into a peace society. When Paul addressed the convention attendees on March 2, 1917, she had already determined the strategy she would advocate, based on her knowledge of the history of the women's movement. Neither of the suggested actions were acceptable in her view. Indeed, Paul had an alternative idea. "Those who wish to work for preparedness, those who wish to work for peace," Paul said, "can do so through organizations for such purpose. . . . Our organization is dedicated only to the enfranchisement of women. . . . We must do our part to see that war, which concerns women as seriously as men, shall not be entered upon without the consent of women."[7]

By the time she spoke to the convention, the question of the organizations' war policy had actually been settled. The staff of *The Suffragist* paved the way by contacting members, encouraging them to support Paul's position and thanking them for their consideration of a difficult choice. Articles and editorials outlined Paul's proposed strategy clearly and straightforwardly, leaving little opportunity to misinterpret or misunderstand exactly what she intended. Florence Bayard Hilles, of Delaware, the daughter of Grover Cleveland's secretary of state, voiced the opinion of most of the delegates: "We are composed of pacifists, militarists, Protestants, Catholics, Jews, Republicans, Democrats, Socialists, Progressives, Populists and every other following. . . . If we for a moment divert our party from the purpose of its organization, we not only weaken it, we destroy it. We must be considered an integral part of this country."[8]

The convention passed the following resolution: "Be it resolved that the NWP, organized for the sole purpose of securing political liberty for women, shall continue to work for this purpose until it is accomplished, being unalterably convinced that in so doing the organization serves the highest interests of the country." The convention also agreed to discontinue the CU and to incorporate all of its members into the NWP. Again the majority of delegates voted with Paul, agreeing that the merger could only serve to strengthen them as they pursued their political goals. The CU, which had served its purpose well, thereby ceased to exist. Alice Paul was elected chairwoman of the new NWP, with Anne Martin as vice-chair and Mabel Vernon as secretary. Burns, Belmont, Kent, and Lewis remained on the Executive Board along with several newcomers representing unenfranchised women in the East.

When the convention adjourned on March 4, the day before Wilson's second inaugural, members staged a massive demonstration at the White House. Intent on delivering the convention resolutions to Wilson, a thousand suffragists, each carrying a purple, white, and gold banner, surrounded the White House. In some respects, the demonstration called to mind the 1913 parade. But now, four years later, there was less of a holiday atmosphere and more an air of gritty determination.

Guards were posted inside the gates every fifty feet and all gates had been locked, making it impossible for the suffragists to enter the grounds. For this to happen required the authorization of Wilson or his advisers. The guards refused even to deliver the resolutions to the president or his aides, as they had done in earlier instances. In a driving, icy rain, the suffragists marched silently around the White House perimeter, attracting a large audience in the process. Journalist Gilson Gardner, writing for the Scripps newspaper chain, later wrote about the event: "A special committee . . . went to the White House gates, but those gates for the first time in two decades were locked. . . . The delegation . . . waited for a long time—which was typical of the attitude of the Administration. . . . Mr. Wilson from the first has kept the women waiting. It is a poor business—both for the women and for Wilson." Less than a month later, on April 6, 1917, the United States officially declared war on Germany. With America now in the war, and given Alice Paul's determination to continue the fight for a federal suffrage amendment, there could be no doubt that she and the president were on a collision course.

NAWSA now found itself in a sticky situation. Carrie Chapman Catt had already announced that NAWSA would support all of the administration's war policies. Within hours of declaring war on Germany, the Democratic caucus met and announced that, for the duration of the war and for six months thereafter, Congress would act upon only those issues that Wilson determined were emergency war measures. Suffrage was not on his list of war measures. NAWSA's war policy was criticized for another important reason. Many suffragists claimed to be pacifists and belonged to anti-war groups such as the Women's Peace Party. Catt and Shaw were among this group. Not only was Catt willing to commit NAWSA to support of the war, but she felt compelled to persuade people to forgo their personal beliefs regarding peace. Catt believed that NAWSA *had* to demonstrate that women were loyal Americans first and foremost. She rejected the idea that pacifists were acting in good conscience to promote the welfare of the country. Catt's policy lacked moral grounding. To pacifists, suspending their beliefs in order to support the war seemed at the very least unnecessary. "To my mind, I didn't need to do it [abandon pacifist beliefs] and it is too evidently a bid for popular favor," one critic declared. Nevertheless, both Catt and Shaw accepted appointments by Wilson to serve on the Council on National Defense. This did little to lessen the perception that the two NAWSA stalwarts were willing to trade principle for advantage. "That 'Look at us, we don't picket—we help the country—please give us the vote,' disgusts me," another critic said. Still another fumed, "Nothing can excuse the Catt-Shaw crowd but their seventy years."[9]

The difference in attitude between Paul and Catt became crystal clear to Congresswoman Jeannette Rankin, the Republican from Montana and the first woman elected to the House of Representatives. Rankin had been a NAWSA member. She was also a lifelong pacifist and continued to be committed to a federal suffrage amendment. When she announced that she could not in good conscience vote in favor of the declaration of war, Catt and other NAWSA leaders began to exert tremendous pressure on her. They told her that a negative vote would set woman suffrage back by twenty years, if not more. It was moral blackmail, plain and simple, and a weaker individual might have given in. But Rankin's reputation among Montanans as someone to be reckoned with was not just talk. She cast her vote against entry into the war. Exhibiting neither sympathy for her predicament nor admiration for her courage, Catt expressed only anger and contempt for her. Catt, never one to let go of a grudge, endorsed Rankin's opponent when the congresswoman ran for the Senate in 1918. The night before the scheduled war vote, Paul also called on Rankin. She told the congresswoman that the NWP had taken no stand on the war. Speaking only for herself, Paul wanted to let Rankin know that she would support her decision, regardless of how she chose to cast her vote. Later, Rankin acknowledged that Paul's was the "only support I received from women in my vote." Paul never asked her to vote one way or the other, nor did she ask how Rankin intended to vote.[10]

For several weeks after the declaration of war, Paul continued to send her volunteers out on the picketing line. They began carrying banners quoting Wilson's statements about securing democracy abroad and pointing out that half the American population was denied democracy at home. The banners were intended to embarrass the president, and they did, especially when they quoted Wilson's war message: "We shall fight . . . for democracy—for the right of those who submit to authority to have a voice in their own government." The pickets were not interfered with by authorities, but they increasingly came under attack by public passersby. Harassment of the picketers escalated from having poles ripped out of their hands to destruction of the banners, and then to pushing and shoving that inevitably caused injuries to some of the women. The authorities continued to refrain from interfering—until the so-called Russian Banner incident.

Wilson sent his envoy, Elihu Root, to the new Russian Republic in an effort to persuade it to stay in the war. Root claimed, in a speech to the Russians, that the United States was a country where "universal, direct, equal and secret suffrage obtained." It flabbergasted Paul that Root would misrepresent the real situation so boldly. Suffragists were outraged. On June 20, 1917, a delegation from the Russian Republic visited the White House to continue talks regarding cooperation. Paul stationed Lucy Burns and Dora Lewis outside the White House gate with an enormous banner addressed to the Russians. "President Wilson and Envoy Root are deceiving Russia . . . ," it read. "The women of America tell you that America is not a democracy. Twenty million women are denied the right to vote. . . . Tell our government that it must liberate its people before it can claim free Russia as an ally." As soon as the Russian delegation passed through the gate, all hell broke loose. Angry crowds tore the banner down, shredding it and harassing the picketers while DC police stood idly by and watched. The next morning, it was front-page news. The *New York Times* declared that the Russians went by so quickly that they could not have read the banner's words. In fact, the Russians did read them. Alice received a note from N. A. Nesaragof, a member of the delegation. He applauded the NWP for its courage "despite the angry crowd" and urged Paul to continue pursuing her goal, noting that "in Russia, a different kind of oppressors did the very same thing the American police do now."

Though Paul and the NWP had become targets of the press as well as the public, she had no intention of quitting. She issued a press release of her own, defending their actions: "It is those who deny justice and not those who demand it, who embarrass the country. . . . The responsibility . . . is with the government and not with the women of America, if the lack of democracy at home weakens government in its fight for democracy three thousand miles away." The situation began unraveling quickly for both the Wilson administration and the NWP. Hurried conferences between the administration and the DC authorities were held, with discussion centered on how best to handle an increasingly embarrassing situation to the detriment of the suffragists and the benefit of the administration. Suggestion strategies ranged from raiding the NWP headquarters at Cameron House to arresting picketers. Shortly thereafter, Paul received a call from the chief of police, Major Raymond Pullman. He advised her that further demonstrations could lead to arrests. Paul had previously taken the precaution of getting legal advice on the NWP's right to picket the White House. She pointed out that picketing was not illegal. Pullman stated unequivocally that the women would be arrested if they attempted to picket again.

Paul knew that this was a pivotal moment. From her past experience in England, she realized that she had to make clear to her volunteers the possible consequences of picketing. She hoped that their decisions regarding picketing would be positive, but she knew that each woman had to make up her own mind on the matter. It was one thing to stand outside the White House with a sign, but quite another to get arrested with unknown consequences. Katherine Morey, a volunteer from Boston, expressed the view of many when she telephoned Alice and said, "We will have to have people *willing* to be arrested, and I will come down and I will be one." True to her word, Morey took the next train to Washington.

Three days later, Paul headed for Pennsylvania to attend a meeting of NWP members. There was an unmistakable undercurrent of tension because the participants were aware that the NWP had reached a critical crossroads. No one could really predict what the police would do, so preparations for a worst-case scenario had been made. At the same time, no one really believed that actual arrests would be made, because there were no legal grounds for doing so. Citizens had the right under the First Amendment to public demonstrations, which included picketing and carrying signs requesting redress of their grievances. As the discussion progressed among those attending the meeting, the housekeeper summoned Paul to take a phone call. When she returned, she quietly informed the gathering that her caller, a newsman, had just reported that the worst had indeed happened. The die had been cast. Lucy Burns and Katherine Morey had been arrested and were being detained at a DC station. Everyone was dumbfounded. No one could believe it had come to this. Yet, as they talked about their response, one thing became clear: they were committed to continuing, in spite of the arrests. In a telephone conversation with Major Pullman, Paul made that very clear. "I feel that we *will* continue," she told him. If he had thought the NWP would cease picketing because of the arrests, he had underestimated Paul's determination to stay the course. This decision to continue picketing marked the beginning of a real militancy in the American suffrage campaign. Refusing to discontinue picketing in time of war defined Paul and her colleagues as "un-American." Critics who had characterized Paul's strategy as militant from the beginning were appalled to learn how far she was willing to go to secure a federal amendment. In their eyes, this was a truly militant stance for which there could be no defense.[11]

Between June 22 and June 26, twenty-seven arrests were made. The picketers were charged with obstructing traffic and released without penalty. But the women refused to be deterred from picketing so the authorities intensified the consequences. Six women arrested on June 27 were fined $25 each for obstructing traffic. Just as Susan B. Anthony had done years earlier, the women refused to pay the fines. They were sentenced to three days in jail. According to the *New York Times,* the sentences were light because there were rumors that the prisoners intended to commence a hunger strike. The *Times* noted that no one could starve to death in three days. But it also warned that authorities were going to impose greater penalties if the picketing persisted. On July 14, sixteen women were arrested and tried. The determined women showed no signs of being intimidated. "Well girls," Florence Bayard Hilles quipped, "I've never seen but one court in my life and that was the Court of St. James. But I must say, they are not very much alike."[12] The women on trial were not reluctant to speak their minds. Elizabeth Rogers said, "[W]e know full well we stand here because the President of the United States refuses to give liberty to American women." Matilda Hall Gardner was even more explicit: "Even should I be sent to jail . . . I would not be in jail because I obstructed traffic but because I have offended politically, because I demanded of this government freedom for women." Nevertheless, when they were found guilty and sentenced to sixty days in Occoquan Workhouse, the penalty stunned them. Occoquan, in suburban Virginia, was notorious for its dismal conditions. No one anticipated such a harsh punishment.[13]

Wilson publicly ignored the situation. His press secretary, George Creel, issued a statement—intended to be humorous—claiming that Wilson was the only person who knew the right attitude to take toward the picketers: "a whimsical smile, slightly puckered at the roots by a sense of the ridiculous." While the president may have been described as being amused, privately he could not ignore the seriousness of the events happening outside the White House gates and in the DC courts. Two visitors to the Oval Office made that particularly clear. Dudley Field Malone, a member of Wilson's administration, spoke with the president immediately after leaving the courtroom. Appalled at the proceedings and the sentence, Malone reminded Wilson that he had campaigned for him in the West in 1916, assuring voters that Wilson not only sympathized with the suffrage cause but would do something about it during his second term. When Wilson objected to the inference that he personally had dictated the arrests and trial, Malone pointedly told him that things of that magnitude never happened without being planned by the District Commissioners. The commissioners were all Wilson appointees and did nothing without informing the administration and securing its okay. Malone informed Wilson that he (Malone) intended to represent the suffragists in their appeal and would therefore tender his resignation. At Wilson's request, he agreed to hold off on the resignation until the president had time to gather more information.

The following day, a longtime Wilson friend from New Jersey, J.A.H. Hopkins, secured an appointment to see the president. He and his wife, Allison Hopkins, had been dinner guests at the White House just days earlier. Now Allison sat in a prison cell in Occoquan. "How would you like to have your wife sleep in a dirty workhouse next to prostitutes?" the distraught Hopkins asked. Wilson feigned shock to learn of the arrests and harsh sentences, claiming he knew nothing about them. When the president asked what he could do, Hopkins had a terse reply: release the prisoners and see that the Susan B. Anthony amendment is passed immediately. Wilson did issue a pardon for the prisoners. Each and every one of them wanted to reject the pardon, until Dudley Malone pointed out that they could refuse to be pardoned but would, in effect, be tossed out of the workhouse. Allison Hopkins issued a public statement saying that she did indeed reject the pardon, a decision with which Paul agreed. "We're very much obliged to the President but we'll be picketing again next Monday. The President can pardon us again if we are arrested on Monday, and again and again. . . . [B]ut picketing will continue and sooner or later, he will have to do something about it."[14]

At the same time, news began circulating that Wilson was considering making suffrage a war measure. Actions taken by the president regarding suffrage were complicated. The war formed a backdrop for a triangle that had been developing since 1914, consisting of Wilson, NAWSA, and the NWP. As a counterpoint to Alice Paul's militant strategy despite the war, Carrie Chapman Catt struck a conciliatory note with Wilson. Thus, Wilson could attribute to NAWSA any concessions made to suffragists on the grounds that NAWSA represented real American womanhood. He may have been capitulating to Alice Paul's demands, but he was not about to lose face in the process. For Wilson, NAWSA was a necessary part of the equation. Free of any pressure from NAWSA, Wilson could, if it suited him, use NAWSA to explain actions that he took in response to Alice Paul's campaign. But despite the rumors circulating, Wilson was not ready to take that next step. While both he and District Commissioner Louis Brownlow discussed the picketing situation and agreed that further arrests were not desirable, the authorities on site were not necessarily apprised of those feelings. But neither man interfered when more arrests were made in the ensuing months. Sentences gradually became harsher, but with no new pardons in the offing.

The war, of course, had a great deal to do with how the picketers were dealt with. In order to get total support for the war, Wilson instituted the policy of "100 percent Americanism," urging Americans to support their country unconditionally. Actions both foolish and threatening were a consequence of that policy. The Espionage Act of

1917, intended to prohibit treasonous acts such as spying, also contained more subtle and dangerous provisions including bans on speech or actions that might aid the enemy. On the silly side, sauerkraut was renamed "Liberty Cabbage" and German measles became known as "Liberty measles." Those engaged in teaching the German language were reported to authorities by neighbors certain that they had seditious intentions. A great many people believed that *any* dissent, for *any* reason, was tantamount to treason. No less than the *New York Times* placed under one umbrella anarchists, strikers, anti-war demonstrators, draft resisters, and, yes, suffragists as well, thereby conveying to readers the implication that *all* dissent was equally meritless and harmful. All of these tactics helped to persuade many people that the suffragists were engaged in dangerous anti-American activities. The extent to which the ideas behind the tactics filtered into the suffrage courtroom became clear when presiding Judge Alexander Mullowney said that he knew that the words on the picketers' banners were "treasonous and seditious." He had no problem meting out harsh sentences for what were, at worst, dubious misdemeanors.

Even given these circumstances, throwing conventional middle-class women into a workhouse did not sit well with a substantial portion of the press and the public. "It is ludicrous for Washington diplomats to pose as teachers of democracy to the people of benighted Russia which has admitted the women of their country to equal political and civil rights," observed a Florida newspaper. Said another New York paper: "The suffrage issue exists. It cannot be met by denial . . . or even imprisonment. The fundamentals of our democratic institutions are at stake." Chief Justice Walter Clark of the North Carolina Supreme Court asserted that "the manhood of this country will never stand for war upon women." And when actor Richard Bennett was asked by the secretary of war to go to France to narrate a propaganda film, Bennett replied, "Why should I work for democracy in Europe when our American women are denied democracy at home? If I am to fight for social hygiene in France, why not begin at Occoquan Workhouse?"[15] The constant stream of criticism, even if it didn't come from the majority of the press and population, was nevertheless daunting enough to produce sporadic efforts at news censorship. The editor of the *Washington Times* spoke to Wilson's secretary, Joseph Tumulty, proposing a "pact and agreement" among all newspapers that the suffrage story be managed in any way Wilson wished. The president thought the editor's suggestion was a good one that could keep suffrage off the front pages. Wilson suggested that if it was discussed at all, "it should be a bare, colorless chronicle. . . . This constitutes part of the news but it need not be made interesting reading."[16]

Throughout the summer and fall, as the picketing continued, so did the arrests. It is somewhat perplexing that Wilson didn't take more proactive steps in making his own views known, if not about suffrage then certainly about the situation with the picketers being arrested and sent to Occoquan. The level of public indignation only got worse. Representative Charles Lindbergh held Wilson directly responsible for the denial of the picketers' rights to petition the government and said so in a public letter. He believed that Wilson had only to say the word and all of that would stop, but "you did not speak the word." On the heels of the Lindbergh letter, Dudley Field Malone made his resignation public, sending more shock waves. The suffrage issue was percolating in the halls of Congress, with both the House and Senate engaged in discussions. On September 24, the House finally voted to establish a woman suffrage committee—and even more importantly, the chairman of the Rules Committee, Edward Pou, waving Wilson's May 14th war-measures letter overhead, announced that suffrage would be on the table as soon as all the other war measures were attended to.[17]

What the women prisoners had to endure at Occoquan was horrific. The prison was overrun with rats large and small that freely entered the cells, terrifying inmates who often had to beat them off as they climbed onto the cots at night. The food, intentionally repulsive, prompted feeble attempts to introduce some levity by holding contests. The winners were those women who counted the most mealworms in their bowls of gruel. While the contests may have been fleeting distractions, the food simply made the prisoners ill.

Prison authorities had no qualms about using race to intimidate the suffrage prisoners. They told the women that they were being held in a section of the jail where African-American male prisoners roamed about freely, regardless of their level of crimes. If they expected suffrage prisoners to plead for their safety, however, they were surely disappointed. Sanitary conditions were abysmal as well, with buckets of dirty water provided to the suffragists to clean themselves. To be sure, none of these conditions were novel to the regular inmates of Occoquan. But when the white, middle- and upper-class suffragists began touring the country on a Suffrage Special train, relating their experience to audiences, the public found it shocking. Paul capitalized on the Occoquan ordeal by means of the Suffrage Special train tour. Picketers who had spent time in Occoquan and could speak personally about the conditions there were enlisted to come on board and, dressed in their prison garb, address audiences along the route. They attracted larger and larger crowds as newspaper stories telegraphed to the next whistle stop what the prisoners had to endure. By the time the Suffrage Special ended its run, everyone knew all the gruesome details. For the authorities, it was all just another battle in their war against women.

A series of incidents in the fall of 1917 brought matters to at least a temporary head. On October 20, DC police arrested Alice Paul and three other picketers. With the notorious leader of the whole picketing debacle—as the authorities viewed it—in custody, an example could now be made of her. After her trial and conviction, Paul was sentenced to seven months in Occoquan, the harshest sentence yet. On October 30, Paul and Rose Winslow began a hunger strike in an effort to gain political prisoner status. The "crimes" of political prisoners—also known as "prisoners of conscience"—are, by definition, political acts against an unfair government rather than criminal acts. Very few requests for political prisoner status are granted because doing so puts the government in a bad light. Lucy Burns, also confined to the prison, undertook this political prisoner campaign virtually under the noses of the authorities. She managed to get a petition, signed by suffrage prisoners, smuggled out of Occoquan and delivered to the district commissioners. Their only response was to see that each of the signers was transferred to solitary confinement. Prison authorities threatened Paul on a daily basis. They told her to stop the hunger strike or risk being confined to the psychiatric ward of Occoquan—or worse, St. Elizabeth's, the public insane asylum. They needed only the recommendation of one doctor to make that a reality. In the meantime, Paul and Rose Winslow were subjected to forced feedings three times a day. Each one was a painful, vomit-inducing, debilitating ordeal—so painful, in fact, that those forced to experience it were often reduced to screams and cries, not always knowing that they themselves were doing the screaming.

Forced feedings further compromised Paul's health, leaving her weak and nauseous. But despite her deteriorating condition, she refused to stop her hunger strike and after three weeks, prison authorities transferred her to the psychiatric ward in the District Jail. She was prohibited from seeing or speaking to anyone not on the staff, and no one was told where she had been taken, including her lawyer, Dudley Field Malone. Malone spent a frantic ten days trying to find out where Paul had been hidden away in the vast prison system. The door to her room had been removed and a prison guard woke her every hour with a bright spotlight, making sleep impossible for more than a few minutes at a time. And for no apparent reason, the windows in her room were boarded up.

The circumstances of her detention terrified the usually unflappable Paul. She came to dread the daily visits from doctors who questioned her repeatedly, especially about her feelings toward Wilson. The head physician was especially threatening. "I believe I have never in my life before feared anything or any human being, but I confess I was afraid of Dr. Gannon. . . . I dreaded the hour of his visit."[18] Gannon continually demanded to know whether Paul regarded Wilson as a personal enemy. If he could get Paul to say that she did view him in this way, the doctors would have grounds to have her declared insane. (Paranoia and persecution complex were sufficient grounds toward this end.) The only straws she could cling to, and what saved Paul, were her inner strength and the kindnesses of some of the psychiatric ward nurses who constantly told her they knew she was not insane.

By November 9, Wilson had received enough complaints to dispatch an investigator, Dr. W. Gwynn Gardiner, with instructions to report to the president regarding the situation. Gardiner's report was a whitewash. Whether he actually conducted his own investigation and chose to misrepresent conditions, or merely accepted the word of prison officials, is not clear. His report exonerated the officials, denied any abuse of prisoners, and stated that forced feedings were an everyday occurrence that were not in the least harmful because the prisoners "took the tube . . . and swallowed it willingly." This, he claimed, produced no more than ordinary discomfort. The descriptions of forced feedings that Rose Winslow smuggled out of Occoquan told a different story. "Don't let them tell you we take this well. Miss Paul vomits much. . . . I do too. . . . We think of the coming feedings all day. It is horrible."[19] Wilson nevertheless accepted the Gardiner report and told Joseph Tumulty to distribute it to anyone concerned about the treatment of the prisoners. This was decidedly not Woodrow Wilson's finest hour.

Even as Paul's confinement continued to play out, prison authorities committed the most outrageous acts of unwarranted abuse against a group of newly arrived suffrage prisoners. The incident, which became known as "The Night of Terror" in suffrage circles, began when the new prisoners were being processed at Occoquan. Without warning, prison superintendent Raymond Whittaker burst into the room followed by a bevy of guards. Stationing himself in the center of the room, Whittaker began ordering the guards to take various prisoners, whom he identified by name, to the cells. It was pure bedlam and totally disorienting. The prisoners feared for their lives. Mary Nolan, a seventy-three-year old Floridian with an impaired leg, found herself being dragged off by two guards, though she told them repeatedly she would go willingly. Dorothy Day (later associated with the Catholic Workers) had her arm twisted behind her back and was slammed down not once but twice over the back of an iron bench. Dora Lewis was thrown into a cell with such force that she was knocked unconscious, and for some frantic minutes her friends thought she had died. The guards also flung Alice Cosu of New Orleans into her cell. Less fortunate than Dora Lewis, Cosu actually suffered a heart attack as a consequence. Repeated pleas to prison guards to have her attended to were ignored, and Cosu went without medical attention until the following morning. Lucy Burns, arrested once again after serving her previous sixty-day sentence, was identified by Whittaker as the ringleader of the group. Whittaker's guards shackled her to the cell bars with her hands above her head. She was left that way until morning, at which point the guards returned, removed her clothes, and left her with only a blanket. The entire attack was unexpected, unprovoked, and carried out with a stunning ferociousness. Inquiries poured into the Oval Office as news of the treatment of the prisoners became known. One NAWSA member sent Wilson a copy of her local paper reporting on Alice Paul. Wilson responded that he thought "our present reply ought to be to the effect that no real harshness of method is being used . . . there being an extraordinary amount of lying about the thing." Ironically, if Wilson had thought about it, he might have questioned more carefully who was doing the lying.[20] Once again, at yet another juncture in the war against women, the president failed to live up to his reputation as an educator, a fighter against corruption, and a progressive.

On November 20, Malone finally found Alice Paul in the psychiatric ward. He obtained a writ of *habeas corpus,* authorizing her transfer out of the ward. Shortly afterward, she was allowed to have a late-night visitor, the first such permission since her incarceration. The visitor, journalist David Lawrence, was a personal friend of Wilson's—though he insisted that he was doing this on his own and had not been sent by anyone. However, the fact that Lawrence gained permission to speak with Paul at this late hour, along with the nature of his discussion, strongly suggests that Wilson not only sent him but cleared the way for his access to Paul. Paul said little, letting Lawrence tell her why this extraordinary meeting had been allowed. "The Administration could easily hire a comfortable house in Washington and detain you all there," Lawrence told her. "But don't you see that your demand to be treated as political prisoners is infinitely more difficult to grant than to give you a federal amendment?" It was a remarkable statement. The Wilson administration had apparently been moved enough by events to consider the implications of granting political prisoners status versus advancing a federal amendment. According to Lawrence, a federal amendment was the path of least resistance. Lawrence then asked about Paul's future intentions. Would she consider suspending picketing if the administration passed the amendment through one house of Congress in the next session, with a promise to see it passed through the other house within a year? Paul was adamant: "Nothing short of passage of the amendment will end our agitation." Lawrence told Paul that, although Wilson would not mention suffrage in his Annual Message, he would make his views known to Congress before the amendment next came up for a vote.[21]

After he left, Paul thought about the message Lawrence had delivered. She surmised correctly that decisions regarding the prisoners were going to be made very quickly. It was the first real crack in Wilson's refusal to consider a federal suffrage amendment.

Within days of Lawrence's late-night visit, the government released all of the suffrage prisoners. Suffrage appeal cases were already working their way through the courts. The government's case was shaky at best, and legal scholars believed that the higher court would condemn the government's action in denying suffragists their First Amendment rights. Then, too, the political climate for suffrage had changed markedly—largely thanks to Alice Paul and the NWP. Since the start of the picketing, Wilson had transformed from a dodger on the issue of suffrage to an active suffrage supporter and, most importantly, a supporter of a federal amendment as well. He would continue to extend himself, with only sporadic bouts of backsliding, in the ensuing months. But for nearly a year, the war on the home front—the war against women—had been waged. Suffragists' rights were being denied. They had been treated appallingly. They were subjected to mental and physical abuse at the hands of authorities. And the Wilson administration willingly conspired with and condoned the actions of those in charge. The administration had, in short, written a sorry chapter in American history. The women involved in the battles conducted themselves with courage and determination. But unnecessary and unjust war, wherever and however it is fought, is truly a poor business. Now, despite the harrowing months behind them, Paul geared up to continue the fight for a federal amendment. Suffragists, she knew, still had a long way to go.

8

Victory and Discord

The year that had just ended, 1917, proved to be an extraordinary one for Alice Paul. She survived the worst that the Wilson administration could churn out. Her own ordeal in the psychiatric ward of the District Jail and the constant threats to admit her permanently were finally put to rest when the physician sent to perform a final mental examination refused to abandon his integrity by falsely declaring Paul mentally impaired. Dudley Field Malone conducted an insistent pursuit to find his client in the labyrinthine system of the District Jail. Wilson capitulated and ordered the release of all the suffrage prisoners. And through his emissary, David Lawrence, he agreed to support a federal suffrage amendment. For all intents and purposes, the war against women came to an end. Even in the face of personal danger to her health, welfare, and future, Paul had refused to halt the campaign to secure a federal amendment, including further picketing if that is what it would take. She remained true to her word.

The picketing campaign had been a monumental success. Success carried a price, however. The consequences of the authorities' reaction to the picketing created dangerous and personal difficulties for the participants. Over the course of the picketing campaign and the Watch-fires of Freedom demonstrations, thousands of women volunteered to take their turn on the picket lines. More than 500 women were arrested and 168 women actually served prison sentences, mostly in Occoquan Workhouse. The bravery of the thousands who volunteered, knowing full well they might be arrested, cannot be overstated. Many of those who were sent to Occoquan found that support from their families—if indeed they had such support to start with—often evaporated quickly. Elderly Louisine Havemeyer, the woman responsible for introducing America to impressionist artists, received message after message from family members who accused her of bringing disgrace down upon all their heads. The one comforting family message came from her young grandson, who wanted to see his "grandmama" again because, as he noted, she was a "real sport." Mary Winsor's aunt told her that her "reckless" actions were harmful to the family's reputation. Rebecca Reyher recalled that "while I was on the picket line, among the people who passed me by were many I had gone to high school with, or previous friends and neighbors, and . . . they turned their noses up at me, practically spat at me." Few family members were as supportive as Thomas Hepburn, the husband of Katherine Houghton Hepburn. When Katherine asked if her picketing might harm his medical practice, he responded, "Of course it will, but do it anyway. If you don't stand for the things you believe in, life is no good. If I can't succeed anyway, then let's fail."[1]

Buoyed by this kind of bravery and determined not to let the Wilson administration drag its feet, Paul continued to send picketers out, both to protest the lack of a federal amendment and to encourage politicians to quickly pass such an amendment. She also began a protest campaign in Lafayette Park, across the street from the White House, dubbed the Watchfires of Freedom. Printed copies of Wilson's speeches on the subject of democracy abroad were routinely burned by NWP members. Lighting fires in safely contained urns, and with great fanfare dropping the copies into the flames, the demonstrators once again attracted massive press coverage. If Wilson and other politicians wanted to ignore them, they could not ignore the resulting media attention.

As support for a federal amendment moved inexorably through the halls of Congress, often with Wilson's behind-the-scenes encouragement, the president finally took the step that, in Paul's eyes, ensured success. Like many politicians, Woodrow Wilson had the ability to transform political necessity into personal advocacy. His wartime speeches showed a growing awareness of the important role that women played in the war effort. However, where suffrage was concerned, Wilson frequently took pains to say that he was responding to the cooperative women of NAWSA and not to the militant NWP. Given the degree to which the NWP's actions regularly dominated press coverage of the issue, it is difficult to deny the pressure that the organization brought to bear upon the president. Paul had said all along that persuading Wilson to support a federal amendment would be the key to their success. She wasn't particularly concerned about who the president credited with his evolving stance; it was enough that he was moving toward support of a federal amendment. By May 1918, the theme so carefully cultivated by Paul—that it was all up to Woodrow Wilson now—seemed finally to have permeated throughout suffrage groups including the NWP, the Democratic National Committee (DNC) Women's Bureau, women voters and citizens, and even the Republicans.

One last egregious instance of backsliding occurred when Paul announced that, in view of the Senate's refusal to bring suffrage to a vote once again in the current congressional session, the picketing campaign would resume. A meeting held at Lafayette Park in August 1918 resulted in the arrest of sixty women. Some were released unconditionally while others were released on bail, to face charges at another time. Even the most cynical of observers were stunned by this turn of events. What could the administration hope to gain by letting the arrests takes place, thereby leading people to believe that Wilson approved of them? The terrible publicity attendant upon the Occoquan episodes just a few months earlier made the current response to demonstrations even more questionable. Several of the women were sentenced to fifteen days in a prison that, in many respects, was worse than Occoquan because it had been closed down for years. Within five days, during which the suffrage prisoners began hunger strikes, and following a multitude of complaints from politicians and citizens alike, the prisoners were released. Paul received a notice from Wilson's military aide saying that future demonstrations in Lafayette Park would not be interfered with.

On Monday, September 30, 1918, Wilson sent word to members of the Senate that he would personally address them in thirty minutes' time. Accompanied by all but one of his cabinet members, the president headed for the Capitol. Presidents rarely invoke their prerogative to directly address a body of Congress on a pending issue. The last president to address members of Congress was Thomas Jefferson. Everyone knew what issue Wilson intended to speak to, but there was an air of tension, nevertheless, as he approached the podium. His speech was both eloquent and powerful. To be sure, the war was already drawing to a close and an armistice would be signed less than two months later, on November 11, 1918. His address to the Senate had less to do with the war itself than with postwar negotiations and his plans for a postwar world, which he fervently hoped would include a League of Nations.

> I regard the extension of suffrage to women as vitally essential to the successful prosecution of the great war . . . in which we are engaged. It is my duty to win the war and to ask you to remove every obstacle that stands in the way of the winning of it. . . . They [other nations] are looking at the great, powerful, famous democracy of the West to lead them to a new day for which they have long waited; and they think in their logical simplicity that democracy means that women shall play their part in affairs alongside men and upon an equal footing with them. . . . I tell you plainly as the Commander in Chief of our armies . . . that this measure is vital to the winning of the war. It is vital to the right solutions which we must settle, and settle immediately. . . . I ask you to place in my hands, instruments, spiritual instruments, which I do not now possess, which I sorely need, and which I have daily to apologize for not being able to employ.

Wilson insisted that "the voices of the foolish and intemperate agitators do not reach me at all." To Paul, that did not matter. She could not have cared less about Wilson's need to minimize her effect on his decisions. But it was significant that, in tying the success of the war to enactment of a federal suffrage amendment, Wilson validated the war policy that Paul had adopted nearly two years earlier. Paul and the NWP had transformed suffrage into an issue of such monumental importance that its passage became imperative in order to maintain public trust in the integrity of the United States both at home and abroad. In the eyes of people throughout the world, woman suffrage had become the measure of America's good intentions and trustworthiness in world affairs. Paul had always understood this. Now, so did Woodrow Wilson.

Wilson, to his credit, pursued every opportunity to persuade Senate Democrats who still refused to budge on the suffrage issue. He sent numerous letters and met with the senators in question several times. He also sent messages to the governors of southern states, which most of the hold-out Democrats represented, urging them to appeal to the senators to change their votes. Finally, on June 4, 1919, the Senate voted 56 to 25 in favor of suffrage and the ratification process officially began. Shortly after the Senate vote, in September 1919, Wilson went on a western-states speaking tour promoting the League of Nations. Severe headaches forced him to return to Washington. Shortly after his arrival back at the White House, he suffered a serious stroke, which left him paralyzed on his left side.

The ratification process took a little over a year. It proceeded fairly rapidly for two reasons. First, legislators in most states knew that their constituents favored woman suffrage. And, second, the process remained free from anti-suffrage protests. The anti-suffragists' efforts grew weaker and weaker over time as more people favored woman suffrage. But up until the final Senate vote, the anti-suffragists continued to lobby for modification of the Susan B. Anthony Amendment. A last-ditch effort was made to attach a time limit for ratification to the amendment wording. If the amendment included a time limit for ratification, the anti-suffragists reasoned, they could continue their opposition and stop the process, even if by only one state. But the Senate roundly denounced the proposal, because everyone knew it was a delaying tactic and lacked merit. Once that happened, the anti-suffragists gave up the fight, conceding that further opposition would be fruitless under the circumstances.

As a result of Wilson's stroke, his health continued to decline throughout the ratification process. But the public never knew how serious things were. Members of his family and his administration neither informed the public nor called for the president's resignation. But they also ensured that other measures important to Wilson, including a League of Nations, did not fall by the wayside. Tennessee was the final state to vote for the amendment, thus making the Anthony Amendment the Nineteenth Amendment to the United States Constitution. On August 26, 1920, Secretary of State Bainbridge Colby signed the proclamation of ratification, bringing to an end the historic crusade begun nearly a hundred years earlier. Among the congratulatory messages received by Alice Paul was one from Chief Justice Walter Clark of North Carolina:

> Will you permit me to congratulate you upon the great triumph in which you have been so important a factor? There were politicians and a large degree of public sentiment, which could only be won by the methods you adopted. . . . It is certain that, but for you, success would have been delayed for many years to come.

Earlier, one congressman had told Dora Lewis and Maud Younger that "all this agitation, the lobbying, the persistence never-ceasing, often to us men very irritating, like grains of sand in the eyes, has nevertheless hastened your amendment by ten years." While the numerous messages were gratifying, Paul never doubted the wisdom of her strategy. The NWP had won over Wilson, Paul had noted several months earlier. "We knew that it, and it alone, would ensure our success. It mean[t] to us only one thing—victory."[2]

With ratification of the Nineteenth Amendment, a long chapter in the fight for equality for American women came to a close and a new chapter began. Since the 1890s, when the rationale for suffrage shifted from an argument based on justice to one based on expediency, most women viewed the ballot as a cure-all for societal ills. In the broadest sense, all suffragists were feminists. But that word served as an umbrella term referring to two distinct strains of feminism: social feminism and ideology-based feminism.

The dividing line between the two groups tended to coincide with their allegiances in the suffrage movement. Most older suffragists (including the majority of NAWSA members, though by no means all of them) were social feminists. The social feminists believed that using their new voting power would result in legislation affecting women workers, reduce or eliminate child labor, and establish wage and hour minimums. In short, they advocated women's traditional societal role, that of mother and nurturer. For the social feminists, there existed an immutable difference between women and men that mitigated women's ability to lay claim to equality in the fullest sense of the word. Most social feminists had little desire to alter long-standing gender roles, as defined by society. If equality could be obtained without disrupting, displacing, or endangering women's traditional place within the family, social feminists did not object. But if they desired equality at all, it was only to the extent that it did not infringe upon their demands for protection for women. Protective legislation, the social feminists believed, was necessary to ensure that women would be treated fairly, especially in the workplace. And, when all was said and done, they viewed the Nineteenth Amendment as a necessary tool to ensure continuation of traditional roles. Any effort to disrupt traditional roles would be opposed by social feminists in the polling booth.

The ideology-based feminists tended to be more radical; they viewed the vote as a crucial first step to full social, economic, and civic equality with men. They wanted to be on an equal footing with their husbands on issues dealing with home and children, they wanted equality in the workplace, and they wanted equality on civic issues—including the court system. The ideology-based feminists took their cues from the original Declaration of Sentiments, penned by Elizabeth Cady Stanton in 1848. In it, she identified the areas in which women were placed at a disadvantage because of the way society was organized. They were concerned not only with women's status in the public sphere but also with their status in the private sphere. Like Doris Stevens, many of these women viewed men—including husbands, fathers, brothers, and sons—as invariably having the upper hand.[3]

The ideological feminists sympathized with many of the same causes advocated by social feminists. But their views regarding equality inevitably placed the two groups on a collision course. Protective legislation desired by the social feminists would not, for example, guarantee that women would be given equal opportunity to pursue education, jobs, equal pay for equal work, the right to property ownership, dominion over their children in cases of divorce, the right to have a say in family planning, or equality in the eyes of the law. More importantly, the ideologists rejected the prevailing belief in women's inferiority by virtue of their reproductive function and physical attributes. For them, biology was not—nor should be—destiny. Like Elizabeth Cady Stanton, the radicals believed that womanhood itself was the crucial factor, and that wifehood and motherhood were merely incidental. These issues were more abstract, and thus less appealing, than the cut-and-dried legislative solutions that could be enacted to eliminate social ills. But ideological feminists, such as Crystal Eastman, understood and articulated the kind of change necessary in an equitable society. As Eastman put it:

> [The problem is] how to arrange the world so that women can be human beings, with a chance to exercise their infinitely varied gifts in infinitely varied ways, instead of being destined by the accident of their sex to one field of activity—housework and child-raising. And second, if and when they choose housework and child-raising, to have that occupation recognized by the world as work, requiring a definite economic reward and not merely entitling the performer to be dependent on some man.[4]

Paul absolutely agreed with this point of view. Throughout the suffrage years, the internalization of feminist ideology had been the characteristic that Paul most hoped to find in potential volunteers. This is not to say that she rejected help from those with a more socially feminist perspective. But the women to whom she turned for important leadership roles were almost always those who believed in Paul's brand of feminism: Mabel Vernon, Crystal Eastman, Mary Beard, Lucy Burns, Sara Bard Field, Inez Milholland, Dora Lewis, Alva Belmont, Louisine Havemeyer, the Hepburns, Doris Stevens. All were feminists. Eastman clearly stated the necessity for a redefinition of how society had to be arranged if women were going to achieve true equality. It could never be obtained solely through enactment of the Nineteenth Amendment. This amendment was certainly a step in the right direction, but further steps had to be taken to truly ensure equality. Such steps were much discussed among women in the months following ratification.

Even before ratification, women had begun to ask "What next?" NWP members, who had organized solely to promote a federal suffrage amendment, asked "What—if *anything*—next?" The ensuing discussion began to sort out those NWP members who considered themselves Paul feminists. In July 1920, Alva Belmont raised the question of how best to proceed at a meeting of the Executive Committee. She favored maintaining the organization, but with a slightly different goal: obtaining full equality for women in all phases of life and making them a power in the life of the state.

The response to Belmont's remarks resulted in NWP members arguing for a variety of future goals. For the first time, it became apparent that NWP members were as disparate in their plans and desires as were women in general. Not all—or even most—NWP members were ready to commit to a new campaign, regardless of the goal. A general feeling of exhaustion permeated the membership. After nearly a decade of lobbying, demonstrating, picketing, imprisonment, and engaging in anti–Democratic Party campaigns that made them the targets of public wrath, the ladies of the NWP wanted to take a long breather. Some of them felt that they had sacrificed enough for women's rights and were ready to let the next generation take the reins. Lucy Burns was both exhausted and angry. "I don't want to do anything more," Burns declared. "I think we have done all this for women and we have sacrificed everything we possessed for them, and now let them . . . fight for it now. I am not going to fight . . . anymore."

Burns undoubtedly thought her life was going to take a very different course when she first arrived in Europe to study. When she returned to America, she and Alice Paul worked together on a day-by-day, hour-by-hour basis to win suffrage. Paul became the strategist and tactician and Burns the chief implementer. Burns organized in the states, helped to coordinate the vast picketing campaign, spent more time in prison than any other American suffragist, endured all of the attendant horrors of her confinement, toured the country with the Prison Special, and in every other way possible helped to achieve the goal that she and Paul had discussed sitting on the police-station billiard table in London more than a decade earlier. Now exhaustion, both physical and emotional, overtook Burns. But fatigue and the desire for a normal life were coupled with bitterness toward those who had sat out the suffrage movement. Single women, Burns believed, had borne the cost of suffrage. Now it should fall to married women to take up the gauntlet. Most members of the NWP were equally exhausted. They may not all have felt exactly as Lucy Burns did, but they, too, retired or simply let their memberships lapse after ratification. Mabel Vernon testified before the House Judiciary Committee in 1925 and reported that the NWP membership had dropped to about twenty thousand. That may have been a generous estimate; but if it were even close to accurate, it would mean that fully two-thirds of the NWP members had resigned or let their membership lapse after 1920 and never rejoined the organization.[5]

At a post-ratification meeting of the NWP leadership, most of the women gathered appeared to be on the same page. For one thing, they were unanimous in insisting that Alice Paul had to remain as leader of the organization. They believed that any attempt to carry on would depend largely on Paul's willingness to continue the work. Paul, however, would not immediately agree to their request. She continued to fight against her physical limitations as she had done throughout the suffrage campaign. On several occasions in those years, Paul had to give in and take to her bed for two or three days to regain strength. At least once, she landed in the hospital because she had allowed herself to become so run down. Now, she could think of nothing more inviting than to return to Paulsdale and put everything out of her mind. She felt such "extreme fatigue" that she thought she could "hardly go on any longer."[6] At the same time, the fact that the NWP still had outstanding debts totaling nearly $10,000 weighed heavily on her. She would not leave creditors in the lurch. Accordingly, she and Maud Younger agreed to take on the responsibility of raising enough money to clear the accounts.

Most Executive Committee members had come to the February 1921 meeting with two agendas. Getting Paul to stay on board was clearly one of these. But second agendas varied widely from person to person. Belmont restated her case for an organization dedicated to equality, but she lacked specifics about how to achieve that equality. Eastman came with the most clearly defined and articulated set of proposals, which addressed fundamental issues including economic and occupational independence, planned parenthood, education, and an endowment for mothers—especially those with economic limitations. Others wanted the new party to focus on world peace, pacifism, protective legislation for women and children, and other similar issues.

Paul continued to avoid making any commitments beyond raising funds to pay the party's remaining debts. Her stock responses to inquiries about her intentions regarding a new NWP were noncommittal. She said that it would be up to "the women who will have to go on with the work, if the organization continues, to decide what they would like to do." She didn't exactly exclude herself from participation, even if it sounded that way. In truth, it was highly unlikely that Paul would withdraw from taking part in the women's movement, however it might be structured. As a journalist friend of Paul's noted in an article in *Century Magazine:*

> Every other woman in Washington I can imagine without a cause. . . . Even over teacups, I think of Paul as a political force, a will bound to express itself politically. . . . I remember a long talk we had in 1921 when she was searching her mind for the next plan to advance the freedom of women. She was overwhelmed by the setting up of the League of Nations, which she regarded as a closed corporation for deciding the fate of women and of the people. . . . She burned with disgust for the inconsequential part women played in international politics.[7]

Over the course of the suffrage years, Paul had given up almost everything not directly related to getting a federal amendment. Relationships with potential beaux, reading for pleasure (which she had enjoyed since childhood), vacations with friends and family members, even just enjoying the company of friends—one by one these activities were put on hold until her life became the cause and the cause became her life. Her complete immersion in women's freedom may not have been the course she consciously chose, but it was the consequence of the gradual relinquishment of each small part of her private life. Despite her protestations that she would not commit to taking on responsibilities in the new organization, Paul reached the point in her life when she could no more turn her back on the next step than she could have withdrawn from the suffrage campaign before that goal became reality. In refusing to make any immediate long-term commitments, Paul gave herself time to consider her options. The plan she settled on was, first, to renew her physical health and resources and settle outstanding debts and, only then, to decide where she personally would be most useful in the women's rights movement.

Paul did, however, agree to one more short-term commitment—namely, a ceremony at the Capitol on February 15, 1921, the anniversary of Susan B. Anthony's birthday. Given her aversion to loose ends, the ceremony gave Paul the opportunity to close out the suffrage chapter of the women's movement with the kind of flourish and pageantry she found so satisfying. Years before, a NAWSA committee had commissioned sculptress Adelaide Johnson to make busts of the three suffrage pioneers: Anthony, Stanton, and Lucretia Mott. The sculptures were meant to be presented to Congress for permanent placement in the Capitol rotunda, but the project ended up on the back burner. Eventually, a member of the original committee, Ida Husted Harper, in an effort to revive the project, approached Carrie Chapman Catt to enlist her help. Catt thought the sculptures were artistically unattractive and refused to become involved. She did, however, give Harper authority to determine what, if anything, should be done with them. Paul had heard about the statues years earlier and talked to Harper about them. In May 1920, Harper turned them over to Paul as no one else had expressed any interest in going forward with the original intent.

Paul proposed to have the suffrage ceremony revolve around the presentation of the statues to Congress. From the start, she had wanted the ceremony to be more than just an NWP event. Invitations were sent to every women's group in the country that had participated in any way in the suffrage movement. Paul hoped that the ceremony would be an opportunity not only to celebrate their collective victory but also to demonstrate the solidarity of the women's movement itself.

More than a hundred women's organizations sent delegates to the ceremony. All of the major suffrage groups were represented, with one exception: Carrie Chapman Catt refused to send anyone from NAWSA. Jane Addams opened the ceremony with a brief address praising the three suffrage pioneers, and Sara Bard Field delivered the keynote address. It was an impassioned speech that electrified the delegates. Like Addams, she praised the work of Anthony, Stanton, and Mott and their dedication to women's freedom. With the power of the vote, women no longer had to accept the age-old challenge to "live a great life for others at the expense of self." Presenting the sculptures to the Speaker of the House, Field said, "Mr. Speaker, I give you Revolution!"[8]

While Field's speech inspired those who heard it, her claims of future solidarity were more wish than reality. The unanimity demonstrated by the women at the Capitol rang down the curtain on the coalition of interests that held together so long as they had a common, single, and easily identifiable goal, such as the federal suffrage amendment. Thereafter, the coalition that might have been the basis for greater gains in the future began to fragment as women gravitated toward those avenues for change that they most identified with. The consequences of a dissolved coalition were not at all apparent at the moment. Still reveling in their recent victory and attendant optimism, the women delegates began to head home. NWP members remained in Washington to attend the national convention arranged by Paul to begin the next morning.

It didn't take long for Paul to determine a new set of goals. Hoping to prepare the delegates for the proposal to be put forth at the convention, she wrote the lead editorial in a special edition of *The Suffragist*, reminding her readers that the Seneca Falls Women's Bill of Rights of 1848 contained a series of demands that went beyond just the right to vote. Indeed, the Bill of Rights also demanded equality for women with men and the removal of policies that kept women legally and socially in a position of second class citizenship. Throughout the suffrage campaign, Paul insisted that all other issues affecting women had to remain subordinate if they were going to succeed. But she always believed that, while the vote would be important to the achievement of complete equality between the sexes, it would not be sufficient. She warned her readers of the danger that suffrage victory carried with it: "Because of a great victory, women will believe that their whole struggle for independence is ended. They still have far to go." The convention, she added, would determine "whether there is any way [the National Woman's Party] . . . can serve in the struggle which lies ahead to remove the remaining forms of woman's subordination."[9] Paul intended her editorial to strike the theme that would dominate the convention debate: equality.

In her opening address to the convention audience, Paul reiterated the equality theme. With her every reference to equality, applause and cheers rolled like waves across the vast convention hall. Minority proposals were placed before the audience, with ample time allocated to discuss each one: Crystal Eastman's list of specifics that she believed the NWP had to address in order to achieve a successful outcome, a proposal championed by Jane Addams to transform the party into a peace organization, and, finally, a "great divide" issue that would ultimately split the women's movement—protective legislation. All three proposals were voted down. Speakers representing various political parties asked the NWP to reorganize along lines that would enable political parties and the NWP to work together. These, too, were voted down, with Rose Winslow delivering the final blow: "Don't let's get respectable. . . . I wish to say that before you can serve, you must have power."[10]

On the final day of the convention, the Minnesota state chairwoman presented the majority proposal. It recommended that that the immediate work of the organization be the removal of the legal disabilities of women with equality as the goal. It also recommended that the NWP Executive Committee be allowed the freedom to pursue whatever program it deemed necessary to implement the spirit and intent of the convention. The new NWP would define itself as an organization dedicated to securing equality for women—that much was clear. But from the earliest discussions regarding the future of the NWP, Executive Committee planners never defined exactly what constituted equality. They assumed that everyone would accept an unarticulated but mutually understood and commonly held presumption of what the word meant. Convention delegates certainly favored equality for women. But the variety of criticisms that were articulated made it clear that not everyone would agree on what equality meant for women and, more importantly, how to achieve it. The same criticisms that had dogged Paul from the very first suffrage parade in 1913—elitism and racism—began to surface once again. Taking into account the criticisms leveled at Paul—albeit by a minority of delegates—*The Nation* later echoed the critics and accused her of being racist, out of touch with the problems of working women, and remiss in not allowing more time to discuss issues.

The woman who introduced the majority report said later that she never saw such a large and enthusiastic crowd deflate so quickly. And, as in 1913, most of the criticisms were a consequence of Paul's desire to keep conflict out of the proceedings. She wanted to leave the NWP in an atmosphere free of dissension and discord. But, perhaps as a reflection of her complete exhaustion after more than a decade of nonstop work, her failure to define precisely what was meant by equality created the very turmoil she sought to avoid. Amidst that turmoil, she characterized African-American women as "spoilers" because they insisted on being allowed to speak to the delegates and she left too many delegates feeling that the convention had been structured to ensure passage of the majority report.

It *was*, as one observer noted, Alice Paul's convention. She called the shots for the most part. And even though she continued to make clear that she did not intend to hold any office in the new NWP, many people were troubled by the way things were going. For one thing, the order in which proposals were introduced and voted on seemed to be orchestrated with the goal of ensuring that the majority proposal always came out on top. By the time delegates heard the majority report, all of the other proposals had been voted against. Moreover, while time was allocated for discussion of each proposal, it was not an open-ended discussion. There was never any intention of allowing debate on each proposal to drag on endlessly. Once the allocated time expired, a vote was taken on that issue. Still, feedback indicated that the overwhelming majority of delegates and attendees favored the proceedings and had nothing but praise for Paul and the NWP. The majority report was, after all, the report of the *majority*. If the majority had voted down their own proposal, that would have been an astounding turn of events.

The majority vote dissolved the old NWP and immediately established a new NWP, which would be dedicated to equal rights for women. The *New York Times* observed that "if there were those present who did not believe in the battle cry of [equal rights] they remained quiet, for they were in the minority."[11] Though Paul achieved her goal of putting the organization on the trail of equality for women, the way it was done was one of the few missteps in her otherwise masterful grasp of politics and strategy. Paul's longtime friend Elsie Hill was elected chairwoman. Paul remained a noncandidate for office. After long deliberation, she had decided to take a leave of absence and attend law school. She reasoned that if she were going to play any role in the quest for equal rights, she'd better be well prepared to do so. Her first commitment, of course, would be to join Maud Younger in raising the money necessary to clear away NWP debts.

Following the convention, the NWP began drawing up blanket equal rights amendments for the states as well as a federal equal rights amendment. Only then did it become clear just how isolated the NWP was, as the only organization advocating equal rights. The most vocal opponents focused their opposition on protective legislation. Without question, such legislation was a valid concern and its defense should not have come as any great surprise. But the bitterness of the opposition did surprise the equal rights activists. For example, Florence Kelley, convinced that equal rights would jeopardize the work of securing protection for women in industry, characterized her one-time ally as a "fiend" who intended only to hinder the women's movement and undo twenty years of labor legislation. (Ironically, the objections to Paul's advocacy for equal rights were almost identical to the arguments raised by her suffrage critics. In both cases, critics always claimed that Paul's ideas and strategies were going to set back the cause and do irreparable harm to women.) Kelley's accusation—leveled not just at Paul but at the entire NWP—reinforced, for many women, the image that had burdened the NWP throughout the suffrage campaign. The party, therefore, had to continue combating charges that it was elitist, intemperate, and unconcerned with the needs of working women. The critics pursued this accusation despite people like Rose Winslow and Maud Younger whose entire careers were for and about women workers. NAWSA, in large part, had helped to forge that image.

Indeed, NAWSA had established itself as the most influential woman suffrage group in opposition to almost everything that Paul did. Under the leadership of Carrie Chapman Catt, NAWSA members staked out their claim as the movers and shakers in the suffrage movement. Following ratification, Catt reorganized NAWSA as the League of Women Voters, whose focus would be to influence legislation benefiting women. To Catt's credit, the League became the most influential women's political coalition going forward from the 1920s. Whether she received the lion's share of credit for the suffrage victory is disputable, however.

When NWP picketers were denied their civil liberties during World War I, NAWSA loudly disassociated itself from the militants. Catt asserted repeatedly that the NWP did not feel a true commitment to suffrage, and she condemned what she invariably referred to as militant activities. By its silence, NAWSA lent its support to the treatment accorded picket prisoners. And Wilson did his part by repeatedly pointing to NAWSA as the quintessential example of American womanhood—an example that, given the organization's work within the system and unflagging patriotism during the war, amply demonstrated that women deserved equal suffrage. Public response to the NWP was more ambivalent than Catt liked to see. Most Americans did not appreciate the treatment of picket prisoners. They viewed the actions of the government as heavy-handed at best and barbaric at worst. Nevertheless, a body of opinion—encouraged by NAWSA and government officials—built up regarding Alice Paul and the NWP. In the minds of many Americans, the NWP was not to be trusted. Furthermore, a surprising number of people overlooked the crucial role played by Alice Paul in getting the federal amendment. The fact that she had succeeded in tying the fate of the war and postwar reconstruction to the fate of suffrage so that Wilson had no other choice but to strongly support a federal amendment was, quite frankly, lost on most Americans. *How* suffrage had been won became less important than the fact that victory had been secured. And because so many people either misunderstood or ignored the mechanics of the suffrage campaign, accepting the conventional wisdom that lay all the credit for victory at NAWSA's doorstep became the path of least resistance.

In truth, this outcome was an injustice to the women's movement. Women had taken control of their own destinies. They had forced the issue. Against all odds, they had won a resounding victory. And how they won that victory was an important consideration, for one fundamental reason: by downplaying the importance of the militant movement in the suffrage campaign, critics had dramatically decreased the probability that women would unite and use the power they now possessed. In these circumstances, women tended to accept the false pronouncement that equal rights would be harmful to women—especially working women. The criticisms of the protective legislationists—however meritorious their cause—had placed Paul and the NWP once again at the center of a conflict that pitted it against virtually every other woman's organization. What also decreased was the likelihood that an equal rights amendment could be obtained in less than the seven decades it took to achieve suffrage.

On the seventy-fifth anniversary of the Seneca Falls Convention, Alice Paul met with the Executive Committee. Though no longer a member of the committee, she had taken responsibility for writing an equal rights amendment for consideration. The amendment, which quickly became known as the Lucretia Mott Amendment, stated its intent and purpose in straightforward terms: "Men and women shall have equal rights throughout the United States and every place subject to its jurisdiction. Congress shall have the power to enforce this article by appropriate legislation." The simplicity of its language was intended to avoid any of the entanglements that equality inevitably touched on. In short, the idea was to make equal rights a single-issue goal, just as suffrage had been. Introduced in Congress in December 1923, the equal rights amendment seemed to be moving quickly in the right direction.

Once the equal rights amendment made its way to Congress, the alarm sounded by Florence Kelley became a call to arms. Those who naively thought that equal rights and protective legislation were not mutually exclusive propositions soon realized the degree to which they were at odds. Both sides believed they were right. The protectionists had been right in the past and the equal rights advocates would be right in the future. For the present, each side failed to recognize the opportunity that was placed in their respective paths. Compromise would have allowed women to strengthen their ranks and consolidate their new power. But neither side considered compromise a viable solution.

It was during the course of a House Judiciary Committee hearing on equal rights in 1925 that Alice Paul found out just how isolated she and the National Woman's Party were. Among all the women's organizations invited to testify, the NWP was the only group advocating the equal rights amendment. Almost every other organization spoke to its own special interests and in the process argued against equal rights. Congressmen, hearing evidence over a three-day period, were persuaded that it would not be as vigorously pursued as the suffrage amendment had been.

Paul took away from the hearings the conviction that the first task of the NWP *had* to be to secure the support of other women's groups before the party could attempt to launch a truly national campaign for equal rights. This would require a far different strategy than that employed for suffrage. For these reasons and over the pivotal issue of protective legislation, the women's movement in the 1920s splintered. What should have been a powerful new force in American life and politics, with the help and leadership of Alice Paul—the one indisputably successful leader and strategist of the suffrage movement—became instead a conglomeration of severely weakened groups that would carry little weight for the legislation they supported. Even Paul had no immediate answer to the central question of how to proceed and gain the support of other women's organizations.

9

The Quest for
Equality for Women

By 1926, Alice Paul had fully thrown herself back into the pursuit for
equality. She continued to avoid the question of retiring from an active
role in the NWP. By then, she had already carried out her decision to go
to law school, earning her LLB from the Washington College of Law in
1922. She went on to earn a master's in law from American University
in 1927 and a doctorate in civil law, also from American University, in
1928. Attending law school didn't detract at all from doing whatever
had to be done in pursuit of equality. Following the congressional hearings in 1925, her immediate goal became the task of gathering information. Paul had to persuade other women's groups, as well as state and
federal legislatures, that protective legislation—though it may have been
a necessary alternative in the past—would actually prevent women from
achieving an equal status in society. Indeed, she believed that protective legislation would ultimately prove to be counterproductive for both
women and men.

The NWP spent the remainder of the 1920s working on two fronts:
it undertook a massive information-gathering program in the states,
and, in concert with its avowed purpose to remove the legal disabilities
against women, it conducted individual state studies that ultimately
produced a series of reports unique in scope and detail. The studies examined the legal position of women in such areas as marriage, divorce,

child custody, employment, education, family planning, and career planning.

Paul perceived the protective legislation issue to be the most pressing. She wanted to meet head-on the fundamental inadequacy of discriminatory legislation regardless of who benefited from its enactment. Toward that end, Paul lobbied vociferously to get NWP representatives on an investigative panel being formed under the direction of Mary Anderson, the head of the Department of Labor's Women's Bureau. The Women's Industrial Conference, at a meeting in January 1926, had requested the panel. Mindful of the debate raging between the equal righters and the protectionists, the conference promoted the Women's Bureau's "comprehensive investigation of all the special laws regulating the employment of women to determine their effects." They hoped that such an investigation would answer, once and for all, the question of whether protective legislation had helped or hindered women workers.[1]

Mary Anderson herself certainly did not advocate equal rights, but in an effort to solicit "well-rounded advice" on the investigation, she appointed three members of the NWP to the Advisory Committee: Alice Paul, Doris Stevens (now Mrs. Dudley Field Malone), and Maud Younger, whose credentials as a labor leader in California were well regarded. The remaining three members included a member of the American Federation of Labor (AFL), a member of the Women's Trade Union League (WTUL), and the legislative counselor of the League of Women Voters. In general, labor unions did not support protective legislation on behalf of special interest groups, including women, immigrants, and ethnic minorities, even though their membership included these groups. The issues that most concerned working women were minimum wages and maximum hours. The unions wanted neither imposed mandated wages nor imposed maximum hours. Mandated wages in particular were most often lower than the wages that unions wanted to negotiate for their members. With a cheaper working force available, employers could choose to hire the less expensive workers. Given that kind of competition, unions found it extremely difficult to compete for the jobs that their mostly male rank-and-file members held.

Ironically, despite the appointment of the three NWP representatives, the conference program committee refused to allow members of the NWP to speak at the meetings. From the start, the meetings were torn by strife and tension. The three protectionists were convinced that Paul, Stevens, and Younger were interested only in promoting the cause of the NWP and unconcerned with conducting an objective inquiry. At issue was the form that the investigation would take. The protectionists favored a technical study conducted by experts and utilizing scientific methods; Paul and her colleagues wanted to hold a series of public meetings in which industrial leaders, women workers, and other interested parties could directly address the pros and cons of protectionism. After four stormy meetings dominated by increasingly bitter acrimony, the three pro-protectionist members resigned in protest, accusing the NWP members of being obstructionist and making serious inquiry impossible. But according to Women's Bureau press releases, the NWP members had cooperated fully and agreed to an investigation carried out by a team of prominent technical investigators. No amount of cooperation seemed likely to result in a congenial working atmosphere since antagonisms had, by this time, become intensely personal. The situation made further committee meetings pointless. As one of the original members exited the meeting room, she took one last shot at Alice Paul: "My experience with the National Woman's Party," she said, "has shown me that it is composed mostly of women who never knew what it meant to work a day in their lives."[2]

Ill-informed as they were, such criticisms only widened the chasm between the NWP and the public. In an effort to put the best face possible on a deteriorating situation, Paul professed to be "delighted" that the protectionists had resigned. "The Women's Bureau will now undoubtedly serve a more useful purpose from the point of view of working women than ever before," she asserted, adding that the "National Woman's Party is the one group in the country which stands for giving working women the same chance in industry as the working men and for basing labor legislation upon the job, and not upon the sex of the worker."[3] Paul's message did not sit well with pro-protectionists.

The Advisory Committee now a complete shambles, Mary Anderson canceled all scheduled meetings with the announcement that they would be fruitless under the circumstances. At the same time, she made clear that the investigative committee would proceed with its inquiry, "according to the usual methods of the Department, and its findings will be available for use by all those, of whatever opinion, who are desirous of securing the facts on the subject." The Women's Bureau industrial technical experts conducted the investigation. In November 1928, the findings were released to the public. The report stated unequivocally that protective legislation had indeed proved beneficial to women workers. Paul disagreed entirely with the conclusions, but she did not believe that the final report bent the data in order to fit a desired set of values. It didn't have to. The investigation was carried out along a fairly narrow line of inquiry. When asked, for example, whether participants believed that protective legislation helped working women, respondents found that the "yes" or "no" responses called for did not leave room for expanding on opinions. The investigators were acting in good faith in conducting an objective inquiry, as they perceived it.

Their report, entitled "Effects of Special Legislation on Women's Work," noted that there were 8.5 million women employed in American industry and, of these, only one-third were covered by special labor laws. "In general," the report further noted, "the regulatory hour laws as applied to women engaged in the manufacturing processes of industry do not handicap the women." The report also pointed out that when the laws were applied to specific occupations, they were, in a "few instances," a handicap to women. Even with that caveat, its overall conclusion was very favorable in its description of protective legislation as a way to smooth the path for women workers. What the report did not discuss were the ways in which protective legislation for women handicapped male workers. That issue was not investigated in the survey. Even so, the report took the wind out of the NWP equal rights sails. The protectionists had clearly won the argument for the time being. And with the onset of the national and then global economic depression that began the following year, Paul could do little except hold the ground already won. Even that, in the darkest days of the depression, proved too difficult a task at times.

Paul and her colleagues began reaching out to women in other organizations. Soliciting converts to equal rights continued at a snail's pace. Even organizations that were founded to eliminate inequalities for professional women did not readily embrace an equal rights amendment (ERA). The American Association of University Women (AAUW), founded by Bryn Mawr's president, M. Carey Thomas, created more equitable conditions for women who wanted to pursue academic careers. But it did not support an equal rights amendment. Decisions to support or reject equal rights often came down to the question of protective legislation and the fear that an equal rights amendment would dismantle all the progress made on behalf of women workers. The AAUW leadership wrote a letter attempting to persuade Congress not to endorse equal rights. It was only when Paul went to Carey Thomas and asked her to intervene that the AAUW leaders withdrew the letter, stating that they were going to study the issue further. The "study" lasted for more than twenty years. More problematic still, not all NWP members favored equal rights. Specifically, some members of the NWP Executive Committee did not believe that equal rights should come before a clearly defined legislative program addressing specific issues affecting women that ranged from legal rights—including property rights and custody of children—to health issues, education, and peace.

Those who opposed equal rights didn't seem to grasp that—with the exception of the peace issue—all of their concerns had to do with legal rights, economic parity, and social justice. Equal rights, in Paul's view, addressed all of these issues in a way that favored women's status. A number of women were convinced that the peace issue ought to be pursued before anything else. Jane Addams, for example, chose to devote all of her efforts to finding peaceful solutions to world conflicts. Addams served as president of the Women's International League for Peace and Freedom and in 1931 won the Nobel Peace Prize.

With no real consensus and lacking the resources to mobilize the new NWP in the same way she had been able to determine strategy in the old NWP, Paul now sought out other venues that would promote equality for women. In the late 1920s, an issue germane to women's equality began picking up traction among international women's organizations. The conventional standard observed by most governments held that a woman from any nation who married a foreign national lost her citizenship rights in her native country. Moreover, any children born to that woman, unless the children were illegitimate, were considered citizens of their father's country. American women who married foreign nationals were stripped of their citizenship and could no longer obtain an American passport. For Paul, this state of affairs was an opportunity to reinforce women's rights internationally. Building relationships with international organizations in order to pursue issues that would result in a step forward in securing equality for women would be worth the investment in time and effort. Paul asked the Executive Committee to endorse an NWP initiative to establish relationships with international organizations, which it readily agreed to do. She also suggested that Doris Stevens would be the ideal person to appoint as their international chairwoman. Once the committee agreed that Stevens should be their point person, Paul asked her to go to Havana, Cuba, to attend the Conference of American Republics as the NWP representative. Stevens readily agreed. She succeeded in getting the conference to accept an Inter-American Commission on Women as a standing committee. The whole point was to set the stage so that the NWP would be in a position to influence proceedings at the upcoming Montevideo Conference of the American Republics.

The Montevideo Conference dealt with the rights and duties of states (by which was meant countries). It was the perfect opportunity to bring up the issue of women's citizenship rights. Stevens, now the chairwoman of the Inter-American Commission on Women, saw to it that the conference did take up the issue. On consideration, it was adopted and ratified by the states represented at the conference. Thereafter, women who had married foreign nationals were no longer denied citizenship in their native countries. They could obtain passports, and their children were recognized as citizens of their mother's native country as well as of their father's. This was a victory for equality for women the world over. For Paul, there was a personal element as well. Her longtime friend and coworker Maud Younger had a sister who'd married a Prussian military officer before World War I. Once the war started, she was declared an enemy alien. After the war, as a widow, she had no source of income, she could not return to the United States with her children, and her only means of survival was the financial support she received from her sister Maud. With the ratification of the Montevideo Conference Treaty in 1934, her rights—and those the rights of thousands of other women whose nationality had been tied to their husbands' native country—were restored.

At about the same time, Paul heard that the World Court at the Hague would take up a Codification of International Laws. She immediately began lobbying to have President Herbert Hoover appoint Emma Wold to the American delegation. Wold was a lawyer working on the states project of gathering data on the status of women. Hoover agreed to appoint Wold, the first American woman to participate on this level at an international conference. Paul now had Emma Wold working on the inside and Doris Stevens, as chairwoman of the Inter-American Commission on Women, working on the outside. Paul also organized a large delegation to see Hoover. The delegates asked Hoover to take the position at the Hague that the United States would support complete equality in every field that might come up in international law within the code. As it turned out, the World Court took up the issue of women's nationality rights first. When it became clear that they were leaning toward accepting the old version of nationality rights, Paul called on Dr. James Brown Scott, the president of the World Organization of International Law, and asked him to intercede with Hoover. Scott discussed with Paul his meeting with Hoover. The president seemed agreeable to Scott's request, but nothing concrete was settled.

Paul urged him to return once more and to strongly suggest that a World Code should not start on a basis of inequality. Hoover subsequently sent word to the members of his delegation stipulating that they not agree to any language that did not support full equality. The US delegation thereafter abstained whenever a vote was taken on code language that did not support equality. Because of the importance of securing the United States' agreement in the decisions regarding a new World Code, the issue was referred to the League of Nations for further consideration. It was a partial victory, but a victory nevertheless.

In the early 1930s, Paul had to deal with another issue—this one involving the NWP itself. Longtime activist and NWP supporter Alva Belmont died in January 1933. Belmont, who lived in Paris at the time of her death, had asked Paul to meet with her before leaving the United

States. What Belmont wanted to talk about was her funeral. She wanted a funeral service that focused on her years as a suffrage activist. She also wanted to be sure that Paul would carry out her wishes, which Paul agreed to. The pallbearers were women with whom she had worked in the suffrage campaign. A contingent of young girls dressed in the suffrage colors of white, purple, and gold lined the steps. It was the kind of event that Paul had become so expert at organizing, filled with iconic imagery. In her will, Belmont left the NWP $100,000 as well as the Sewell-Belmont House on Constitution Avenue, which had become the party headquarters. She also stipulated in her will that the money had to be used solely for NWP work and that the deed to the building would revert to Belmont's estate if the NWP chose to allow male members to join the party. The reason for this stipulation had to do with what happened to the American Red Cross, founded by Clara Barton. When Barton lost control of the organization and installed an all-male board, the Red Cross dropped all references to Barton and her pivotal organizational role. Even her portrait was removed from the premises. Belmont did not want that to happen to the NWP. Paul could not have guessed that the terms of Alva Belmont's will would initiate an internal power struggle within the NWP several years later.

The Montevideo success along with the World Court codification of international law deliberations convinced Paul that she needed to devote more time to international relations, at least until American women became more inclined to revisit equal rights in numbers large enough to sway the politicians at home. For the next few years, she continued to do just that. In 1938, she founded the World Woman's Party (WWP), with headquarters in Geneva, Switzerland. By that time, Adolph Hitler was already asserting his power both inside and outside of Germany. In violation of the Versailles Treaty negotiated after World War I, Germany had begun to rearm in earnest. Hitler annexed Austria, made inroads into Poland and Czechoslovakia, and began his genocidal war against Jews and other groups he considered unfit to be included in the "master race."

The war in Europe started on September 1, 1939. Paul had established the WWP headquarters in the Villa Bartholoni on the shores of Lake Geneva. It quickly became a point of refuge for Jews and their families, including feminists, who had been forced to flee their own countries. With Paul's help, they were able to secure temporary shelter. More importantly, Paul helped them find American sponsors and passports and arranged for their safe passage to the United States.

Among the families Paul helped were the Mullers from Karlsruhe, Germany. Mr. Muller, a professor of Latin, English, and Ancient Greek at the local Gymnasium, helped prepare students for university. In 1938, Professor Muller lost his job because he was Jewish. On November 9, 1938, known as *Kristallnacht*—the night of broken glass—brown-shirted Nazi thugs marauded throughout Germany, smashing windows in homes identified as occupied by Jews and arresting scores of people. Professor Muller was arrested by the German Gestapo and taken to Buchenwald Concentration Camp. A Swiss government official, a close friend of the family, interceded on Muller's behalf. He was released on the condition that he leave Germany before year's end. When the Mullers left Germany on December 31, 1938, they relocated to a Swiss mountain village. Less than a year later, they moved to Geneva, where they sought help from the League of Nations. Mrs. Muller began volunteering at the WWP because of her interest in women's rights. Paul invited the family to reside at Villa Bartholoni. The Mullers eventually were able to immigrate to the United States. Through the auspices of the Jewish Agricultural Society, they were relocated, coincidentally, to New Jersey, Paul's home state.[4] Years later, the Mullers would repay Paul for her support and kindness in an unexpected way.

As the situation in Europe became more and more restrictive, thanks to the Nazis, Paul decided to return to the United States and continue WWP operations from there. In the spring of 1941, only months before the United States entered the war, Paul relocated to Washington, DC, where she continued to maintain her relations with international groups. Off and on over the next three decades, Paul lived at the NWP headquarters in the Sewell-Belmont House. She also had a small cottage in Connecticut that she sometimes shared with Elsie Hill during the time they were both working to get an equal rights clause in the Human Rights covenant of the United Nations charter.

When Paul returned from Europe, she faced an internal NWP struggle that led to an attempted coup. It had to do with Alva Belmont's will, specifically her bequest to the NWP. Sometime during the early 1940s, Doris Stevens decided to bring legal charges against Paul and the NWP, claiming that Alva Belmont had promised to leave her $50,000 in her will. Moreover, Stevens accused Paul of influencing Alva Belmont when the two met to discuss her funeral plans. Stevens believed that Paul had persuaded Belmont to give the $50,000 to the NWP. Stevens continued to insist that she was entitled to the money. The lawsuit touched off one of the NWP's strangest episodes—an instance in which a group of disaffected members, who either were led by Stevens or took advantage of her situation to convince Stevens to participate, attempted to take over the NWP.[5]

Paul knew nothing about Belmont's promise to Stevens. She also thought it quite possible that Belmont did make such a promise because there were occasional instances in the past when Belmont did not follow through on a commitment. But she intended to abide by the terms of the Belmont bequest. Paul liked Stevens and even believed her claim, but she would not give her $50,000. Stevens's resentment festered for a long time before she decided to file the lawsuit against Paul and the NWP. She also fell in with younger NWP members who had not been part of the suffrage struggle, settled, by then, more than two decades earlier, and who had never worked with Alice Paul. These women believed that Paul was nothing more than an autocratic tyrant who had to be removed from the NWP. They established an insurgent group, identified themselves as the real NWP, held meetings, and maintained elaborate minutes, all with the intention of building a body of evidence that would stand up in a court of law. They were even bold enough to hold their meetings in the library of the Sewell-Belmont House. They walked off with all of the membership records, which they used to contact NWP members. And they called for a national convention at the same time that the NWP had scheduled its annual convention. When Paul and the Executive Board discovered the plot, they made every effort to assure members, and everyone else who might be concerned, that the insurgents did not speak for the NWP, nor did they have any authority to do so. After months of wrangling, the insurgents actually attempted to take physical control of the headquarters building. Paul and her colleagues got wind of what was about to happen and hired private detectives to provide protection. Doris Stevens and her chief collaborator showed up with about twenty others and attempted to make good on their plan to take over the headquarters. They almost succeeded. When they identified themselves as NWP members, the hired detectives graciously held the door open for them. The attempted coup took place on the final night of the NWP convention, so there was a fairly large group of members spending the night at the headquarters. A stand-off took place, with NWP loyalists preventing insurgents from making them leave, and insurgents refusing to leave the building. Someone finally called the police, and the insurgents, perhaps realizing they had no ability to oust Paul and her colleagues, abandoned their plan to take over the building.

Not ready to throw in the towel, the insurgents shortly thereafter sent a small delegation to the NWP bank. The emissaries presented documents claiming that their board members had appointed a new treasurer and wanted the bank to draw up the necessary paperwork that would enable only that person to withdraw NWP funds, then amounting to about $250,000. The banker examined the papers and had no reason to doubt their story, but insisted that they had to have the official NWP seal on the documents before their instructions could be followed through. The insurgents left the bank and went directly to the office of the NWP lawyer, where the seal was kept. Paul was called by the lawyer, Burnita Shelton Matthews, an NWP member and long-time friend of Paul. At that point, Paul told her what had transpired. It was clear that the insurgents wanted to gain access to NWP funds. Despite the insurgents' insistence, Matthews refused to give up the seal. Once again, the insurgents were thwarted in their attempt to pull off the coup. The lawsuit filed by Stevens came to trial in November 1947 and was dismissed, ending the insurgents' efforts to take control of the NWP and exonerating Paul of the charge that she had used her influence with Belmont to prevent Stevens from receiving a $50,000 promised inheritance.

The attempted coup, with its combined elements of audacity and desperation, as well as a peppering of Keystone Cop–style humor, certainly ranks as one of the oddest episodes in the history of the NWP. But aside from its comical aspects, it was an indication of how far removed the younger-generation NWP members were regarding Paul's leadership style. If she reflected on this to any great extent, she did not share her reflections in any significant way.

Throughout this period, Paul managed to get congressional supporters for an equal rights amendment into both houses of Congress as well as onto party platforms. But the legal difficulties tied up NWP funds, including the party endowment, until the lawsuit was settled. As a consequence, efforts to make headway in the equal rights struggle were limited. Since the NWP remained the only organization advocating for equality, everything accomplished either domestically or internationally on behalf of American women could be traced back to Paul and the NWP. Almost all women's organizations still opposed equal rights and continued not only their fight to retain the protective legislation laws already passed but also their efforts to expand them.

The anti–equal rights supporters included, notably, Eleanor Roosevelt, a staunch protectionist advocate. During the time her husband, Franklin, was president of the United States, his New Deal administration program supported protective legislation for working women. And because he also supported labor unions, the unions didn't see any reason to change their stance on protective legislation. When World War II ended and talks began regarding establishment of the United Nations, Eleanor Roosevelt, a United States delegate on the Human Rights Commission, was appointed chairwoman of the Commission. She brought to that body's deliberations her firm belief that women still had a need for protective legislation. While they hammered out a Human Rights Covenant to the United Nations charter, Roosevelt consistently opposed sex equality as part of the definition of human rights because such equality would mean an end to protectionism. She was so respected that whenever she made a recommendation, the Commission delegates almost always deferred to her.

Alice Paul believed that the Declaration of Human Rights could be another crucial opportunity to further the cause of equality for women. The fact that Roosevelt opposed including equality in the final product did not deter Paul in the least. As always, she refused to take no for an answer. Taking up residence in New York's University Club for the duration, she and Elsie Hill traveled every single day to Lake Success, New

York, where the Human Rights Commission did its work. They took seats behind the delegates and talked to everyone they could, sometimes on a daily basis if it seemed the delegate favored their position. Their first goal was to work on getting delegates to vote to establish a full committee on the status of women. Paul and Hill were able to persuade a delegate from Chile to propose that equality for women be included in the language of the Commission's covenant. "Mrs. Roosevelt *staunchly* and very vigorously opposed it."[6] Press coverage focused on the question of why Eleanor Roosevelt would not favor equality for women. It turned out to be the first crack in Roosevelt's resolve to keep equality for women at bay. A few days later, she addressed the delegates: "I want to make clear I am being criticized for opposing an equal rights for women section being added to this proposal by Figaroa [the delegate], from Chile. I want to state that, in all events, I have withdrawn my opposition to the equal rights for women amendment."

Getting approval for the full committee was the next step—which Roosevelt also opposed. She was willing to compromise and thus agreed to establish a Subcommittee on the Status of Women. The Subcommittee reported to the chair of the Human Rights Commission—that is, Eleanor Roosevelt. She had the final say in what was reported to the General Assembly for consideration. In order to circumvent this obstacle, the Subcommittee had to be raised to the status of a full committee. Paul and Hill had the ear of a delegate from India, Sir Ramaswami Mudaliar. "I remember so well. . . . Medaliar presided and day after day we would go down and stay till late at night. . . . And never would our subject come up. . . . One day Mrs. Roosevelt announced that she could no longer attend any meetings. . . . So the next meeting . . . Meduliar brought up the question of making the subcommittee into a full committee and giving it all the rights under the Status of Women Commission that the Human Rights Commission had. He had . . . purposefully . . . waited until Mrs. Roosevelt was no longer there to make any opposition."[7] The long months of sitting in on every Human Rights Commission meeting were successful in all respects. When the issue of full committee status arose at any of these meetings, a delegate from the United States said, "My instructions say that whenever it comes up, the United States delegation *strongly* supports the raising of the Status of Women Subcommittee to a full commission." In 1951, the delegates voted favorably to establish a Status of Women Commission. In the end, equality of women was addressed directly in the Preamble and, indirectly, through the language of the Articles, in each and every Article of the Human Rights Declaration. Paul and Hill were the only people representing a woman's organization to show up every day, lobby the delegates, and advocate inclusion of equality for women in the United Nations Charter.

For the remainder of the 1950s, Paul seemed finally to slow down. She was in her sixties by then, a time when most of her peers had either died, were contemplating retirement, or had already retired. Retirement was not in Paul's lexicon, however. She continued to lobby politicians to make sure that the ERA would be introduced into each new session of Congress. Even with the United Nations Charter success, there had been no obvious shift in women's attitude toward equal rights. Working from her Connecticut cottage, Paul continued to communicate with women's organizations, hoping to change their minds regarding equal rights. The veneer of calm that seemed to define the 1950s could barely contain the vast discontent that pervaded political, social, and cultural issues by decade's end.

The 1960s in the United States proved to be tumultuous, electrifying, unpredictable, frightening, and exhilarating. This was the decade that witnessed a civil rights revolution, the hippie culture, and massive antiwar demonstrations as more and more Americans became dissatisfied with the nation's involvement in Viet Nam and challenged those who believed America had to stop Communism at all costs. It was also the era of the Black Panthers movement, Model Cities, the War on Poverty, Woodstock, and the emergence of the modern women's movement. Lines were constantly being drawn and redrawn: young versus old, black versus white, peace versus war, antiwar protesters versus silent majority, hard hats versus college kids, civilians versus the military, poor versus rich, male versus female, and advocates of change versus the status quo. One president was assassinated; another was forced to announce that he would not seek a second term; a civil rights icon was struck down, as was an advocate for social change—all either revered or despised by large segments of the population. Few people who lived through the decade were unaffected by it.

In 1960, Alice Paul was seventy-five years old. As she had done throughout the decade of the 1950s, she continued to work tirelessly wherever she saw an opportunity to promote equality for women, though by now she had slowed down physically. She still possessed the razor-sharp intellect that had enabled her to map out the successful suffrage strategy—and that she had brought to bear on all of her efforts since. When the Kennedy administration proposed a Civil Rights Act in 1962, she immediately set to work to ensure that the language of the Act would not exclude women, as it did in its first incarnation. In the wake of Kennedy's assassination in 1963, President Lyndon Johnson picked up the Civil Rights initiative. More than Kennedy, Johnson had the ability to push through a bold civil rights act. He was a southerner, in his mannerisms he was a "good old boy," and he knew how to convince recalcitrant members of Congress to do his bidding. But without the unstoppable Alice Paul and the NWP, it is likely that prohibitions against discrimination based on sex would not have made it into the final version of the Civil Rights Act of 1964.

Initially, the biggest challenge was to overcome civil rights activists' opposition to including sex discrimination in the bill. The argument against consideration of sex discrimination had changed little since the Civil War, when the issue had to do with African-Americans and women's rights: "It is the Negro's hour." But once again, Paul refused to take "no" for an answer. Her hand was still on the plow and would remain there steadily until women had full equality. As her mother had advised her decades earlier, she was obliged to stay the course until she reached "the end of the row." It was a long row but she was not about to abandon it.

NWP members worked feverishly through all their usual channels and connections to find someone in Congress who would take the lead in introducing an amendment to include discrimination based on sex as part of the bill. Paul really wanted sex to be included as a criterion in all of the Titles included in the comprehensive civil rights bill, but she determined that the best place to start would be with Title VII, which had to do with employment. She had already instructed NWP members working with her to call every woman's organization they could think of to try and get more support. Without exception, they were turned down by everyone. At almost the last moment, Paul approached longtime friend and supporter Howard Smith of Virginia and asked him to introduce an amendment to Title VII. Smith agreed to do so. When Smith proposed the amendment, another huge debate was initiated, but in the end his amendment carried. Title VII provided that

> [t]he terms "because of sex" or "on the basis of sex" include, but are not limited to, because of or on the basis of pregnancy, childbirth, or related medical conditions; and women affected by pregnancy, childbirth, or related medical conditions shall be treated the same for all employment-related purposes, including receipt of benefits under fringe benefit programs, as other persons not so affected but similar in their ability or inability to work, and nothing in section 2000e-2(h) of this title [section 703(h)] shall be interpreted to permit otherwise. This subsection shall not require an employer to pay for health insurance benefits for abortion, except where the life of the mother would be endangered if the fetus were carried to term, or except where medical complications have arisen from an abortion: Provided, that nothing herein shall preclude an employer from providing abortion benefits or otherwise affect bargaining agreements in regard to abortion.[8]

Although Title VII remained the only part of the bill to include discrimination based on sex, it nevertheless represented a huge victory because the Civil Rights Act of 1964 was a landmark piece of legislation. Smith's amendment to include "sex" in Title VII was viewed by some as a cynical attempt to defeat the bill because he opposed the Civil Rights Act. But that argument is questionable in light of Smith's twenty-year history of sponsoring an equal rights amendment. In any case, without Paul and the NWP, women would have been left out of the Act entirely, which would have been a big step backward in the effort to secure equality.

By the end of the 1960s, the political winds had changed markedly for women. For one thing, women's organizations had begun to reconsider

the issue of equality for women. Despite the unwillingness of these organizations to support Paul and the NWP during the Civil Rights controversy, protective legislation did little to ameliorate the difficulties that
women faced in their daily lives. The 1963 publication of Betty Freidan's book *The Feminine Mystique* had sparked a growing conversation
among women. Freidan spoke to the discontent that many women felt
regarding what they perceived as a confining role as wives and mothers.
What women wanted, she argued, did not lie in rejecting the traditional
role society chose for them. If women wanted to focus on home and
children, that would always be a valid option. But women also wanted
to be able to expand into areas that would satisfy their desire to participate outside of the home. Freidan's observations echoed Crystal Eastman's discussion, nearly fifty years earlier, of what women wanted. In
1966, Freidan, along with twenty-eight other women and men—including Shirley Chisholm and Pauli Murray, the first African-American
Episcopal priest—founded the National Organization for Women
(NOW). NOW fully supported an equal rights amendment, and by
1970 traditional opponents of an ERA, including labor unions, had
changed their view and supported it as well. The last major women's
organization to support the ERA, the American Association of University Women, which had opted to perform a "study" of the issue decades
earlier, finally consented in 1972.

When NOW was founded, Alice Paul and a great many NWP
members joined the organization immediately, mainly because of
NOW's support of an equal rights amendment. Paul and Freidan met
and discussed the amendment that Paul had written back in 1923, the
Lucretia Mott Amendment. Subsequently, the Women's Bureau succeeded in getting a rider attached to it, the Hayden Rider, which would
have prohibited repeal of any protective legislation measures and ultimately weakened the ERA. Paul spent the next few months working on
behalf of removing the Hayden Rider. Freidan seemed to be indifferent to the rider, making Paul's task that much harder. In the end, Paul
prevailed by convincing representatives from the Women's Bureau that
trying to get the ERA passed at this point with the Hayden Rider attached would be like starting all over again. The Hayden Rider was

dropped, and the only other change made was to rename the equal rights amendment the Alice Paul Amendment.

By the time of the NOW convention, during which the "new" amendment was voted on, Paul had the support of another committee member. When the committee reported that it had decided to retain the Alice Paul Amendment as currently written, without the Hayden Rider, a huge debate ensued. People began bringing up all kinds of issues, including abortion, which, as far as Paul could see, had nothing to do with the ERA as a piece of legislation. As Paul had noted long ago during the suffrage campaign, "I think if we get freedom for women, then they are going to do a lot of things that I wish they wouldn't do; but it seems to me that it isn't our business to say what they should do with it. It is our business to see that they get it." In the end, when a vote was taken by the convention, the ones who carried the day were the NWP members who had joined the NOW. They never imagined when they joined that it would be their votes that counted.

It took another two years for the equal rights amendment to pass both Houses of Congress. During that time, Paul once again employed some of the old suffrage tactics, particularly button-holing politicians to secure their support. When the ERA did pass in 1972, however, it included a seven-year time limit for ratification. This was bad news as far as Paul was concerned. Similar efforts to place a time constraint on the suffrage amendment had been roundly rejected because congressmen recognized the time limit as a delaying tactic that could mean defeat of the amendment if the anti-suffragists succeeded in persuading enough states not to ratify. There weren't enough votes to remove the time constraint from the ERA. But Paul remained determined that, with unrelenting pressure, women could ensure that the necessary number of states would ratify the amendment before the time limit elapsed.

Women were confident that the legislation sent out by the 92nd Congress to the states would be ratified very quickly. By the end of 1973, thirty states had ratified the amendment. But while initial ratification seemed to proceed very rapidly, the ERA advocates underestimated the strength of the chief anti-ERA spokesperson, Phyllis Schlafly. Schlafly—a lawyer, conservative, political activist, author, public speaker, wife, mother, and founder of the Eagle Forum—opposed the ERA. She claimed that it would deny Social Security benefits to widows, make women eligible for the military draft, and force them to use unisex bathrooms. The arguments Schlafly repeated over and over again were meant to frighten women who did not want their traditional societal roles to change. She argued that she was protecting housewives and mothers from the feminists, who, she claimed, disparaged them. Most women, she said, believed that their roles as housewives and mothers was the natural order—the way society should be organized.

Schlafly's arguments were specious and misleading, if not outright lies, but she could be a very persuasive speaker. She ignored the critics who exposed the apparent hypocrisy of her position. Some of the critics pointed out that Schlafly was able to have it all: family and career. And she did so, they said, by fighting those who said they were trying to get it for her. Although Schlafly claimed that she always deferred to her husband, giving up speaking opportunities when he said she had been away from home too long, a review of her speaking engagements in the years following passage of the ERA reveals that she apparently did not pass up many invitations. She became the face and the voice of the opponents of an ERA amendment. With the time limit approaching, Congress passed a one-time extension for an additional thirty-nine months. The legislation was then three states short of ratification. But the moment seemed to have passed for women and an ERA. With Schlafly and her Eagle Forum continuing to play on the fears of women who were not at all sure how the ERA would be a benefit and with state legislators in the remaining states falling back on politics instead of the merits of the amendment, the time expired and the ERA failed to become a constitutional amendment.

During the ratification extension period, Alice Paul, then approaching ninety years of age, had been living in her Connecticut cottage for some time. She depended on her neighbors to look out for her. But as her health deteriorated, she began to need full-time care. She had few resources to draw upon, and most of her family had already passed on. Due to her reduced circumstances, Paul was confined to a nursing home in Ridgefield, Connecticut. By chance, the family she had helped to immigrate to America when she was in Switzerland—the Mullers—read an article about her in a local newspaper. Mrs. Muller quickly insisted that her lawyer son call on a Quaker judge whom they knew, to see what could be done for Paul. The Mullers succeeded in getting Paul transferred to a more congenial facility in Moorestown, an institution that Paul's family had endowed years earlier. The Mullers visited Paul in Moorestown. Mrs. Muller was grateful that she could provide some little assistance to her friend and former mentor.

In 1974 Alice Paul suffered a stroke that left her incapacitated, and on July 9, 1977, at the age of ninety-two, she died. To the very end, she expressed complete confidence that the ERA would be ratified.

10

Epilogue

Alice Paul remained convinced, up to the very end, that the equal rights amendment would be ratified before the time extension expired. Sadly, that was not to be the case. Had she been younger and in possession of the woman-power and organizational resources that were hers during the suffrage movement, the ERA might be a constitutional amendment today. But there was no one else with her singular drive, focus, and ability to take on that task. Ratification failed three states short of the required number.

While her quest for equality failed for the moment, Paul's legacy remains an essential part of American history. Historian William O'Neill rightly characterized Paul as "the one truly charismatic figure" in the suffrage movement. Not just those who agreed with her, but many who professed to be put off by her, were persuaded to follow her, even to prison, because of her dedication and passion for equality. She showed women, by her own example, that they could take control of their destinies—that they did not have to stand and wait, hoping to be rewarded in the end.

Her strategy for achieving suffrage with the Nineteenth Amendment shaved years off of that struggle. She wasn't afraid of being called a militant or a feminist, and she never doubted the direction she had chosen to follow in her life: "I have never doubted that equal rights was the right direction."[1] She was also modest to a fault about her contribution to equality: "I always feel the movement is a sort of mosaic. Each of us puts in one little stone and then you get a great mosaic at the end."[2] But she accomplished much, much more than placing one little stone. Paul lobbied for her beliefs with integrity, honesty, and courage. Unlike modern-day lobbyists who believe that exchanging money for votes does no harm to a democracy, Paul believed that democracy was the ultimate prize and that democracy mandated equality. For her, the real danger to a democratic society was willingness to sacrifice principle in favor of expediency.

Thanks to Paul's commitment to suffrage, women earned the vote years earlier than they otherwise might have. She was able to force Woodrow Wilson to support a suffrage amendment as a necessity in winning World War I, though he had previously and adamantly vowed not to deal with suffrage because he didn't consider it a war measure. And thanks to Paul's unflagging efforts to secure equality, women were represented in many international and national treaties and laws that they might otherwise have been left out of, including the Declaration of Human Rights in the United Nations Charter and the Civil Rights Act of 1964. It was Paul who orchestrated a successful campaign so that women doctors who wanted to do their part in World War II were able to serve in military hospitals. And it was Paul who used her contacts to promote women as United States delegates in international conferences, where they had never been able to serve before. Paul also helped to support the appointment of women as federal judges. Her relentless pursuit of equality eventually succeeded in persuading millions of American women to change their minds and finally recognize equal rights as a priority. Because of the groundwork that she laid, decade after decade, the modern women's movement, represented by NOW, was able to move an equal rights amendment through Congress in an astoundingly short period of time.

Crystal Eastman once observed that history was rife with men and women whose every waking moment was devoted to an impersonal cause. But Eastman found in Paul a rare combination of qualities. In Eastman's view, Paul had a passion for service and sacrifice along with the shrewd calculating mind of a born politician. She also possessed the ruthless driving force, sure judgment, and phenomenal grasp of detail that characterized great entrepreneurial success. *Ruthless* is not a word that described Alice Paul. But she was that leader, that passionate human being, that unflagging champion who dedicated her life to the cause of equality for women. During the suffrage campaign, Paul gave up any semblance of a private life. For her, private life and public life were one. She was not a self-aggrandizer. She asked everything for her cause and nothing for herself. Time and again, from her earliest suffrage days to her later equal rights activity, Paul would look directly at someone and, in her quiet manner, ask that person to take up some task or other in order to further the cause. More often than not, whether that person agreed or disagreed with Paul, the task was completed in exactly the manner requested. It was never about Paul herself but always about the cause. That is probably why, when Paul suffered a stroke and had to be hospitalized and then sent to a nursing home, there were no women's groups sufficiently aware of her financial situation to ensure that her last days were comfortable and spent in dignity. Were it not for the Mullers, who did come to her assistance, Paul might have died well before her life could be celebrated by those who owed her so much.

Many women today believe that a constitutional amendment for equal rights is no longer a necessity and that feminism is anachronistic. Alice Paul challenged such beliefs all her life. "Most reforms, most problems are complicated," she said. "But to me there is nothing complicated about ordinary equality."[3] She was well aware that, without the protection of a constitutional amendment, laws designed to protect women's equality and rights not only could be but *would* be changed at the whims of Congress, state legislatures, and presidents. When a nation rejects the rightness of "ordinary equality," it is incumbent upon all of us to question why. That is Alice Paul's legacy.

PRIMARY SOURCES

THE NINETEENTH AMENDMENT TO THE UNITED STATES CONSTITUTION

The right of citizens of the United States to vote shall not be denied or abridged by the United States or by any State on account of sex.

Congress shall have power to enforce this article by appropriate legislation.

THE PROPOSED EQUAL RIGHTS AMENDMENT, OR "ALICE PAUL AMENDMENT"

Section 1. Equality of rights under the law shall not be denied or abridged by the United States or by any State on account of sex.

Section 2. The Congress shall have the power to enforce, by appropriate legislation, the provisions of this article.

Section 3. This amendment shall take effect two years after the date of ratification.

LETTER TO CHAIRMAN OF THE HOUSE JUDICIARY COMMITTEE

May 1, 1917
Hon. Edwin Y. Webb
Chairman Judiciary Comm.
U.S. House of Representatives

Dear Sir,

It seems to me right to ask you to help the cause of Woman Suffrage just now at this Session of Congress by an irresistible and favorable report on the Federal Suffrage Amendment Bill. My father trained me in my childhood days to expect this right. I have given my help to this—and worked for its coming a great many years. It seemed as if the hour would come for this great act of justice and that this Congress doing most needed things for the whole world ought not to overlook the appeal of the women of our land.

YOURS MOST SINCERELY,

MARY O. STEVENS

ASSOCIATION OF THE ARMY NURSES OF THE CIVIL WAR

STATEMENT OF MARY NOLAN, DICTATED ON HER RELEASE
FROM PRISON, IN PRESENCE OF DUDLEY FIELD MALONE.
EXCERPTED FROM DORIS STEVENS, *JAILED FOR FREEDOM,*
PP. 196-199.

The Night of Terror

Suddenly the door literally burst open and Whittaker [Superintendent of the District of Columbia Jail] burst in like a tornado, some men followed him. We could see a crowd of them on the porch. They were not in uniform. They looked as much like tramps as anything. They seemed to come in—and in—and in. . . . Mrs. Lewis [Dora Lewis, Philadelphia] stood up. Some of us had been sitting and lying on the floor, we were so tired. She had hardly begun to speak, saying we demanded to be treated as political prisoners, when Whittaker said:

"You shut up. I have men here to handle you." Then he shouted "Seize her!" I turned and saw men spring toward her, and then one screamed "They have taken Mrs. Lewis."

A man sprang at me and caught me by the shoulder. I am used to remembering a bad foot, which I have had for years, and I remember saying, "I'll come with you, don't drag me. I have a lame foot." But I was jerked down the steps and away into the dark. I didn't have my feet on the ground. I guess that saved me. I heard Mrs. Cosu [Alice Cosu], who was being dragged along with me, call "Be careful of your foot."

We were rushed into a large room. . . . Punishment cells is what they call them. Mine was filthy. It had no window save a slip at the top and no furniture but an iron bed covered with a thin straw pad, and an open toilet flushed from outside the cell. . . .

In the hall outside was a man called Captain Reems. He had on a uniform and was brandishing a thick stick and shouting as we were shoved into the corridor, "Damn you, get in here."

I saw Dorothy Day [later of the Catholic Workers] brought in. She is a frail girl. The two men handling her were twisting her arms above her head. Then suddenly they lifted her up and banged her down over the arms of an iron bench—twice. As they ran past me, she was lying there with her arms out, and we heard one of the men yell, "The suffrager! My mother ain't no suffrager! I'll put you through."

At the end of the corridor they pushed me through a door. Then I lost my balance and fell against the iron bed. Mrs. Cosu struck the wall. Then they threw in two mats and two dirty blankets. There was no light but from the corridor. The door was barred from top to bottom. The walls and floors were brick or stone cemented over. Mrs. Cosu would not let me lie on the floor. She put me on the couch [i.e., the iron bed] and stretched out on the floor on one of the two pads they threw in. We had only lain there a few minutes, trying to get our breaths, when Mrs. Lewis, doubled over and handled like a sack of something, was literally thrown in. Her head struck the iron bed. We thought she was dead. She didn't move. We were crying over her as we lifted her to the pad on my bed, when we heard Miss Burns [Lucy Burns] call:

"Where is Mrs. Nolan?"

I replied, "I am here."

Mrs. Cosu called out, "They have just thrown Mrs. Lewis in here too."

At this, Mr. Whittaker came to the door and told us not to dare to speak, or he would put the brace and bit in our mouths and the straitjacket on our bodies. We were so terrified. We kept very still. Mrs. Lewis was not unconscious, she was only stunned. But Mrs. Cosu was desperately ill as the night wore on. She had a bad heart attack and was then vomiting. We called and called. We asked them to send our own doctor, because we thought she was dying. . . . They (the guards) paid no attention. A cold wind blew on us from the outside and we three lay there shivering and only half conscious until morning.

"One at a time, come out," we heard someone call at the barred door early in the morning. I went first. I bade them both goodbye. I didn't know where I was going or whether I would ever see them again. They took me to Mr. Whittaker's office, where he called my name.

"You're Mary Nolan," said Whittaker.

"You're posted," said I.

"Are you willing to put on a prison dress and go to the workroom," said he.

I said "No."

"Don't you know now that I am Mr. Whittaker, the superintendent?" he asked.

"Is there any age limit to your workhouse?" I said. "Would a woman of seventy-three or a child of two be sent here?"

I think I made him think. He motioned to the guard.

"Get a doctor to examine her," he said.

I took off my coat and hat. I just lay down on the bed and fell into a kind of stupor. It was nearly noon and I had had no food offered me since the sandwiches our friends brought us in the courtroom at noon the day before.

The doctor came and examined my heart. The he examined my foot. It had a long blue bruise above the ankle, where they had knocked me as they took me across the night before. He asked me what caused the bruise. I said, "Those fiends, when they dragged me to the cell last night." It was paining me. He asked if I wanted liniment and I said only hot water. They brought me that and I noticed they did not lock the door. A negro trusty was there. I fell back again into the same stupor.

The next day they brought me some toast and a plate of food, the first I had been offered in over 36 hours. I just looked at the food and motioned it away. It made me sick. . . . I was released on the sixth day and passed the dispensary as I came out. There were a group of my friends, Mrs. Brannon [Lucy Brannan] and Mrs. Morey and many others. They had on coarse striped dresses and big, grotesque heavy shoes. I burst into tears as they led me away.

SIGNED: MARY I. NOLAN

NOVEMBER 21, 1917

THE PHYLLIS SCHLAFLY REPORT

The Debates About ERA

The Equal Rights Amendment was presented to the American public as something that would benefit women, "put women in the U.S. Constitution," and lift women out of their so-called "second-class citizenship." However, in thousands of debates, the ERA advocates were unable to show any way that ERA would benefit women or end any discrimination against them. The fact is that women already enjoy every constitutional right that men enjoy and have enjoyed equal employment opportunity since 1964.

In the short term, clever advertising and packaging can sell a worthless product; but, in the long term, the American people cannot be fooled. ERA's biggest defect was that it had nothing to offer American women.

The opponents of ERA, on the other hand, were able to show many harms that ERA would cause.

1. ERA would take away legal rights that women possessed—*not* confer any new rights on women.

    A. ERA would take away women's traditional exemption from military conscription and also from military combat duty. The classic "sex discriminatory" laws are those which say that "male citizens of age 18" must register for the draft and those which exempt women from military combat assignment. The ERAers tried to get around this argument by asking the Supreme Court to hold that the 14th Amendment already requires women to be drafted, but they lost in 1981 in *Rostker v. Goldberg* when the Supreme Court upheld the traditional exemption of women from the draft under our present Constitution.

    B. ERA would take away the traditional benefits in the law for wives, widows and mothers. ERA would make unconstitutional the laws, which then existed in every state, that impose on a husband the obligation to support his wife.

2. ERA would take away important rights and powers of the states and confer these on other branches of government which are farther removed from the people.

    A. ERA would give enormous power to the Federal courts to decide the definitions of the words in ERA, "sex" and "equality of rights." It is irresponsible to leave it to the courts to decide such sensitive, emotional and important issues as whether or not the language applies to abortion or homosexual rights.

3. Section II of ERA would give enormous new powers to the Federal Government that now belong to the states. ERA would give Congress the power to legislate on all those areas of law which include traditional differences of treatment on account of sex: marriage, property laws, divorce and alimony, child custody, adoptions, abortion, homosexual laws, sex crimes, private and public schools, prison regulations, and insurance. ERA would thus result in the massive redistribution of powers in our Federal system.

4. ERA's impact on education would take away rights from women students, upset many customs and practices, and bring government intrusion into private schools.

    A. ERA would force all schools and colleges, and all the programs and athletics they conduct, to be fully coeducational and sex-integrated. ERA would make unconstitutional all the current exceptions in Title IX which allow for single-sex schools and colleges and for separate treatment of the sexes for certain activities. ERA would mean the end of single-sex colleges. ERA would force the sex integration of fraternities, sororities, Boy Scouts, Girl Scouts, YMCA, YWCA, Boys State and Girls State conducted by the American Legion, and mother-daughter and father-son school events.

    B. ERA would risk the income tax exemption of all private schools and colleges that make any difference of treatment between males and females, even though no public monies are involved. ERA is a statement of public policy that would apply the same rules to sex that we now observe on race, and it is clear that no school that makes any racial distinctions may enjoy tax exemption.

5. ERA would put abortion rights into the U.S. Constitution, and make abortion funding a new constitutional right. *Roe v. Wade* in 1973 legalized abortion, but the fight to make abortion funding a constitutional right was lost in *Harris v. McRae* in 1980. The abortionists then looked to ERA to force taxpayer funding. The American Civil Liberties Union filed briefs in abortion cases in Hawaii, Massachusetts, Pennsylvania and Connecticut arguing that, since abortion is a medical procedure

performed only on women, it is "sex discrimination" within the meaning of the state's ERA to deny tax funding for abortions. In the most recent decision, the Connecticut Superior Court ruled on April 19, 1986 that the state ERA requires abortion funding. Those who oppose tax funding of abortions demand that ERA be amended to prevent this effect, but ERA advocates want ERA *only* so long as it includes abortion funding.

6. ERA would put "gay rights" into the U.S. Constitution, because the word in the Amendment is "sex" not women. Eminent authorities have stated that ERA would legalize the granting of marriage licenses to homosexuals and generally implement the "gay rights" and lesbian agenda. These authorities include the *Yale Law Journal*, the leading textbook on sex discrimination used in U.S. law schools, Harvard Law Professor Paul Freund, and Senator Sam J. Ervin, Jr. Other lawyers have disputed this effect, but no one can guarantee that the courts would not define the word "sex" to include "orientation" just as they have defined "sex" to include pregnancy.

7. In the final years of the ERA battle, two new arguments appeared. Both were advanced by the ERA advocates, but they quickly became arguments in the hands of the ERA opponents.

   A. ERA would require "unisex insurance," that is, would prohibit insurance companies from charging lower rates for women, even though actuarial data clearly show that women, as a group, are entitled to lower rates both for automobile accident insurance and life insurance. This is because women drivers have fewer accidents and women live longer than men. Most people found it a peculiar argument that "women's rights" should include the "right" to pay higher insurance rates.

   B. ERA would eliminate veterans' preference. This rests on the same type of legal argument as the abortion funding argument: since most veterans are men, it is claimed that it is "sex discriminatory" to give them benefits. Naturally, this argument was not acceptable to the veterans, and their national organizations lobbied hard against ERA.

THE PHYLLIS SCHLAFLY REPORT

NOVEMBER 1981

THE CASE FOR AN EQUAL RIGHTS AMENDMENT

Shirley Chisholm, "I Am for the Equal Rights Amendment."

In 1968, Shirley Anita St. Hill Chisholm became the first African-American woman elected to Congress. Four years later, in 1972, she launched a bid to become the Democratic nominee for president of the United States—another first for an African-American woman. Throughout her career in Congress, Chisholm was a staunch advocate of women's rights and civil rights. On August 10, 1970, she delivered a speech on the floor of the US House of Representatives urging support for the equal rights amendment. That speech appears below.

Mr. Speaker, House Joint Resolution 264, before us today, which provides for equality under the law for both men and women, represents one of the most clear-cut opportunities we are likely to have to declare our faith in the principles that shaped our Constitution. It provides a legal basis for attack on the most subtle, most pervasive, and most institutionalized form of prejudice that exists. Discrimination against women, solely on the basis of their sex, is so widespread that is seems to many persons normal, natural and right.

Legal expression of prejudice on the grounds of religious or political belief has become a minor problem in our society. Prejudice on the basis of race is, at least, under systematic attack. There is reason for optimism that it will start to die with the present, older generation. It is time we act to assure full equality of opportunity to those citizens who, although in a majority, suffer the restrictions that are commonly imposed on minorities, to women.

The argument that this amendment will not solve the problem of sex discrimination is not relevant. If the argument were used against a civil rights bill, as it has been used in the past, the prejudice that lies behind it would be embarrassing. Of course laws will not eliminate prejudice from the hearts of human beings. But that is no reason to allow prejudice to continue to be enshrined in our laws—to perpetuate injustice through inaction.

The amendment is necessary to clarify countless ambiguities and inconsistencies in our legal system. For instance, the Constitution guarantees due process of law, in the 5th and 14th amendments. But the applicability of due process of sex distinctions is not clear. Women are excluded from some State colleges and universities. In some States, restrictions are placed on a married woman who engages in an independent business. Women may not be chosen for some juries. Women even receive heavier criminal penalties than men who commit the same crime. What would the legal effects of the equal rights amendment really be? The equal rights amendment would govern only the relationship between the State and its citizens—not relationships between private citizens. The amendment would be largely self-executing, that is, and Federal or State laws in conflict would be ineffective one year after date of ratification without further action by the Congress or State legislatures.

Opponents of the amendment claim its ratification would throw the law into a state of confusion and would result in much litigation to establish its meaning. This objection overlooks the influence of legislative history in determining intent and the recent activities of many groups preparing for legislative changes in this direction.

State labor laws applying only to women, such as those limiting hours of work and weights to be lifted would become inoperative unless the legislature amended them to apply to men. As of early 1970 most States would have some laws that would be affected. However, changes are being made so rapidly as a result of title VII of the Civil Rights Act of 1964, it is likely that by the time the equal rights amendment would become effective, no conflict in State laws would remain.

In any event, there has for years been great controversy as to the usefulness to women of these State labor laws. There has never been any doubt that they worked a hardship on women who need or want to work overtime and on women who need or want better-paying jobs, and there has been no persuasive evidence as to how many women benefit from the archaic policy of the laws. After the Delaware hours law was repealed in 1966, there were no complaints from women to any of the State agencies that might have been approached.

Jury service laws not making women equally liable for jury service would have been revised. The selective service law would have to include women, but women would not be required to serve in the Armed Forces where they are not fitted any more than men are required to serve. Military service, while a great responsibility, is not without benefits, particularly for young men with limited education or training.

Since October 1966, 246,000 young men who did not meet the normal mental or physical requirements have been given opportunities for training and correcting physical problems. This opportunity is not open to their sisters. Only girls who have completed high school and meet high standards on the educational test can volunteer. Ratification of the amendment would not permit application of higher standards to women.

Survivorship benefits would be available to husbands of female workers on the same basis as to wives of male workers. The Social Security Act and the civil service and military service retirement acts are in conflict. Public schools and universities could not be limited to one sex and could not apply different admission standards to men and women. Laws requiring longer prison sentences for women than men would be invalid, and equal opportunities for rehabilitation and vocational training would have to be provided in public correctional institutions. Different ages of majority based on sex would have to be harmonized. Federal, State, and other governmental bodies would be obligated to follow nondiscriminatory practices in all aspects of employment, including public school teachers and State university and college faculties.

What would be the economic effects of the equal rights amendment? Direct economic effects would be minor. If any labor laws applying only to women still remained, their amendment or repeal would provide opportunity for women in better-paying jobs in manufacturing. More opportunities in public vocational and graduate schools for women would also tend to open up opportunities in better jobs for women.

Indirect effects could be much greater. The focusing of public attention on the gross legal, economic, and social discrimination against women by hearings and debates in the Federal and State legislatures would result in changes in attitude of parents, educators, and employers that would bring about substantial economic changes in the long run.

Sex prejudice cuts both ways. Men are oppressed by the requirements of the Selective Service Act, by enforced legal guardianship of minors, and by alimony laws. Each sex, I believe, should be liable when necessary to serve and defend this country. Each has a responsibility for the support of children.

There are objections raised to wiping out laws protecting women workers. No one would condone exploitation. But what does sex have to do with it? Working conditions and hours that are harmful to women are harmful to men; wages that are unfair for women are unfair for men. Laws setting employment limitations on the basis of sex are irrational, and the proof of this is their inconsistency from State to State. The physical characteristics of men and women are not fixed, but cover two wide spans that have a great deal of overlap. It is obvious, I think, that a robust woman could be more fit for physical labor than a weak man. The choice of occupation would be determined by individual capabilities, and the rewards for equal works should be equal.

This is what it comes down to: artificial distinctions between persons must be wiped out of the law. Legal discrimination between the sexes is, in almost every instance, founded on outmoded views of society and the pre-scientific beliefs about psychology and physiology. It is time to sweep away these relics of the past and set further generations free of them.

Federal agencies and institutions responsible for the enforcement of equal opportunity laws need the authority of a Constitutional amendment. The 1964 Civil Rights Act and the 1963 Equal Pay Act are not enough; they are limited in their coverage—for instance, one excludes teachers, and the other leaves out administrative and professional women. The Equal Employment Opportunity Commission has not proven to be an adequate device, with its power limited to investigation, conciliation, and recommendation to the Justice Department. In its cases involving sexual discrimination, it has failed in more than one-half. The Justice Department has been even less effective. It has intervened in only one case involving discrimination on the basis of sex, and this was on a procedural point. In a second case, in which both sexual and racial discrimination were alleged, the racial bias charge was given far greater weight.

Evidence of discrimination on the basis of sex should hardly have to be cited here. It is in the Labor Department's employment and salary figures for anyone who is still in doubt. Its elimination will involve so many changes in our State and Federal laws that, without the authority and impetus of this proposed amendment, it will perhaps take another 194 years. We cannot be parties to continuing a delay. The time is clearly now to put this House on record for the fullest expression of that equality of opportunity which our founding fathers professed. They professed it, but they did not assure it to their daughters, as they tried to do for their sons.

The Constitution they wrote was designed to protect the rights of white, male citizens. As there were no black Founding Fathers, there were no founding mothers—a great pity, on both counts. It is not too late to complete the work they left undone. Today, here, we should start to do so.

In closing I would like to make one point. Social and psychological effects will be initially more important than legal or economic results. As Leo Kanowitz has pointed out:

"Rules of law that treat of the sexes per se inevitably produce far-reaching effects upon social, psychological and economic aspects of male-female relations beyond the limited confines of legislative chambers and courtrooms. As long as organized legal systems, at once the most respected and most feared of social institutions, continue to differentiate sharply, in treatment or in words, between men and women on the basis of irrelevant and artificially created distinctions, the likelihood of men and women coming to regard one another primarily as fellow human beings and only secondarily as representatives of another sex will continue to be remote. When men and women are prevented from recognizing one another's essential humanity by sexual prejudices, nourished by legal as well as social institutions, society as a whole remains less than it could otherwise become."

BLACKPAST.ORG (1970)

STUDY QUESTIONS

1. What factors do you think led to the defeat of the ERA?
2. Alice Paul was often criticized for keeping the reins of her suffrage campaign tightly in her own hands, yet her goal was political equality. Is it possible to achieve a truly democratic end if the means are a concentration of power in the hands of one leader?
3. Alice Paul's strategy for winning woman suffrage attracted far fewer supporters than the strategy of the NAWSA. What do you think explains this?
4. Offer a defense, or a criticism, of the government's harsh treatment of the suffrage prisoners.
5. Analyze Alice Paul's militant strategy for winning an equal rights amendment. Did it help or hurt the cause? What alternative strategy might have been put forward?
6. In the 1920s, a central debate among women activists was whether to pursue an equal rights amendment or to fight for an extension of protective legislation for women workers. Give the pros and cons of both positions.
7. Consider the arguments made by the anti-suffrage forces. Were the same arguments used by those who opposed the ERA? What similarities and what differences can you discover in the opposition to these two movements?

NOTES

CHAPTER ONE

1. *Conversations with Alice Paul,* p. 16.
2. Ibid.
3. Herendeen, "What the Hometown Thinks of Alice Paul," p. 45.
4. *Conversations with Alice Paul,* pp. 16–18.
5. Ibid.
6. Ibid., pp. 7–8.
7. Ibid., pp. 27–30.
8. Ibid., pp. 19–20.
9. Ibid., pp. 20–21.
10. Ibid., p. 21.
11. Ibid.
12. Ibid., p. 34.
13. Ibid., p. 48.

CHAPTER TWO

1. "Letter Written by Mrs. Belmont to a Friend," ca. December 1918, *The Papers of the National Woman's Party 1913–1920: The Suffrage Years,* Manuscript Division, Library of Congress, Washington, DC.
2. Irwin, "The Adventures of Feminism," p. 456, Inez Haynes Irwin Papers, Schlesinger Library, Radcliff College, Cambridge, MA.
3. Statement of Katherine Houghton Hepburn, n.d., Florence Ledyard Cross Kitchelt Papers, Schlesinger Library, Radcliff College, Cambridge, MA.
4. *Philadelphia Inquirer,* January 21, 1910.
5. *New York Times,* November 30, 1909.
6. "Woman Suffrage at Moorestown," *Friends' Intelligencer,* February 19, 1910, pp. 121–122.
7. Ibid.
8. Taft quoted in *New York Times,* April 14, 1910.
9. Frances Squire Potter to William Howard Taft, April 15, 1910.
10. Harper et al., *The History of Woman Suffrage,* vol. 5, p. 271.

11. Statement of Katherine Houghton Hepburn, n.d., Kitchelt Papers, Schlesinger Library, Radcliff College.

12. Frederick Sullens to Lily Wilkinson Thompson, April 6, 1913, Lily Wilkinson Thompson Papers, Mississippi State Archives, Jackson, MS.

13. Showalter, *These Modern Women: Autobiographical Essays from the Twenties,* pp. 86–92.

CHAPTER THREE

1. Irwin, *Up Hill with Banners Flying,* p. 31; *New York Times,* March 4, 1913.

2. Irwin, *Up Hill with Banners Flying,* p. 66.

3. Ibid., p. 68.

4. Ibid., p. 11. See also Mabel Vernon: *Speaker for Suffrage,* pp. 157–158, and Kirchwey, "Alice Paul Pulls the Strings," p. 332.

5. Herendeen, "What the Hometown Thinks of Alice Paul," p. 45.

6. Irwin, *Up Hill with Banners Flying,* pp. 14–15.

7. *Conversations with Alice Paul,* p. 110.

8. Irwin, *Up Hill with Banners Flying,* p. 16.

9. Ibid., p. 18.

10. Ibid., ch. 4.

11. *New York Times,* March 4, 1913.

12. *Senate Suffrage Committee Report,* pp. 77–85.

13. *New York Times,* March 4, 1913.

14. *Washington Post,* March 5, 1913.

15. Ada Ralls to Alice Paul, April 4, 1913, NWP Papers.

16. *Jackson Daily News,* April 7, 1913; Frederick Sullens to Lily Wilkinson Thompson, April 8, 1913, Thompson Papers.

17. William A. Clark to Alva Belmont, April 7, 1913, National Woman's Party Papers (hereafter NWP Papers).

18. *The Suffragist,* vol. 1, November 15, 1913.

CHAPTER FOUR

1. Stevens, *Jailed for Freedom,* p. 13; Alice Paul to Mary A. Burnham, June 12, 1914, cited in Katzenstein, *Lifting the Curtain,* p. 138.

2. Harper et al., *History of Woman Suffrage,* vol. 5, pp. 380–381; *Conversations with Alice Paul,* p. 98.

3. *The Suffragist,* vol. 1, December 6, 1913.

4. Peck, *Carrie Chapman Catt,* pp. 239–240.

5. *Conversations with Alice Paul,* p. 115.

6. *New York Times,* January 5, 1914.

7. Carrie Chapman Catt to Emma Gillette, August 9, 1916, NAWSA Papers; Random Notes Taken at the Discussion Between the National American Woman Suffrage Association and the Congressional Union, February 12, 1914, NWP Papers.

8. *The Suffragist,* vol. 1, December 6, 1913.

9. Lucy Burns to Alice Paul, January 23, 1914, NWP Papers.

10. Charlotte Whitney to Mrs. William Kent, September 11, 1915, NWP Papers.

11. Alice Paul to Eunice R. Oberly, February 19, 1914, NWP Papers.

12. *The Suffragist,* vol. 2, March 21, 1914.
13. Report of the Congressional Union, 1914, NWP Papers.

CHAPTER FIVE

1. Mary Ritter Beard to Alice Paul, August 23, 1914, NWP Papers.
2. *Congressional Record,* 63rd Congress, 1st Sess., February 4, 1914.
3. Antoinette Funk to Anna Howard Shaw, January 21, 1914, NAWSA Papers; Alice Paul to Harriet Taylor Upton, June 17, 1914, and Report of the Congressional Union, 1914, NWP Papers.
4. Report of the Congressional Union, 1914, pp. 26–27, NWP Papers; *The Suffragist,* vol. 3, July 15, 1914; *New York Times,* July 1, 1914.
5. Ibid.
6. Ibid.
7. *New York Tribune,* August 30, 1914.
8. Sara Bard Field quoted in Irwin, *Up Hill with Banners Flying,* pp. 83–85.
9. *Republican Herald,* October 15, 1914.
10. *Seattle Sunday Times,* reported in Irwin, *Up Hill with Banners Flying,* p. 90.
11. Irwin, *Up Hill with Banners Flying,* pp. 83–85.
12. Quoted in the Report of the Congressional Union, 1914, pp. 51–52, NWP Papers.
13. *Congressional Record,* vol. 51, part 17, pp. 1228–1229.
14. Alice Paul to Mary Beard, November 4 and 9, 1914, NWP Papers.

CHAPTER SIX

1. Alice Paul, *Minutes of the National Advisory Committee Meeting,* March 31, 1915, NWP Papers.
2. Report of the 1914 NAWSA Convention by Harper et al., *History of Woman Suffrage,* vol. 5, pp. 424–425.
3. Alice Paul to Carrie Chapman Catt, June 24, 1915, NWP Papers.
4. Margaret Kessler to Elizabeth Kent, November 1915, NWP Papers.
5. Mabel Vernon, *Speaker for Suffrage,* p. 144.
6. *Sara Bard Field: Poet and Suffragist,* interview conducted by Amelia R. Fry, Berkeley Oral History Project, Bancroft Library, University of California at Berkeley, 1979, p. 249.
7. Quoted in Irwin, *Up Hill with Banners Flying,* p. 114.
8. *Conversations with Alice Paul,* pp. 202–203, 326.
9. *Congressional Quarterly Guide to U.S. Elections,* p. 491; Irwin, *Up Hill with Banners Flying,* pp. 152–154.
10. Report of the Proceedings of the National Woman's Party Convention; *New York World,* June 7 and 8, 1916.
11. See *The Suffragist,* vol. 4, November 25, 1916, p. 6; and *Campaign Text-Book 1916,* NWP Papers.
12. *New York Times,* November 10 and 12, 1916.
13. The quotes from *San Francisco Examiner, Wichita Eagle, Utica* (New York) *Dispatch, Flagstaff* (Arizona) *Sun, and Oroville* (California) *Mercury* all appear in *The Suffragist,* vol. 4, November 25, 1916, pp. 4–8.

CHAPTER SEVEN

1. Blatch and Lutz, *Challenging Years,* pp. 275–276.
2. Ibid., pp. 276–277.
3. Edna Buckinan Kearns to Alice Paul, August 1917 (emphasis in original document), NWP Papers.
4. Mrs. Victor DuPont to Alice Paul, February 27, 1917; Mrs. Avery Ferry Coonley to Alice Paul, January 31, 1917; Alice Paul to Mrs. Carl Sprague, June 19, 1917, NWP Papers.
5. *New York Times,* January 15, 1917; *New Republic,* December 8, 1917, p. 115; *The Nation,* September 6, 1917, p. 237.
6. Helen Woodrow Bones to Jessie Woodrow Wilson Sayre, January 16, 1917, Wilson Collection, Princeton University.
7. Alice Paul to State Chairmen, February 8, 1917, NWP Papers.
8. Florence Bayard Hilles quoted in Irwin, *Up Hill with Banners Flying,* pp. 278–279.
9. Peck, *Carrie Chapman Catt,* pp. 265–271; O'Neill, *The Woman Movement,* p. 80; Lillian Holt to Alice Parke Lock, February 16, 1917, Alice Parke Lock Papers.
10. *Conversations with Alice Paul,* pp. 174–177.
11. N. A. Nesaragof to Alice Paul, June 21, 1917, copy of letter in Wilson Papers. Irwin, *Up Hill with Banners Flying,* pp. 214–215; *Conversations with Alice Paul,* pp. 213–216, 264.
12. Florence Bayard Hilles, in Stevens, *Jailed for Freedom,* p. 100 (see also pp. 103–104).
13. *The Suffragist,* vol. 5, July 21 and 28, 1917; *New York Times,* June 28 and July 15, 16, and 17, 1917.
14. Alice Paul, quoted in the *Baltimore Sun,* July 20, 1917.
15. Letter from Richard Bennett to Newton D. Baker, September 22,1917, reprinted in Irwin, *Up Hill with Banners Flying,* p. 151.
16. Woodrow Wilson to Joseph P. Tumulty, Memo, November 10, 1917, Wilson Papers.
17. Congressman Charles A. Lindbergh to Woodrow Wilson, August 27, 1917, and Dudley Field Malone to Woodrow Wilson, September 7, 1917, Wilson Papers.
18. *Conversations with Alice Paul,* pp. 197, 225–226, 230–234.
19. W. Gwynn Gardiner to Woodrow Wilson, November 9, 1917, Wilson Papers; Letter from Rose Winslow, ca. November 1917, smuggled out of District Jail, NWP Papers.
20. Mrs. S. G. Harrison, Democratic Club of Alameda to Woodrow Wilson, November 18, 1917, Wilson Papers.
21. The Lawrence meeting was reported by Alice Paul to the best of her recollection of what transpired between her and David Lawrence. The quotes attributed to Lawrence were reconstructed by Paul from her memory. See also Louisine Havemeyer, "Prison Special," *Scribner's Magazine,* June 1922, pp. 640–673. Wilson's biographer, Arthur S. Link of Princeton University, in an interview with the author in June 1981, concurred that it was probable that Wilson sent Lawrence to talk with Paul. Link said that Wilson had, from time to time, used Lawrence as an unofficial emissary in situations where it was not advantageous to use normal channels of communication.

CHAPTER EIGHT

1. Havemeyer, "The Prison Special: Memories of a Militant," pp. 661–667; Mary Winsor to Mary Howard, July 13, 1917, The Papers of Mary Winsor, Schlesinger Library of Radcliffe College, Harvard University; Reyher interview, *Search and Struggle for Equality,* pp. 48–50;

memoir by Katherine Houghton Hepburn, undated, Florence Ledyard Cross Kitchelt Papers, Schlesinger Library of Radcliffe College.

2. *New York Times,* January 10, 1918.

3. Doris Stevens Memoirs, n.d., Doris Stevens Papers, Schlesinger Library, Radcliff College, Cambridge, MA.

4. Crystal Eastman, "Now We Can Begin" (December 1920), reprinted in Cook, *Crystal Eastman on Women and Revolution,* pp. 53–54.

5. *Conversations with Alice Paul,* p. 257; *Hearings of the House Judiciary on the Equal Rights Amendment,* 68th Congress, 2nd Sess. (Washington, 1925).

6. *Conversations with Alice Paul,* pp. 256, 307.

7. Evans, "Women in the Washington Scene," p. 514.

8. Speech of Sara Bard Field at the Capitol Ceremony, February 15, 1921, NWP Papers.

9. *The Suffragist,* vol. 10, January–February 1921, p. 339.

10. Report of the National Convention of the National Woman's Party, February 15–18, 1921, NWP Papers.

11. *New York Times,* December 26, 1920, and January 15–18, 28, and 29, 1921.

CHAPTER NINE

1. *Survey,* June 15, 1926, copy in Mary Van Kleeck Papers, Sophia Smith Collection, Smith College Library, Northampton, MA; *New York Times,* January 20, 1926.

2. Quoted in *New York Times,* May 10–12, 1926, and *The World,* May 11, 1926.

3. Press Release, National Woman's Party, May 11, 1926, NWP Papers.

4. Fuentes, "Three United States Feminists—A Personal Tribute."

5. *Conversations with Alice Paul,* pp. 568–572.

6. *Conversations with Alice Paul,* pp. 606–611.

7. Ibid., pp. 606–611.

8. United States Equal Employment Opportunity Commission, *Title VII of the Civil Rights Act of 1964.*

CHAPTER TEN

1. *Conversations with Alice Paul,* pp. 400–423.

2. Ibid.

3. Ibid.

ANNOTATED BIBLIOGRAPHY

PRIMARY SOURCES

For students interested in learning more about advances made by and for women in the nineteenth and twentieth centuries, or who wish to do their own research, there is no shortage of available primary and secondary sources to explore. Primary sources are materials that may include personal papers, letters, diaries, interviews, and memoirs; papers that relate to the organization and activities of groups (e.g., the National Woman's Party and the National American Woman Suffrage Association); organization publications; membership rolls; fundraising documents; contemporary newspaper and magazine reports including drawings, cartoons, and photographs; and government documents and audio and/or visual recordings including speeches, filmed events, broadcasts, and songs. In short, any contemporary material related to a particular event, group, or individual that a student may wish to investigate would be considered a primary source. Secondary sources include books and articles usually based on primary-source materials that provide a narrative interpretation of the author's opinions and conclusions about his or her subject.

A great deal of primary-source information can now be found on the Internet. Exploring available Internet sources begins, of course, with a search engine inquiry. Google (www.google.com) and Yahoo (www.yahoo.com) are probably the most popular search engines. Other excellent engines are Bing (www.bing.com), Alta Vista (www.altavista.com), and Ask (www.ask.com). Keywords are important to narrow down the scope of information and sites retrieved by search engines. Some excellent sources for research on women's rights can be found at the Library of Congress (www.loc.gov). The Library of Congress has vast holdings on virtually every conceivable topic, and there is a surprising amount of information available online. The LOC has an online digital collection (www.loc.gov/library/libarch-digital.html) and an extensive online photographs collection (www.loc.gov/pictures). The University of California at Davis has compiled an excellent list of resources at The History Project site (http://historyproject.ucdavis.edu). The History Project has sections listing collections by geographic region in the United States. Some of the collections are available online, but of even greater value are the collections in geographic locations accessible to the researcher. The History Project also includes narratives of a variety of topics along with bibliographies, documentary sources related to each topic, and suggested study questions. The University of California at Berkeley has made available online all of the interviews conducted in the Berkeley Suffrage Oral History Project (http://bancroft.berkeley.edu/ROHO/project /suffragist). Participants in the project interviewed Alice Paul, Mabel Vernon, Sara Bard Field,

Rebecca Hourwich Reyher, and others in the 1970s, providing researchers with hundreds of pages of recollections in their own words. Other websites that are well worth investigating include American Women's History: A Research Guide, Middle Tennessee State University (http://frank.mtsu.edu/~kmiddlet/history/women.html); Digital Women's Collections Online (http://scriptorium.lib.duke.edu/women/digital.html); Documenting the American South: The Southern Experience in Nineteenth-Century America (http://metalab.unc.edu/docsouth/); H-Net: Humanities and Social Studies online, Michigan State University (http://www.h-net.msu.edu); Harvard University, Cambridge, MA (http://harvard.edu); Institute for Research on Women and Gender, University of Michigan (http://www.umich.edu/~irwg); National Women's History Project (http://www.nwhp.org); New York Public Library (http://nypl.org); and Viva Link (http://www.iisg.nl/~womhist/vivalink.html). These references, in turn, will lead to many other sources available through organizations, libraries, and universities throughout the country.

Manuscript Collections

Manuscript collections are generally held in government archives, college and university libraries, and private libraries. The papers and manuscripts used in research for this book included all three kinds. Notes give the reader some insight into how valuable this kind of research can be. Although I haven't listed all of them herein, many are cited, including the Library of Congress (NWP and NAWSA Papers, government documents, the Congressional Record), the University of California, Berkeley (Oral History Collection), Princeton University (Wilson Papers), and the Schlesinger Library in Boston.

Suffrage Interviews

- Sara Bard Field: *Poet and Suffragist,* interview conducted by Amelia R. Frye 1959–1963, Suffragist Oral History Project, University of California at Berkeley (1979).
- Elsie Hill: interview conducted by Morton Tenczar, July 30–August 7, 1968, Oral History Project, University of Connecticut at Storrs.
- Burnita Shelton Matthews: *Pathfinder in the Legal Aspects of Women,* interview conducted by Amelia R. Frye, 1973, Suffragists Oral History Project, University of California at Berkeley (1975).
- Alice Paul: *Conversations with Alice Paul,* interview conducted by Amelia R. Frye, 1972–1973, Suffragist Oral History Project, University of California at Berkeley (1976).
- Alice Paul: "I Was Arrested, Of Course . . . ," interview conducted by Robert S. Gallagher, American Heritage.com, History's Homepage: *American Heritage Magazine* 25, no. 2 (February 1974).
- Jeannette Rankin: activist for world peace, *Women's Rights and Democratic Government,* interview conducted by Malca Chall and Hannah Josephson, 1972–1974, Suffragists Oral History Project, University of California at Berkeley (1974).
- Rebecca Hourwich Reyher: *Search and Struggle for Equality and Independence,* interview conducted by Amelia R. Frye and Fern Ingersoll, Suffragists Oral History Project, University of California at Berkeley (1977).
- Mabel Vernon: *Speaker for Suffrage and Petitioner for Peace,* interview conducted by Amelia R. Frye, 1972–1973, Suffragist Oral History Project, University of California at Berkeley (1976).

Memoirs

Another valuable source of information are memoirs written by individuals who were directly involved in the suffrage movement. These also provide a perspective not often found in other print media. Memoirs cited in the notes are included below.

Harriot Stanton Blatch and Alma Lutz, *Challenging Years: The Memoirs of Harriot Stanton Blatch* (New York: G. P. Putnam, 1940).
Carrie Chapman Catt and Nettie Rogers Shuler, *Woman Suffrage and Politics: The Inner Story of the Suffrage Movement* (New York: Charles Scribner's, 1926).
Sarah T. Colvin, *A Rebel in Thought* (New York: Island Press, 1944).
Inez Haynes Irwin, *Up Hill with Banners Flying* (Penobscot, ME: Traversity Press, 1964).
Caroline Katzenstein, *Lifting the Curtain: The State and National Woman Suffrage Campaign in Pennsylvania as I Saw Them* (Philadelphia: Dorrance, 1955).
Elaine Showalter, ed., *These Modern Women: Autobiographical Essays from the Twenties* (Old Westbury, NY: The Feminist Press, 1978).
Doris Stevens, *Jailed for Freedom* (New York: Boni & Liveright, 1920).
Edith Bolling Wilson, *My Memoir* (Indianapolis: Bobbs-Merrill, 1939).

Government Publications

District of Columbia, *Annual Report of the Commissioners of the District of Columbia, Year Ended June 30, 1917,* vol. 1, Miscellaneous Reports, Washington 1917.
District of Columbia, *Annual Report of the Commissioners of the District of Columbia, Year Ended June 30, 1918,* vol. 1, Miscellaneous Reports, Washington, 1919.
Senate Suffrage Committee Report, United States Congress, US Senate Report No. 53. Report of the Committee of the District of Columbia, United States Senate, Pursuant to S. Res. 488 of March 4, 1913, Directing Said Committee to Investigate the Conduct of the District Police of the District of Columbia in Connection with the Woman Suffrage Parade on March 3, 1913, 63rd Congress, 1st Sess., May 29, 1913, Washington, 1913.
United States Congress, *Congressional Record,* 63rd Congress, 1st Sess. through 68th Congress, 2nd Sess., Washington, 1914–1925.
___, *Hearings of the House Committee on the Judiciary on the Equal Rights Amendment,* 68th Congress, 2nd Sess., Washington, 1925.
___, *Hearings on the Senate Committee on Woman Suffrage, 1916,* Washington, 1916.
___, *House Committee Hearings on Federal Woman Suffrage, January 3–7, 1918,* Washington, 1918.
___, US Senate Report No. 35, *Woman Suffrage,* 64th Congress, 1st Sess., January 8, 1916, Washington, 1916.
___, US Senate Report No. 53, Report of the Committee of the District of Columbia, United States Senate, Pursuant to S. Res. 499 of March 4, 1913, Directing Said Committee to Investigate the Conduct of the District Police and Police Department of the District of Columbia in Connection with the Woman Suffrage Parade on March 3, 1913, 63rd Congress, 1st Sess., May 29, 1913, Washington, 1913.
___, *Women in Congress,* Washington, 1976.

Newspapers and Periodicals

Scores of newspapers and periodical were researched for this project. The *New York Times,* the *New York World,* the *Washington Post,* and the *Philadephia Inquirer* provided valuable day-to-day reports on suffrage activities. Local newspapers from around the country also yielded such information but with a local/community perspective. Periodicals, including *Scribner's, Harper's, The Nation,* and the *Atlantic Monthly,* are equally valuable for their opinion pieces not always found in straight reportage. Many of these publications are now online and readily available.

Contemporary Articles

Charles A. Beard, "Woman Suffrage and Strategy," *New Republic* 1 (December 12, 1914): 22–23.

___, "The Woman's Party," *New Republic* 9 (July 29, 1916): 329–331.

Mary Ritter Beard, "The Legislative Influence of Unenfranchised Women," *Annals of the American Academy of Political and Social Science* 56 (November 1914): 54–61.

Clara Mortenson Beyer, "Do Women Want Protection? What is Equality?" *The Nation* 116 (January 31, 1923): 116.

Alice Stone Blackwell, "Women's 75-Year Fight," *The Nation* 117 (July 18, 1923): 53–55.

Harriot Stanton Blatch, "Do Women Want Protection? Wrapping Women in Cotton Wool," *The Nation* 116 (January 31, 1923): 115–116.

Elizabeth Brooks, "Future Suffrage Policy," *New Republic* 9 (December 9, 1919): 97.

Winifred Harper Cooley, "The Younger Suffragists," *Harper's Weekly* 58 (September 27, 1913): 7–8.

Eugene Debs, "Susan B. Anthony," *Pearson's Magazine* 38 (July 1917): 5–7.

Elizabeth Glendower Evans and Carol A. Rehfisch, "The Women's Party—Right or Wrong?" *New Republic* 13 (September 26, 1923): 123–124.

Ernestine Evans, "Women in the Washington Scene," *Century Magazine* 155 (September 1923): 507–517.

Zona Gale, "What Women Want in Wisconsin," *The Nation* 115 (August 23, 1922): 184–185.

"Gift to the Republicans," *New Republic* 13 (January 12, 1918): 301.

Alice Hamilton, "Protection for Women Workers," *The Forum* 72 (August 1924): 152–160.

Mrs. J. Borden Harriman, "Women in Washington," *The Forum* 72 (July 1924): 45–60.

Louisine Waldron Havemeyer, "The Suffrage Touch: Memories of a Militant," *Scribner's Magazine* 71 (May 1922): 528–539.

___, "The Prison Special: Memories of a Militant," *Scribner's Magazine* 71 (June 1922): 661–676.

Anne Herendeen, "What the Hometown Thinks of Alice Paul," *Everybody's* 41 (October 1919): 45.

"How the Women Voted," *World's Work* 33 (December 1916): 118–119.

Frances Keller, "Women in British and American Politics," *Current History* 17 (February 1923): 831–836.

Florence Kelley, "The New Woman's Party," *Survey* 11, no. 5 (March 5, 1921): 827–828.

Edna Kenton, "Four Years of Equal Suffrage," *The Forum* 72 (July 1924): 37–44.

Freda Kirchwey, "Alice Paul Pulls the Strings," *The Nation* 112 (March 2, 1924): 332–333.

"Labor's Position on Woman Suffrage," *New Republic* 6 (March 11, 1916): 150–152.

Anne H. Martin, "Equality Laws vs. Women in Government," *The Nation* 115 (August 16, 1922): 165–166.

Emmeline Pankhurst, Emmeline Pethick-Lawrence, and F.W. Pethick-Lawrence, *Suffrage Speeches from the Dock: Conspiracy Trials, Old Bailey, May 15–22, 1912,* Pamphlet, Sophia Smith Collection, Smith College.

Helen Ring Robinson, "What About the Woman's Party?" *The Independent* (September 1916): 381–383.

"Special Feature: The Equal Rights Amendment," *Congressional Digest* 3 (March 1924): 192–207.

Doris Stevens, "The Blanket Amendment: A Debate," *The Forum* 72 (August 1924): 145–152.

"The Spokesman for Suffrage in America," *McClure's Magazine* 29 (July 1912): 335–337.

"Three Cheers for the Poor," *New Republic* 13 (January 26, 1918): 364–365.

Clara Wold, "We Don't Want Nothin' New: A Suffragist's Interview with a Delaware Legislator," *The Independent* 102 (April 17, 1920): 79–80, 115.

"Woman Suffrage and Congress," *The Independent* 84 (December 27, 1915): 522.

"Woman Suffragists and Party Politics," *New Republic* 9 (December 9, 1916): 138–140.

Maud Younger, "The Diary of an Amateur Waitress: An Industrial Problem from a Worker's Point of View," *McClure's Magazine* 27 (March 1907): 543–552 and 28 (April 1907): 665–677.

———, "Taking Orders: A Day as a Waitress in a San Francisco Restaurant," *Sunset Magazine* 21 (October 1908): 518–522.

———, "Revelations of a Woman Lobbyist," *McCall's Magazine* 50 (September-October-November 1919).

HISTORICAL ACCOUNTS

Virginia Bratfisch, *The Non-Violent Militant: Alice Paul* (Santa Monica: Women's Heritage Series, 1971).

Elizabeth Colbert, "Firebrand Phyllis Schlafly and the Conservative Revolution," *The New Yorker* (November 7, 2005).

Blanche Weisen Cook, ed., *Crystal Eastman on Women and Revolution* (New York and London: Oxford University Press, 1978).

Robert Dallek, *Lyndon B. Johnson, Portrait of a President* (New York: Oxford University Press, 2004).

Crystal Eastman, "Alice Paul's Convention," in Blanche Weisen Cook, ed., *Crystal Eastman on Women and Revolution* (New York and London: Oxford University Press, 1978).

Carol Felsenthal, *The Biography of Phyllis Schlafly: The Sweetheart of the Silent Majority* (New York: Doubleday & Co., 1981).

Jo Freeman, "How Sex Got Into Title VII: Persistent Opportunism as a Maker of Public Policy, " *Law and Inequality: A Journal of Theory and Practice* 9, no. 2 (March 1991): 163–184.

Sonia Pressman Fuentes, "Three United States Feminists—A Personal Tribute," *Jewish Affairs* 53, no. 1 (Johannesburg, South Africa, 1998).

Ida Husted Harper et al., eds., *The History of Woman Suffrage*, vols. 5–6 (New York: Foster and Wells, 1922; reprinted in 1981).

Cynthia Harrison, *On Account of Sex, The Politics of Women's Issues, 1945–1968* (Berkeley: University of California Press, 1992).

Hannah Josephson, *Jeannette Rankin, First Lady in Congress* (Indianapolis: Bobbs Merrill, 1974).

Joseph P. Lash, *Eleanor: The Years Alone* (New York: New American Library. 1985).

Arthur S. Link, *Wilson: Campaigns for Progressivism and Peace 1916–1917* (Princeton: Princeton University Press, 1965).

Arthur S. Link and William M. Leary, "The Election of 1916," in Arthur Schlesinger et al., eds., *The History of American Presidential Elections 1789–1968*, vol. 3 (New York: McGraw-Hill, 1971).

Christine Lunardini, "Jane Addams," in *The American Peace Movement in the Twentieth Century* (Santa Barbara, CA: ABC-CLIO, 1994).

William O'Neill, "Feminism as a Radical Ideology," in Alfred F. Young, ed., *Dissent: Explorations in the History of American Radicalism* (DeKalb: Northern Illinois University Press, 1968).

___, *The Woman Movement: Feminism in the United States and England* (Chicago: Quadrangle Books, 1969).

Mary Grey Peck, *Carrie Chapman Catt: A Biography* (New York: Octagon Books, 1975).

Rosalind Rosenberg, *Divided Lives, American Women in the Twentieth Century* (New York: Hill and Wang, 1992).

Elizabeth Cady Stanton et al., eds., *The History of Woman Suffrage*, vol. 1 (New York: Foster and Wells, 1922; reprinted in 1981).

SECONDARY WORKS AND ARTICLES

The history of women in America has been well documented by historians and writers in the years following the emergence of the modern women's movement. No longer one of the stepchildren of American history, women's history is an essential factor in getting America's story right. In all categories—politics, race, culture, economics, law, work, science, medicine, war, peace, social change—women have influenced in important ways the shape and culture of the nation from its very inception. Listing all of the relevant resources in one bibliographical essay is no longer possible. The task now is to find a sampling of books and articles that will provide an overview of a particular topic and lead the reader to other works when more information is desired. Hopefully, this annotated bibliography of secondary books and articles accomplishes that end.

There are a number of excellent books and articles that review the history of suffrage, women's rights, and feminism in the nineteenth and twentieth centuries. Eleanor Flexner's pioneering work follows the women's movement from Seneca Falls to the passage of the Nineteenth Amendment; see her *Century of Struggle* (Cambridge, MA: The Belknap Press of Harvard University, 1959). See also Carol Berkin and Mary Beth Norton, *Women of America: A History* (Boston: Houghton Mifflin, 1979). Amy T. Butler's *Alice Paul and Ethel M. Smith: Two Paths to Equality in the ERA Debate 1921–1929* (New York: State University of New York Press, 2002) illuminates the conflict between Paul's version of the ERA debate and Smith's desire to achieve equality without damaging protection for women in industry. William E. Chafe's *The American Woman: Her Changing Social, Economic and Political Roles, 1920–1976* (New York: Oxford University Press, 1972) examines women's changing role in society. Chafe focuses on the post–Nineteenth Amendment era and discusses how political participation influenced social change. Chafe's *Women and Equality: Changing Patterns in American Culture* (New York: Oxford Books, 1977) is equally informative on these issues. Eleanor Clift's *Founding Sisters and the Nineteenth Amendment* (Hoboken, NJ: John Wiley & Sons, 2003) is a collection of biographical sketches of prominent American women. Nancy Cott's *The Grounding of Modern Feminism* (New Haven: Yale University Press, 1987) looks at how feminism evolved in the 1920s. Ellen DuBois's *Feminism and Suffrage: The Emergence of an Independent Women's Movement in America 1848–1869* (Ithaca: Cornell University Press, 1978) covers the women's movement from Seneca Falls to the emergence of national suffrage organizations. Edward James and his colleagues published a massive four-volume biographical dictionary titled *Notable American Women: A Biographical Dictionary* (Cambridge, MA, and London: The Belknap Press of Harvard University, 1971–1980)—a resource that should be one of the first stops for anyone wanting to know more about these women who fueled such massive change in America. Indeed, these volumes contain hundreds of biographical sketches of American women in a variety of fields and organizations. Aileen Kraditor's *The Ideas of the Woman Suffrage Movement 1890–1920* (New York: Anchor Books, 1971) provides an excellent analysis of how the argument and rationale for suffrage changed over time. Christopher Lasch's *The New Radicalism in America* (New York: Alfred A. Knopf, 1965) is an intellectual history of the era. Christine Lunardini and Thomas J. Knock's "Woodrow Wilson and Woman Suffrage: A New Look," *Political Science Quarterly* 95 (Winter 1980–1981): 655–671, examines Wilson's evolution regarding the suffrage issue. William J. O'Neill, in *Everyone Was Brave: The Rise and Fall of Feminism in America* (Chicago: Quadrangle Books, 1969), argues that feminism failed in the 1920s. June Sochen's *Movers and Shakers, American Women Thinkers and Activists 1900–1970* (New York: Quadrangle Books, 1972) takes a more positive view of women activists from the beginning of the century to the modern women's movement. And Mary Walton's *A Woman's Crusade: Alice Paul and the Battle for the Ballot* (New York: Palgrave Macmillan, 2010) presents a fresh look at Alice Paul.

Moving beyond the suffrage era, Susan Ware's *Beyond Suffrage: Women in the New Deal* (Cambridge, MA: Harvard University Press, 1981) highlights women's roles in Roosevelt's administration. Blanche Weisen Cook's biography of Eleanor Roosevelt—*Eleanor Roosevelt: Vol. 2, The Defining Years 1933–1938* (New York: Viking Penguin, 1999)—illustrates the First Lady's influence on politics and support for protective legislation for women. Following World War II, women seemed to recede from public attention or activity. But books such as Leila Rupp and Verta Taylor's *Survival in the Doldrums: The American Women's Rights Movement 1945 to the 1960s* (New York: Oxford University Press, 1987) disprove this, with attention given to the work of Alice Paul and the National Woman's Party during these years. The modern women's movement and the emergence of women's liberation in the late 1960s have produced a wealth of informative and analytical work on issues from feminism to the equal rights amendment. Betty Freidan's *The Feminine Mystique* (New York: W.W. Norton, 2001), originally published in 1967, is widely accepted as the book that launched the modern women's movement. Ruth Rosen's *The World Split Open: How the Women's Movement Changed America* (New York: Penguin Books, 2000) examines the connections between the civil rights movement and women's liberation, as well as divisions within the movement itself. Rosen analyzes how the women's movement affected social and cultural change within America. Sarah Evans's *Personal Politics: The Roots of Women's Liberation in the Civil Rights Movement and the New Left* (New York: Vintage Books, 1980) provides an excellent explanation of the religious dimension of the civil rights movement. Finally, both Jane Mainsbridge's *Why We Lost the ERA* (Chicago: University of Chicago Press, 1988) and Mary Frances Berry's *Why the ERA Failed: Women's Rights and the Amending Process of the Constitution* (Bloomington: Indiana University Press, 1988) provide cogent analyses of the politics of ratification and why the ERA fell short by three states.

INDEX